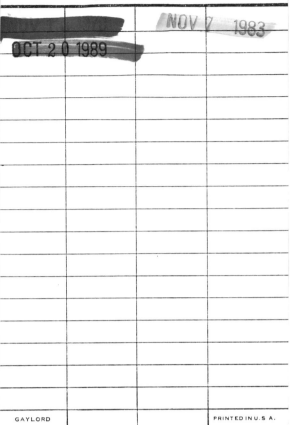

ESSAY ON
PRACTICAL MUSICAL COMPOSITION

DA CAPO PRESS MUSIC REPRINT SERIES

GENERAL EDITOR: FREDERICK FREEDMAN

Vassar College

AN ESSAY ON PRACTICAL MUSICAL COMPOSITION

*According to the Nature of That Science and the
Principles of the Greatest Musical Authors*

BY

AUGUSTUS FREDERIC CHRISTOPHER KOLLMANN

New Introduction by Imogene Horsley
Stanford University

DA CAPO PRESS • NEW YORK • 1973

Library of Congress Cataloging in Publication Data

Kollmann, August Friedrich Christoph, 1756-1829.
An essay on practical musical composition.

(De Capo Press music reprint series)
Reprint of the 1799 ed.
1. Composition (Music) I. Title.
MT40.K77   1973   781.6'1   70-75288
ISBN 0-306-71295-4

This Da Capo Press edition of
An Essay on Practical Musical Composition
is an unabridged republication of the
first edition published in London in 1799.

Copyright © 1973 by Da Capo Press, Inc.
A Subsidiary of Plenum Publishing Corporation
227 West 17th Street, New York, New York 10011

Introduction

Although it came out in two editions, 1799 and 1812, this treatise was not very important in its day. It is an excellent book, a clear and practical explication of eighteenth-century forms and styles, but it was published in England at a time when native musical creativity was at a low ebb, and it had little influence on the Continent. Today, however, it holds great value for American students since it presents, in English, the German approach to the teaching of composition in the classical period.

August Friedrich Christoph Kollmann was born in Engelböstel, Hanover, in 1756 (the same year Mozart was born) and received a solid musical training in the German tradition. Among his teachers was J. Christian Böttner, an organist in the tradition of J. S. Bach. Kollmann himself might have followed the regular pattern of German church musicians had not George III of England called him to London in 1782[1] to serve as schoolmaster to the Germans there; he was also appointed chapel keeper for the Royal German Chapel in St. James, and when a small organ was added to the chapel in 1792, he also served as organist. Once settled in England, he remained there until his death in 1829, leading an active musical life—performing, composing, teaching, and writing about music in the language of his adopted country.[2]

As a composer, Kollmann was neither prolific nor very distinguished. His works show a clear understanding of the art of music and a mastery of compositional techniques. They lack, however, what was then called "genius." His penchant for writing works that analyze well (such as his *Symphony,* [1789] and *Twelve Analyzed Fugues... with Double Counterpoint at all Intervals,* op. 10 [1812, 1823]) and for toying abstractly with formations found in the musical system within which he worked *(The Melody of the Hundredth Psalm with ...a Hundred Different Harmonies in Four Parts,* op. 9 [1809]; *A Rondo on the Chord of the Diminished Seventh* [1810]) seems more in keeping with the theoretical approach of many of our contemporaries than with the composers of the late eighteenth century.

He even produced a number of compositions which might be labelled *Gebrauchsmusik*—such works as *A Divertimento for Three Performers at One Pianoforte* (ca. 1810). Perhaps the most engaging work of this kind is *A Family Piece for Piano* which he printed in the second (and last) issue of his short-lived periodical, *The Quarterly Musical Register* (April 1812).[3] The piece is written for two players at a time—Number 1, who uses only one hand; and Number 2, more skilled, who employs both hands. It is, furthermore, in rondo form and is arranged so as to permit a continual turnover of performers. First, Number 1 drops out and is replaced. Then, once the new Number 1 is settled, the original Number 2 retires and a new Number 2 takes over. The music is composed so that this is managed without interrupting the flow of the piece, and by the time the rondo is finished six people have had a chance to play. One can sense the experienced schoolmaster in Kollmann's final comment: "and to bring in *more than six* performers the piece may be repeated. In the latter manner, a *whole school* may be agreeably employed by this piece."

As a composer and theorist, Kollmann followed the style and forms of the late eighteenth century. As a performer and music lover, he also cherished the music of J. S. Bach and, along with the leading English proponents of Bach's music—Samuel Wesley (1766-1837) and his German-born and trained colleague, Karl Friedrich Horn (1762-1830)—constantly sought to have it heard and understood by the English public. The musical examples at the back of this book include the *Prelude and Fugue* in C Major from Volume II of the *Well-Tempered Clavier,* the *Trio Sonata for Organ in E flat Major,* and all the riddle canons from the *Musical Offering;* this is the first publication of these works in England. His edition of Bach's *Chromatic Fantasia* (London: 1806) is probably the first in which the arpeggios are written out in the manner later adopted by Felix Mendelssohn and Hans von Bülow.[4] A projected edition, with analyses, of the *Well-Tempered Clavier* never materialized, but in later years Kollmann claimed that it was the threat of its appearance that spurred on Carl Czerny to bring out his edition of the work.[5]

It may have been this devotion to Bach's music that led Kollmann to adopt Kirnberger's harmonic theory, since Kirnberger claimed to base his teaching on that of Bach.[6] At a time when Rameau was dominating the scene, Kollmann brought out *An Essay on Musical Harmony* (London: 1796; Utica, N.Y.: 1817),[7] which was based on Kirnberger's method. Several years later he wrote *A New Theory of Musical Harmony* (London: 1806; 1812; 1823), in which he carried these ideas even further than Kirnberger himself.

The *Essay on Musical Harmony* is more than a harmony textbook. It provides a thorough grounding in both harmony and invertible counterpoint, and gives practice in the invention and development of musical ideas. Thus it was meant to give the student a mastery of the techniques necessary to a composer. A mastery of the materials in the book on harmony was considered a prerequisite to the study of the *Essay on Practical Musical Composition.*

While today's scholar need not study the *Essay on Musical Harmony* before he reads this book, he must be acquainted with Kollmann's special use of certain terms in order to understand his meanings. The use of "leading chord" for the dominant harmony is so logical that it needs no explanation. His meaning of "imitation," however, is not the same as ours; it is used to identify the restatement of a theme or "subject" in another voice part immediately upon its first presentation, and also its appearance later on in the course of the composition. Furthermore, these "imitations" may be modifications of the theme, and these changes include variations and developments as well as more mechanical treatments such as inversion, augmentation, and the like.[8]

Although he considered "periodical order" or the "compound rhythm" of a piece which is built up of a number of musical periods to be the source of "the principal beauties of a composition," Kollmann's conception of a "musical period" is less rigidly defined than those of many of his contemporaries.[9] For him it is primarily a rhythmic unit. He finds a period divisible into "strains," inner divisions which end with weaker cadences than the period itself, and smaller divisions—the caesurae—which are set off by short pauses. But he does not consider it necessary to end the period with a perfect cadence. Rather, he finds a perfect ending appropriate only at the end of periods which end the larger divisions of a movement or the movement itself. In this respect, his analytical method can be applied to the constructions of composers such as Domenico Scarlatti and C.P.E. Bach, as well as to the works of Haydn and Mozart.

Despite his mention of the inner divisions of a period, he does not give the type of sophisticated description of their possible interrelations that we find in the textbooks of some of his contemporaries.[10] There is no tendency to limit the term to works in the mature classical style, and his examples are often taken from works which some scholars do not consider to be fully periodic in structure. One example of a period which he cites is the first four measures of the *F-minor Prelude* from Volume II of the *Well-Tempered Clavier*. This he considers to be a complete period, containing two strains and four caesurae, although we, today, depending upon later definitions, would not consider it a period at all. Yet throughout the text on composition he constantly refers to works by Haydn, Mozart, and Clementi as well as to works by earlier composers. Like many practical teachers he draws his ideas from the music and the theorists he knows best, and we may conclude that he tried to make generalizations that cover a wide spectrum of eighteenth-century music.

Kollmann also published a number of small manuals on keyboard playing, *basso continuo,* and so on,[11] but only his harmony books and this text are of significance. As its title suggests, this book is a practical text giving the student the material needed to practice writing in the forms and genres actively used at that time. Kollmann does not theorize; he presents substantiated information about the composition of musical works. His work draws heavily upon German theory books of the mid- and late-eighteenth century, and while he may not always cite his sources specifically,[12] this is clearly due to his dealing with what he conceives to be common knowledge within the profession. Certainly, the ideas originated in practice and in the minds of the writers who recorded them. Kollmann derives many of his ideas from his own musical experience, and his comments upon those theorists he does cite are thoughtful and illuminating. He possessed a penetrating and analytical mind that, combined with a perceptive understanding and love of the new and old music of his century, makes this book fascinating reading for anyone interested in the music of that day.

It is the constant reference to actual compositions as illustrations of his descriptions that makes this so useful, especially since his musical terms by themselves are rarely self-explanatory, and the modern reader would tend to interpret them according to his own musical experience, rather than in the musical context to which they refer. A number of the examples he cites are given in the plates at the back of the book but, as he says in the introduction, he includes here only those which were not readily available to the reader. The composers whose works he felt were easily accessible include: C.P.E. and J.S. Bach, Clementi, Corelli, Geminiani, Handel, Hasse, Haydn, Mozart, as well as the lesser-known Georg Benda, Leopold Kozeluch, Ignaz Pleyel, Johann Schobert, and G. H. Stoelzel.

Another composer who is frequently cited is Kollmann himself. He has provided four analyzed fugues (plates 14—20), with analyses printed on the score, which are also discussed in the text (pp. 45—49). Although fugue and canon were no longer major forms, they were still included in the composer's education, and the section on fugue is interesting because it shows the type of fugue taught to composers of the classical period. It is expecially valuable for the scholar because it is based upon Marpurg's *Abhandlung von der Fuge* (see note 12) and provides us with eighteenth-century English equivalents of Marpurg's terms, explained by Kollmann with precision and clarity.

His treatment of fugue is lengthy because it involves so many fixed technical details. He devotes much less space to the developing homophonic forms because there were at that time only a few general prototypes and the inner details of the forms were not yet conventionalized. Since it is these forms that interest us most, it is disappointing to find that so few of the examples cited are printed in the book. Only the examples for a single section, a *Poco presto* by Kollmann (plate 1; text, p. 3) and two rondos by C.P.E. Bach (plates 1—9; p. 6) are given.

Today we are all aware that the term "sonata form" is a nineteenth-century invention; when Kollmann uses the word "sonata" it is in regard to its identification by medium of performance and style, and usually refers to a set of movements. What we know as sonata form he and his contemporaries referred to as the large binary form, or the form in two large sections as he designates it on page 5 of this book.

The lesser divisions which we make in sonata form are also different from those made by Kollmann. It was Anton Reicha, in 1824, who first used terms borrowed from rhetoric—exposition, bridge, development—to designate sections defined by their musical-psychological character in the unfolding of the form.[13] The term "recapitulation" was not yet used for the final section which brought back the exposition in the tonic key, but Reicha does speak of this section as a unit identified with the exposition, moving in the direction of the later three-part division into exposition, development and recapitulation. But for Reicha, the overall form was still binary—*le grand coupe binaire* was the name he gave it.

For Kollmann the form could be divided into four subsections, which do not coincide with the divisions made in the nineteenth century for they are made entirely according to key.[14] Their relation to the inner divisions commonly used today is as follows:

Kollmann's Divisions	*Modern Divisions*
Subsection I	First Theme Group and Bridge
Subsection II	Second Theme Group
Subsection III	Development
Subsection IV	Recapitulation

It is interesting to note that in the 1812 edition of the *Essay on Practical Composition* Kollmann retains these same subsections made according to key but has moved in the direction of functional terms based on literary form.[15] His first subsection is now likened to a "proposition" and the fourth subsection "once more resumes the first proposition and still enlarges upon it from such *nearest* points of view as are chiefly in the principal key and its fourth."
In both editions he cites as an example of this form the first movement of his *Symphony for*

the Pianoforte, a Violin, and a Violoncello, with analytical explanations of the Subjects and Imitations, the Counterpoint Inversions, and the Rhythmical order it contains, Opus VII (1789). It was probably all too readily available then, and is equally difficult to lay one's hand on today. For this reason it is reproduced here. It is especially interesting because it is one of the very few movements which is analyzed specifically as an example of this form in the eighteenth century.[16]

From the point of view of nineteenth-century theory, in which a new theme was expected at the beginning of the second theme group, this example is highly irregular, for the two subjects of the movement (labelled I and II on the score by Kollmann) are presented in the first eight measures and are used as the basis of the rest of the movement. Yet this is not surprising when we remember that theorists recording the practices of their time tend to stress only those elements that are fixed in the music they know. Among the "modern" composers of the 1790's, Kollmann was most familiar with, and most admiring of, Haydn, and he mentions with great admiration the Salomon Symphonies, which he had heard and knew in published form. Of these twelve symphonies, six—numbers 96, 98, 99, 100, 103, 104—start the new key area with the same theme that opened the first theme group, and some of the others have expositions that are decidedly irregular by later standards. And, of these six, at least four—numbers 98, 99, 100, 103—have a final section that would certainly not fit the nineteenth-century description of a "recapitulation" but fit very well Kollmann's definition of his "fourth subsection."

After the division into subsections based on key, Kollmann's main formal preoccupation is with the larger rhythm created by the lengths of the musical periods it contains. Here, on the score, he has marked off each period by indicating the measure number of the last full measure in that period. In many cases the cadence which marks the end of the period will be found in the measure immediately following that in which the number is marked. The binary character of the movement is emphasized by the fact that he starts his numbering again after the double bar which ends the first section, the first measure of the second section counting as "one" again. The measure counts are cumulative, each number representing the total number of measures which have accumulated since the beginning of that section.

Except for the indications of the beginnings of the four subsections —the exact extents of which are given precisely on page 5 of this book—the notations on the score, including such words as "ditto", are those found on the original print.

The work has been scored from parts. In the original the analysis was printed only on the piano part, and it has been left there. Clearly, a notation such as "I Violin" means that the first subject is stated in the violin. These entries were sketched in small notes in the piano part, but have been omitted here. As stated above, there are only two subjects and these are always indicated by the Roman numerals I and II. "L. C." stands for Leading Chord (see above). When Kollmann puts *"Cresc."* (crescendo) in the score he always inserts *"il"* somewhere between *"Cresc."* and the next dynamic marking to which the crescendo extends; these have been omitted from the score. All other abbreviations have been replaced by complete words.

*These slurs found only in piano reduction (m. 7).

*See measures 79 & 80 in fourth subsection.

xi

xvi

xvii

*Kollmann counts measures in section 2 separately, starting after the repeat sign.

xxiii

XXV

104

128

xxviii

There is no need to comment on the development techniques this movement was intended to illustrate, as Kollmann has identified by number the subject which is the source of each of his "imitations." But the emphasis on invertible counterpoint deserves mention. Scholars investigating the contrapuntal usages of the late eighteenth and nineteenth centuries have tended to stress their use of fugue and canon, yet the most frequently used contrapuntal device in these times is invertible counterpoint. Mozart uses it constantly. Though Beethoven was slow at learning the conventions of fugue in his studies with Albrechtsberger, he mastered invertible counterpoint quickly and began using it right away in his compositions.[17] It is a device used by Wagner as well as by Schumann and Brahms; in fact, it is an ideal device for a style which stresses one predominant melody, since it makes possible the shifting about of the main melody and the component melodies of its accompaniment.

Since the inversions in the first movement of Kollmann's *Symphony* are rather simple, a section from the second movement is included here. This section is built up out of a fragment of quadruple counterpoint. It shows the stylistic simplicity of much of the invertible counterpoint used in homophonic music and illustrates why this device is so seldom recognized—the secondary parts are so simple that one simply does not think of it as being coutrapuntal, let alone being in invertible counterpoint. It is in sharp contrast to Baroque usage where there is a tendency to combine subjects of near equality. Here it is simply a practical device, not an exhibition of skill.

SECTION FROM THE SECOND MOVEMENT OF A.F.C. KOLLMANN'S SYMPHONY
FOR THE PIANOFORTE, A VIOLIN, AND A VIOLONCELLO...OPUS VII

xxx

The remainder of the book is easy to understand and pleasantly informative, requiring no further explanations. For some scholars a short comparison of the 1812 edition with this one may be useful. Copies of both are available at The Library of Congress. There is considerable rewriting and clarifying of the text in the late edition, but the basic organization and content are retained. The plates of examples at the end of the book are the same. However, it is worthwhile to discover the changes that *are* made since in most cases—such as the changes in the detailing of sonata form mentioned earlier—these changes are due to new developments in the field of music.

The most notable changes are the dropping out of the names of composers whose works have gone out of style and the adding of new names. The mention of just a few can give a clue to the speed with which new compositions circulated at the turn of the nineteenth century.

By 1812, Kollmann had become acquainted with G. B. Martini's book on fugue, the *Esemplare, o sia saggio fondamentale pratico di contrapunto* (Bologna: 1774–76). He comments that it has good examples, but does not show one how to write a fugue. [18]

In the section on the concerto, beyond the additions made in the description of the form (which are analagous to those made in the description of sonata form discussed above) there is a change in the composers listed as models. The names Corelli, Geminiani, Dr. Arne and Stanley are dropped, and Kollmann simply names Handel, adding "and other ancient composers." No modern composers are named, although he mentions changes that have taken place in concerto form. [19]

The most consistent additions found throughout the book are the citations of a great many more works by Mozart, and the appearance of the name of Beethoven in a number of places. One of the most interesting places where notable changes have been made is the list of good pieces recommended for the study of keyboard style. New composers have been added, and, as one might expect, works by one old composer—J.S. Bach—are listed as well, because they were becoming available in music shops. The new list is quoted here, so that it can be compared with the list given on page eleven of this edition. [20]

1. The following ones by *Johann Sebastian Bach,* all of which are first rate works:
   The well-tempered Clavier, or 48 Preludes and Fugues; being two in every major and minor key.
   Fantasia Chromatica: in D minor.
   Six grand Suites de Pieces, called his English Suites.
   Six lesser Suites de Pieces, called his French Suites.
   Exercises pour le Clavecin, Op. I
   An Air with 30 Variations, for a Harpsichord with two sets of keys.
2. *Emanuel Bach's* different sets of Sonatas, without accompaniments.
3. *Handel's* Suites de Pieces, chiefly Part I.
4. *Haydn's* Sonatas, and Variations, without accompaniments.
5. *Mozart's* Fantasia, Sonatas, and Variations, of the same kind.
6. The Solo works of *Beethoven, Clementi, J.B. Cramer, Dussek, Steibelt, Woelfl,* and similar other distinguished Composers.

Further comparative study of the two editions yields many such interesting tidbits, but taken as a whole, there are not enough fundamental changes in the later edition to have kept it abreast of the times. It is the first edition, here reprinted, that will interest most scholars, because it offers the practical insight that only a contemporary can give to the musical world of the late eighteenth century.

Imogene Horsley

Stanford University
Stanford, California

[1] Most dictionaries indicate 1782, undoubtedly stemming from John S Sainsbury's *A Dictionary of Musicians From the Earliest Times*, 2 vols. (London: Sainsbury, 1824; reprint: New York: Da Capo Press, 1966). Hans F. Redlich, "The Bach Revival in England (1750–1850); A Neglected Aspect of J.S. Bach," *Hinrichsen's Musical Year Book* VII (1952), 290, claims the year to be 1784. This date is reiterated in his article on Kollmann in Friedrich Blume, ed., *Die Musik in Geschichte und Gegenwart*, 14 vols. (Kassel: Bärenreiter, 1949–63), VII, 1410–12.

[2] Perhaps the earliest biographical entry to appear in a music dictionary is the two-column (autobiographical?) entry in Sainsbury's *Dictionary*, op. cit., II, 22–30. Curiously, the entry gives Kollmann's name as: Augustus Frederick Charles Kollmann.

[3] For information on this periodical, see the unsigned article, "Notes on an Old Musical Journal: *The Quarterly Musical Register*," *The Musical Times* XLVIII [=776] (October 1907), 645–8. Redlich's remark, "The Bach Revival..." op. cit., 292, that the *Quarterly Musical Register* survives in a unique copy is no longer true; other copies can be found in the New York Public Library, and The Boston Public Library.

[4] "Notes on an Old Musical Journal: *The Quarterly Musical Rewiew*," op. cit.

[5] Kollmann's analyzed edition of the complete *Well-Tempered Clavier* has caused considerable confusion among scholars, details of which can be gleaned from Redlich's discussion, op. cit., 291–8. Perhaps most important to mention here is that Kollmann initially announced his "analyzed edition" with printed specimen, in Chapter XI, Section 21 of his *Essay* here reprinted.

[6] Erwin R. Jacobi, "Harmonic Theory in England After the Time of Rameau," *Journal of Music Theory* I/2 (November 1957), 126–46; and "Augustus Frederic Christopher Kollmann als Theoretiker," *Archiv für Musikwissenschaft* XIII/3–4 (September–December 1956), 263–70.

[7] The Utica edition holds a special interest in that it was published under patronage of the Oneida Musical Society (now defunct, but perhaps the most active musical organization in the Mohawk Valley during the first half of the nineteenth century), and it was one of the earliest extensive (about 300 pages) theoretical works to be published anywhere in the United States. While one might expect a Boston, New York, or Philadelphia imprint for the Kollmann, the Utica imprint comes as no real surprise, because the area, including Oneida County, was extremely active in the "singing school" tradition. Indeed, Thomas Hastings (1784–1872), writer of the influential *Dissertation on Musical Taste* (Albany: 1822; reprint: New York: Da Capo Press, 1970), is among the eighty-four subscribers to Kollmann's work. Interestingly enough, Kollmann's *Essay on Musical Harmony* may have had a stronger influence in the United States, (where theoretical works of this caliber were sorely lacking) than it had in England.

[8] *An Essay on Musical Harmony*, Chapter XV.

[9] *Ibid.*, Chapter III.

[10] See Leonard G. Ratner, "Eighteenth-Century Theories of Musical Period Structure," *The Musical Quarterly* XLII/4 (October 1956), 439–54.

[11] Complete list in Hans F. Redlich's article on Kollmann in *MGG*, loc. cit., 1410-12.

[12] Those cited are: J.J. Quantz, *Versuch einer Anweisung die Flöte traversiere zu spielen* (Berlin: 1752); F.W. Marpurg, *Abhandlung von der Fuge* (Berlin: 1753); J.G. Sulzer, *Allgemeine Theorie der Schönen Künste* (Leipzig: 1771–74); J.P. Kirnberger, *Die Kunst des reinen Satzes* (Berlin: 1771–79); and J.G. Albrechtsberger, *Gründliche Anweisung zur Composition* (Leipzig: 1790).

[13] In his *Traité de haut composition musicale*, 2 vols. (Paris: 1824), II, 296–300.

[14] This is in line with eighteenth-century German theory. For further details, see Leonard G. Ratner, "Harmonic Aspects of Classic Form," *Journal of the American Musicological Society* II/3 (Fall 1949), 159–68; and William S. Newman, *The Sonata in the Classic Era* (Chapel Hill: The University of North Carolina Press, 1963), 391–3, et passim.

[15] *An Essay on Practical Composition* (1812 ed.), 3. At about the same time Reicha, in *Traité de melodie* (Paris: 1814) uses "exposition" but not the other terms found in the abovementioned *Traité*...

[16] Two others are to be found in Francesco Galeazzi, *Elementi teoricopratici di musica* (Rome: 1796), II (see Bathia Churgin, "Francesco Galeazzi's Description [1796] of Sonata Form," *Journal of the American Musicological Society* XXI/2 [Summer 1968], 181–99) and Georg Simon Löhlein, *Clavier-Schule*, 3rd edition (Leipzig: 1779), I, 183f.

[17] John V. Cockshoot, *The Fugue in Beethoven's Piano Music* (London: Routledge & Kegan Paul, 1959), 21 et passim.

[18] Page 17 of the 1812 edition.

[19] Page 14 of the 1812 edition; page 21 of the 1799 edition.

[20] Page 8 of the 1812 edition.

ESSAY ON
PRACTICAL MUSICAL COMPOSITION

AN

ESSAY

ON PRACTICAL

MUSICAL COMPOSITION,

ACCORDING TO THE

NATURE OF THAT SCIENCE

AND THE

PRINCIPLES OF THE GREATEST MUSICAL AUTHORS.

———————

BY

AUGUSTUS FREDERIC CHRISTOPHER KOLLMANN,

ORGANIST OF HIS MAJESTY'S GERMAN CHAPEL AT ST. JAMES'S.

———————

London:

PRINTED FOR THE AUTHOR, (FRIARY, ST. JAMES'S PALACE,) AND TO BE HAD OF HIM;

AT MR. DALE'S, NO. 19, CORNHILL, AND NO. 132, OXFORD STREET;—AT MESSRS. LONGMAN, CLEMENTI, AND CO. NO. 26, CHEAPSIDE;—AT MR. SMART'S, THE CORNER OF ARGYLL STREET, OXFORD STREET; AND AT THE OTHER PRINCIPAL MUSIC SHOPS; ALSO AT MR. LOW'S, NO. 7, BERWICK STREET, SOHO.

M,DCC,XCIX.

Entered at Stationers' Hall.

TO

THE KING'S

MOST EXCELLENT MAJESTY,

THE FOLLOWING ESSAY

IS MOST HUMBLY DEDICATED (WITH PERMISSION),

BY

HIS MAJESTY'S

MOST DUTIFUL

AND MOST DEVOTED SUBJECT AND SERVANT,

AUGUSTUS FREDERIC CHRISTOPHER KOLLMANN.

SUBSCRIBERS.

Her Majesty THE QUEEN.

Her Royal Highness the PRINCESS OF WALES.
His Royal Highness the DUKE OF YORK.
Her Royal Highness the DUCHESS OF YORK.
Her Royal Highness PRINCESS AUGUSTA.
Her Royal Highness PRINCESS ELIZABETH.
Her Royal Highness PRINCESS MARY.
Her Royal Highness PRINCESS SOPHIA MATILDA OF GLOUCESTER.

A.

MR. ADAMS, Professor of Music, Hampstead.
Theodore Aylward, Muf. Doct. Professor of Music of Gresham College

B.

N. Baker, Muf. Bac. Stafford.
Mr. Birchall, Six Copies.
Mess's. Broderip and Wilkinson, Six Copies.
Barrington Buggin, Esq.
John Buddle, Jun. Esq.
Capt. Burnaby, 1st Regt. of Guards.
Charles Burney, Muf. Doct. F. R. S.
Mr. Busby.

C.

J. W. Calcott, Muf. Bac. Oxon. Organist of St. Paul's, Covent Garden, and the Asylum.
The Rev. Mr. Carrington.
Miss Child.
Mr. Clouting, Organist of Eyr, Suffolk.
Mr. Collins, Greenwich.
Messrs. Corri, Duffek, and Co.
Mr. Cramer, Musical Instrument Maker to their Majesties.

D.

Mr. Dale, Three Copies.
Capt. Duff, 1st Regt. of Guards.

E.

Mr. Eley.

F.

Mr. Fletcher, Birmingham.
John Nicholas Forkel, Philof. Doct. Director of Music at Gottingen.
Mr. Forster.

G.

Miss Greenhead.
Mr. G. Griesbach. ⎤
Mr. C. Griesbach. ⎬ Musicians to their Majesties.
Mr. W. Griesbach. ⎦
Mr. Groombridge, Organist of Hackney.

H.

Mr. Hachmeister, Organist at Billwerder, near Hamburgh.
Richard Hare, Esq. Bath.
Henry Hafe, Esq.
Mr. Hempel.
Mr. J. Hempel.
Miss Hempel.

b   Mr.

Mr. W. Horſley.
Mr. Hullmandel.

J.

Miſs Jackſon.
Mr. Jones, Organiſt of the French Chapel, Soho, and the Swediſh Chapel, Welcloſe Square.

K.

Mr. Kauntz, Three Copies.
Mr. Kemp, Organiſt of the Cathedral, Exeter.
Mr. Killick, Organiſt, at Graveſend.
Mr. Koehler, Muſical Inſtrument Maker to their Royal Highneſſes the Prince of Wales and Duke of York.
Mr. G. Kollman, Organiſt of St. Catherine's, Hamburgh.
Mr. C. Kollman, Hameln.
Mr. J. Kollman, Organiſt at Luneburgh.

L.

The Counteſs of Loudoun, Two Copies.
His Excellency Baron Lenthe.
Mr. Leffler, Organiſt of St. Catharine's, Tower, and the German Lutheran Chapel, Strand.
The Rev. Mr. O. T. Linley, Minor Canon of the Cathedral of Norwich.
Meſſrs. Longman, Clementi, and Co. Six Copies.
Mr. Lyndham.

M.

Mr. Mackintoſh.
James Martin, Eſq. M. P.
Mr. Miller, Maſter of the Eaſt York Band, Deal.
Mr. J. Moeller, Jun. Muſician to their Majeſties.
Colonel Morris, Coldſtream Guards.
Mr. Mumler.

N.

Mr. Neild, Hertford.
M. Neilſon, Profeſſor of Muſic, Nottingham.
Mr. Nicol, Bookſeller to His Majeſty.

P.

The Honourable George Pomeroy.
The Hon. and Rev. John Pomeroy, Dublin.
Mr. J. Perry.
Mr. S. Pierce, Exeter.
Mr. Preſton, Three Copies.
The Rev. Dr. Prettyman, Archdeacon of Lincoln.
Mr. Prince, Brighton.

R.

The Rev. Mr. R. Roberts, Mitcham.
Mr. W. Rudge, Wolverhampton.
W. Ruſſel, Eſq.

S.

Madame de Salis.
J. de Salis, Eſq.
Mr. Salomon.
Mr. J. Sidney, Jun. Muſician, Maidſtone.
T. Sikes, Eſq. Hackney.
Mr. Smart, Three Copies.
Mr. G. T. Smart, Organiſt of St. James's Chapel.
The Rev. Mr. C. J. Smyth, Minor Canon of the Cathedral of Norwich.
H. Smyth, Eſq. Charwelton, near Brackley.
Maſ. W. Southbrook, Knightſbridge.
John Spencer, Eſq. Wheatfield.

T.

Henry Thompſon, Eſq. Deal.
Mr. Thomſon, Muſician.
Mr. E. Tidy, Jun.
John Townſhend, Eſq.
Richard Twiſs, Eſq.

W.

Mr. S. Webbe.
James White, Eſq. Exeter.
Henry Whitehead, Eſq.
Mr. James Wild, Jun. Mancheſter.
Mr. J. Windſor, Organiſt of St. Margaret's Chapel, Bath.
Mr. Wood.
Mr. Wood, Hackney.
Mr. Woodhall, Jun. Scarbro'.
Mr. Wornum, Three Copies.

PREFACE.

IN the following Sheets I prefume to lay before the Public, a Second Effay, being that mentioned at the beginning of the Introduction to my *Effay on Mufical Harmony*, and by which I complete my doctrine of the Science of Mufic in general.

I fhould have nothing particular to obferve in this place, if I did not feel, (and I truft it will ftrike the difcerning Reader,) that by this Effay I have ventured into a department of much greater depth than the former, and that confequently it has been difficult, to explain and exemplify in the one volume, to which I found it expedient again to confine myfelf, all that I thought neceffary for the ftudy of Practical Compofition. But to prevent the natural fufpicion, of my having either crowded matter upon matter without a fufficient explanation, or of having entirely omitted many ufeful articles for want of room; I beg leave to fay a few words refpecting the Plan which I have purfued in writing the prefent work.

With regard to Doctrines, I have endeavoured not to wafte much room with defcriptions of the mere Forms, which have been hitherto introduced in the different forts of mufical pieces; but rather to teach the Principles on which every remarkable branch of compofition depends, and according to which the known forms of a piece may be varied, as well as new forms invented. By this method I have endeavoured to explain Sonatas, Symphonies, and other pieces of compofition, without giving whole pieces of each fort.

With regard to Examples, I have chiefly felected for my purpofe fuch pieces as have either not yet been printed, or as are fcarce and not generally known ;

known; and only referred to fuch others, as I fuppofe to be either univer-fally known in this country, or eafily to be obtained. But I have taken pains to explain and exemplify every thing in fuch a manner, as to render it intelligible, without thofe works to which I refer, or which I only mention; and that confequently the Reader will not be under the neceffity of procuring them for the fake of underftanding this work.

Whether the above plan be proper or improper, or whether I have been fuccefsful in purfuing it, or not, I humbly fubmit to the decifion of the difcerning Reader; and flatter myfelf that the little merit which may be found in this Effay will be admitted, or its imperfections corrected, with the fame candour which I have hitherto experienced in the reception of my former Effay.

A LIST

A LIST OF THE CONTENTS OF THE WORK,

CALCULATED TO GIVE THE READER A GENERAL IDEA OF THE WHOLE AS WELL, AS TO DIRECT HIM WHERE TO FIND EVERY THING IN PARTICULAR.

———————

INTRODUCTION.

CHAPTER I. OF THE PLAN FOR A PIECE TO BE COMPOSED.

I. *Of the Plan in general.*

§ 1. EXPLANATION.
    II. *Particulars in the said Plan.*
§ 2. General remarks.
    A. *Length and Disposition of a Piece.*
§ 3. Length, in the whole, and in its component parts.
§ 4. Disposition.
    B. *Modulation of a Piece.*
§ 5. Two particulars pointed out.
§ 6. Modulation of every Movement.
§ 7. In short pieces.
    Exemplified under No. 1, 2, 3, 4, 5, 6, 7, 8, 9. N. B. Setting out, elaboration, and return.
§ 8. Modulation to foreign keys.
    Examples under No. 1 & 2.
§ 9. In longer pieces.
§ 10. Modulation of those of more than two short sections.
    Of four, five, and more sections.
§ 11. Those of one or two long sections.
    1, Outlines of an elaborate Movement.
    2, Other particulars.
    Demonstrated according to an Allegro.
§ 12. Exceptions.
§ 13. Relation of Key and Mode between the several movements.
    C. *Character of a Piece.*
§ 14. As prescribed or optional.
§ 15. Means by which characteristics may be brought into a piece.
    What characteristics are proper or not.
§ 16. Optional characteristics in particular.

    D. *The Instruments or Voices for which a piece is to be composed.*
§ 17. Two particulars pointed out.
    E. *The number of Parts, particular Performers, &c.*
§ 18. The Number of Parts.
§ 19. Particular Performers.
§ 20. Particular Places or Occasions.
§ 21. Utility of the plan in question.

———————

CHAPTER II. OF SONATAS.

§ 1. Introduction.
    I. *Of Sonatas in general.*
§ 2. General explanations.
§ 3. Different sorts of Sonatas mentioned.
§ 4. Their proper length.
§ 5. Their number of movements and sections. Their Modulation.
    II. *Of the different Sorts of Sonatas in particular.*
    A. *Sonatas for one Solo Instrument only.*
§ 6. In general.
§ 7. Solos, and rules for them.
§ 8. Those for the Organ.
§ 9. Those for stringed keyed instruments.
    Good works, mentioned under No. 1, 2, 3, 4, 5, 6, 7, 8, 9.
§ 10. Solos for the Harp, or other Instruments.
    B. *Sonatas with Accompaniments.*
§ 11. Definitions.
§ 12. Of principal parts and accompaniments.
§ 13. Obligato, and ad libitum accompaniments.
    C. *Concerting Sonatas without accompaniments.*
§ 14. Definitions.
§ 15. Of Duetts, on one or two Instruments.
§ 16. Of Trios.
§ 17. Of Quatuors.
§ 18. Of Quintetts.
§ 19. Of Sextetts, &c.

c
III. *Of*

III. *Of Sonatinas.*
§ 20. Definition and explanation.
§ 21. Different forts of Sonatinas.
§ 22. Characteriftic Sonatas and Sonatinas.

CHAPTER III. OF SYMPHONIES.

§ 1. Definition.
    I. *Of Symphonies in general.*
§ 2. Different forts pointed out.
    A. *Of characteriftic Symphonies.*
§ 3. Thofe of a prefcribed character.
§ 4. Examples.
§ 5. A fecond clafs of them.
§ 6. The laft clafs ; containing Overtures.
    B. *Of free Symphonies.*
§ 7. Definition.
§ 8. Different forts of them.
§ 9. Their Harmony, and Paffages.
§ 10. Their Modulation.
    II. *Of Symphonies for an Orcheftra.*
§ 11. Two particulars pointed out.
§ 12. Conftruction of their Subjects.
§ 13. Diftribution of the harmony between the
    different inftruments.
    1, In Unifons.
    2, In Tuttis.
    3, In Solos.
§ 14. Harmonies of five and more parts.
§ 15. Obfervation refpecting real or duplicate
    parts.
III. *Of Symphonies for one, or only a few inftru-
    ments.*
§ 16. Particulars of them.
§ 17. Different forms of them.
    Examples.

CHAPTER IV. OF CONCERTOS.

§ 1. Definition, and general explanation.
    I. *Of Concertos in general.*
§ 2. Particulars pointed out.
    A. *Length and Character of Concertos.*
§ 3. Their proper Length.
§ 4. Their Character, as prefcribed or optional.
    B. *Number and Nature of their Movements.*
§ 5. In general.
§ 6. Three Movements analyzed.
    Firft movement.
§ 7. Second movement.
§ 8. Third movement.
§ 9. Accompaniments of the Solos.

    C. *The fancy Cadences.*
§ 10. Three rules.
§ 11. Examples, and an Obfervation.
II. *Of Concertos in regard to the principal and
    other Inftruments for which they are fet.*
    A. *Of thofe for one principal Inftrument.*
§ 12. Particulars explained.
    B. *Thofe for two or more principal Inftruments.*
§ 13. Five particulars explained.
    Concertantes.
§ 14. Concerti Groffi.
    C. *Thofe for Solo inftruments, without accompani-
    ments.*
§ 15. Explanation and Examples.

CHAPTER V. OF FUGUES IN GENERAL.

§ 1. Introduction.
§ 2. Definitions.
§ 3. Origin of Fugues.
§ 4. Imitations in them.
§ 5. Antient modes.
§ 6. Counterpoints, and parts.
§ 7. Sorts of Fugues pointed out.
    I. *Of proper or improper Fugues.*
§ 8. Explanations.
    II. *Of ftrict or free Fugues.*
§ 9. Explanations.
§ 10. Simple and double Fugues.
III. *Of Fugues in regard to the interval in which
    the anfwer is made.*
§ 11. Thofe in all intervals in general.
§ 12. Two particulars pointed out.
§ 13. Fugues in the Fifth or Fourth.
§ 14. Thofe in the Octave or Unifon.
§ 15. Thofe in the Third or Sixth.
§ 16. Thofe in the Seventh or Second.
V. *Of Fugues, in regard to the different forts of
    Imitation.*
§ 17. The different Imitations mentioned.
    VI. *Of Fugues in two and more Parts.*
§ 18. Real and additional parts.
§ 19. Real parts only.
§ 20. Additional parts.

CHAPTER VI. OF SIMPLE FUGUES.

§ 1. Introduction.
    I. *Particulars of a Simple Fugue.*
§ 2. Seven particulars pointed out.
                  A. *Of*

A. *Of the Subject.*

§ 3. Definition and explanation.

§ 4. Three particulars explained, viz: 1, Length; 2, Contents; 3, Beginning and ending.

§ 5. Particular considerations.

B. *Of the Answer.*

§ 6. Definition.

§ 7. Two general rules.

§ 8. Division of the scale as authentic and plagal.

§ 9. How the one part must answer the other. Two rules, and Examples.

§ 10. How a full octave must be answered. Two rules, and Examples.

§ 11. Answers in which the division of the Scale need not be attended to. Two Rules, and Examples.

§ 12. Answers to chromatic and enharmonic Subjects.
    1, Rules, and Examples, respecting chromatic answers.
    2, An Observation respecting enharmonic ones.

§ 13. Of more than one regular Answer to a Subject. Extraordinary liberties mentioned.

§ 14. Liberties in regard to the different Sections of the Fugue.

C. *Of the Order of the Replies.*

§ 15. Definitions.

§ 16. Two rules; and a table of replies.

§ 17. Three particulars.
    1, Order of replies in the different sections. Four rules.
    2, Shape or form of the replies in the succeeding sections. Two rules.
    3, Distance of the different replies. Replies at full distance. Those in various restrictions. Per arsin et thesin.

D. *Of the Counter Harmony.*

§ 18. Definition.

§ 19. Explanation, and two rules.

E. *Of the Intermediate Harmony.*

§ 20. Definition, and two particulars explained.

§ 21. Proper or improper intermediate Harmony.

F. *Of the different Sections of a Fugue.*

§ 22. Definition.

§ 23. Complete or incomplete, distinct or indistinct sections explained.

G. *Of the Modulation of a Fugue.*

§ 24. Three particulars explained.
    1, Modulation in general.

2, Modulation in regard to the different Sections.

3, Ditto in regard to different Cadences.

II. *Construction of a whole simple Fugue.*

§ 25. Introduction.

A. *Construction of a Fugue with regard to its Sections.*

§ 26. Two distinctions made.
    1, Fugues of three sections. Particulars of every section explained.
    2, Those of more than three sections. Also particulars explained.

B. *Construction of a Fugue with regard to its Parts.*

§ 27. Two particulars pointed out.

§ 28. Distance between the different parts. Two rules.

§ 29. Qualities required in the different parts. Two qualities explained.

III. *Fugues analyzed according to the above Principles.*

§ 30. Introduction to the Author's four fugues.

§ 31. Explanation of the characters used in the analysis.

§ 32. The Author's first fugue analyzed.

§ 33. — — second — —

§ 34. — — third — —

§ 35. — — fourth — — Remark respecting the other fugues given in the plates.

CHAPTER VII. OF DOUBLE FUGUES.

§ 1. Introduction.

I. *Of Double Fugues, or Fugues of two Subjects.*

§ 2. Two forts pointed out.

§ 3. Those with a mere Counter Subject.

§ 4. Three rules for them.

§ 5. Those with two independant Subjects. A Rule and Examples explained.

II. *Of Triple Fugues, or Fugues of Three Subjects.*

§ 6. Different forts mentioned.

§ 7. Those of one principal subject explained. One of three independant subjects. Examples explained. N. B. Remark on B, A, C, H.

III. *Of Quadruple Fugues, or Fugues of Four Subjects.*

§ 8. Three forts mentioned. An Example explained.

IV. *Of Quintuple and Sextuple Fugues.*

§ 9. Remarks on both.

§ 10. An example of a sextuple fugue.

§ 11. The invention of Subjects for double fugues.

§ 12. The

§ 12. Four Rules given, with some remarks.
§ 13. The examination of Subjects, with regard
    to their qualifications for double fugues.
    Two rules given.
    Remarks respecting the object in question.
§ 14. An example of an Enharmonic fugue.

CHAPTER VIII. OF CANONS.

§ 1. Definitions.
§ 2. Introduction.
        I. *Of Canons in general.*
§ 3. Sorts of Canons in general.
§ 4. Simple, Double, and Compound Canons.
§ 5. Resolved, and unresolved or ænigmatical
    ones.
§ 6. Finite and infinite canons.
    Also canons per tonos.
§ 7. Polymorphos, or those calculated for many
    resolutions.
II. *Of Canons, in regard to the different Sorts of
    Imitation.*
§ 8. Particulars pointed out.
§ 9. In regard to the Interval, or Intervals of the
    Replies.
§ 10. Strict or free Canons.
§ 11. Equal, reverse, and retrograde Canons.
§ 12. Canons by augmentation or diminution.
    Also by selected, and interrupted Imitation.
§ 13. Replies at equal or unequal distances.
III. *Of Canons, in regard to the Number and
    Quality of Parts.*
§ 14. Of real and other parts.
§ 15. Those without accompaniments.
§ 16. Those with accompaniments.
§ 17. Those with added thirds.
§ 18. Those to a given Melody.

CHAPTER IX. OF THE CONSTRUC-
TION AND RESOLUTION OF CA-
NONS.

        I. *Of their Construction.*
§ 1. Introduction.
    A. *Of the Construction of Simple Canons.*
§ 2. Three particulars pointed out.
    1. *The Interval in which the Reply is made.*
§ 3. Canons in the Unison, or Octave.
    Two sorts distinguished.
§ 4. Those which consist of equal divisions.

An example explained.
Other remarks.
§ 5. Those of unequal divisions.
    1, A first sort explained in five rules.
    2, A second sort explained in two rules.
§ 6. Canons in the second or any other interval
    above or below.
§ 7. Canons per tonos.
    2, *The Motion in which the Reply is made.*
§ 8. Three sorts of motions pointed out.
§ 9. Construction of Canons in Reverse motion.
    Also those in mixed, equal, and reverse mo-
    tion.
§ 10. Canons in Retrograde motion.
    Two rules for them.
§ 11. Reverse Retrograde canons.
    Two rules for them.
    An Observation at N. B.
    3, *The different Lengths of Notes in which the
    Reply is made.*
§ 12. Construction of canons by Augmentation or
    Diminution in general.
§ 13. Canons by augmentation.
    Six rules for those by simple augmentation.
    Of those by double or triple augmentation.
§ 14. Canons by Diminution.
    Three rules for them.
§ 15. Those with intermixed, augmented, and di-
    minished replies.
4. *The Number and Quality of the Parts of a Canon.*
§ 16. Construction of those of Real parts.
§ 17. How accompaniments may be set to them.
§ 18. How parts may be added in Thirds.
§ 19. Construction of canons over a given Me-
    lody.
    B. *Of the Construction of Double Canons.*
§ 20. Introduction.
§ 21. Construction of those of Two Subjects.
§ 22. Construction of those of Three or Four
    Subjects.
§ 23. Construction of Compound Canons.
    Varieties to which they shew the way.
§ 24. Of those called polymorphos.
    Method of constructing them.
        II. *Of the Resolution of Canons.*
§ 25. Definition; and a remark.
§ 26. The method of resolving canons.
III. *A Survey of all the Canons given in this Work.*
§ 27. A general Canon per tonos analyzed.
    A. *Canons on the Subject of Fugue I, Plate XIV.*
    The Author's ten Canons explained.
        B. *Canons by Dr. Burney.*
    An Observation.

Canon

Canon I, II, III, explained.

    c. *Canons by Kirnberger.*

An Obfervation.

Canon I, II, explained.

    D. *Canons by Emanuel Bach.*

Two Canons explained.

    E. *Canons by Fafch.*

Three Canons explained.

    F. *Canon by Marpurg.*

One Canon explained.

    G. *Canons on the Royal Subject, by Sebaft. Bach.*

An Obfervation.

Nine Canons explained.

    H. *Canons by Bevin.*

An Obfervation.

Five Canons explained.

    I. *Canons by Handel.*

An Obfervation.

Two Canons explained.

    K. *Canon by C. H. Graun.*

The Canon explained.

CHAPTER X. OF VOCAL MUSIC.

§ 1. Definition, and general Remarks.

    I. *Of Vocal Mufic in general.*

§ 2. Four general Rules given.

Rule I. How paffages ought to be calculated for human voices in general.

    1, In regard to facility.

    2, In regard to fetching breath.

Rule II. How parts fhould be calculated for the fort of voice for which they are fet.

    1, In regard to Compafs.

    2, In regard to Treble, Alto, Tenor, or Bafs.

Rule III. The Harmony and Melody muft correfpond with the Text in its general charaâer.

Rule IV. The Mufic muft correfpond with every particular charaâeriftic of the Text.

    See the three following Sections.

§ 3. Metre of the Text and Rhythm of the Mufic.

    In general, and in particular cafes.

§ 4. Expreffing of Words.

    In general; and in regard to more than one verfe to one and the fame melody.

§ 5. The Sorts of Letters confidered.

    Five Remarks, refpecting Vowels, Diphthongs, and Confonants.

    II. *Of the different Sorts of Vocal Mufic.*

§ 6. Introduction and general explanation.

    A. *Of Recitatives.*

§ 7. Introduction.

§ 8. Two Sorts of Recitatives pointed out.

§ 9. Thofe with a mere Thorough Bafs accompaniment.

Three particulars to be obferved in them, viz.

    1, Time and Rhythm.

    2, Modulation.

    3. Declamation.

§ 10. An Example by *Graun.*

§ 11. How Recitatives fhould be accompanied.

§ 12. Thofe with accompaniments for divers Inftruments.

§ 13. Thofe intermixed with Ariofos.

§ 14. Double, triple, and quadruple Recitatives.

    B. *Of Airs.*

§ 15. Introduction.

    a. *The inventing of a proper Melody.*

§ 16. Three Rules.

b. *The fupporting of a Melody, by a proper Harmony and Accompaniment.*

§ 17. In general.

§ 18. The Harmony of an Air.

    N. B. Refpecting the Accompaniment, fee § 26.

c. *The different Forms in which Airs may be compofed.*

§ 19. Introduction, and two forts pointed out.

§ 20. The Plain Song, and fimple Air.

§ 21. Thofe for one or more pieces of the Text. Examples explained.

§ 22. Other forms of an Air pointed out.

§ 23. Of fingle Airs.

§ 24. Of Airs in connection with other pieces.

§ 25. The number of the Parts of an Air. Duetts, Tercetts, Quartetts, &c.

§ 26. Accompaniments of an Air. Real or duplicate Parts.

§ 27. Of Bravura Songs. Their fancy Cadences.

    c. *Of Choruffes.*

§ 28. In general.

§ 29. Of plain and imitative Choruffes.

§ 30. Of fimple and double ones.

§ 31. Of Semi choruffes.

§ 22. The Accompaniments of Choruffes.

CHAPTER XI. OF INSTRUMENTAL MUSIC.

§ 1. Introduction.

    I. *Of Inftrumental Mufic in general.*

    A. *In regard to every particular Inftrument.*

§ 2. Three particulars pointed out.

§ 3. Compafs and Scale of Inftruments.

    1. *Stringed Bow Inftruments.*

    The Violin.

      Viola.

      Violoncello.

      Violono.

    2. *Wind Inftruments.*

    The Hautboy.

The

The Clarinett.
    German Flute.
    Baſſoon.
    Serpent.
    Trumpet.
    French Horn.
    Trombono.
§ 4. Clefs in which they are written.
§ 5. The nature of their ſounds.
    1, Continuing or ceaſing ſounds.
    2, Loud or ſoft ones.
    3, Harſh or mild ones.
    4, Grave or acute ones.
§ 6. The paſſages for which inſtruments are cal-
    culated.
    B. *Of the Combination of different Inſtruments.*
§ 7. In general.
§ 8. Which Inſtruments agree together.
§ 9. Which produce the beſt variety.
    II. *Of certain Sorts of Inſtrumental Muſic in*
    particular.
      A. *Of that for an Orcheſtra.*
§ 10. Definition and two particulars.
§ 11. What Harmonies are proper for an Or-
    cheſtra.
    Alſo what Melodies and Paſſages.
§ 12. What Combinations of Inſtruments are good.
    1, In the whole.
    2, In particular paſſages.
      B. *Of Pieces for a Military Band.*
§ 13. Introduction.
§ 14. Two particulars conſidered.
    1, The diſtribution of the Harmony.
    2, The uſe that may be made of different In-
    ſtruments.
§ 15. The pieces which are ſet for a military band.
    2, Pieces of Duty.
    The March, the quick March, and the Troop.
    2, Occaſional pieces.
    A remark reſpecting pieces for Sundays.
      c. *Of Pieces for the Organ.*
§ 16. Introduction.
§ 17. Four particulars pointed out.
§ 18. The nature of Organ Sounds.
    N. B. A remark reſpecting Stops.
§ 19. The temperament of the Scale.
    As proper; and improper.
§ 20. The conſtruction of the Fingerboard.
§ 21. A work by *Sebaſtian Bach* mentioned.
§ 22. The different ſets of Keys.
    Manuals; and Pedals.
§ 23. Of Pedals in general.
§ 24. Improper methods of ſupplying the want of
    them.

§ 25. A mere ſupporting baſs for Pedals.
§ 26. Obligato baſſes for Pedals.
§ 27. Middle parts, or an inverted upper part for
    Pedals.
    Accompaniments on 3 or 4 ſets of Manuals.
§ 28. An Organ Trio for only one ſet of Keys.
§ 29. Of the Swell.

CHATEPR XII. OF STYLE AND NA-
    TIONAL MUSIC.

§ 1. Introduction.
§ 2. Of the places for which muſic is compoſed.
    I. *Of the different Styles of Compoſition.*
§ 3. Of the Church Style.
    Pſalmody. Figurative pieces.
§ 4. Of the Chamber Style.
    In Inſtrumental, or vocal pieces.
§ 5. Of the theatrical Style.
    Obſervation reſpecting Dances.
§ 6. Pieces for the open Field.
§ 7. Styles in regard to the different occaſions,
    for which muſic is compoſed.
    An Obſervation reſpecting miſcellaneous
    Concerts.
§ 8. Varieties of the above Styles.
    Antient and modern Style.
    Style of Authors, and of Nations.
    II. *Of National Muſic.*
§ 9. Introduction.
    A. *Of National Muſic in general.*
§ 10. Remarks reſpecting Italian, German, French,
    and Engliſh national Styles.
    A concluſion drawn from the above.
B. *Of characteriſtic National Pieces in particular.*
§ 11. Introduction.
§ 12. Importance of the ſtudy of National pieces.
§ 13. Of the Allemande.
§ 14.   Bouree.
§ 15.   Ciaconne.
§ 16.   Courante.
§ 17. Of the Gavotte.
§ 18.   Gique.
§ 19.   Loure.
§ 20.   Paſſacaille.
§ 21.   Paſſepied.
§ 22.   Paſtorale.
§ 23.   Polonoiſe.
§ 24. Of the Rigaudon.
§ 25.   Sarabande.
§ 26.   Siciliano.
§ 27. Waltzer.
§ 28. Others in general.
§ 29. Concluſion.

INTRODUCTION.

INTRODUCTION.

§ 1. THAT Rules can be given for musical composition, and ought to be attended to, if a musical work shall deserve the name of a piece of art or science, I have endeavoured to shew in the Introduction to my *Essay on Harmony*. But I know that Treatises of that Art are seldom found so useful as diligent Students wish to find them, and this chiefly on account of their not being studied in a proper manner. I shall therefore in this place attempt to point out *a Method*, according to which musical Treatises in general, and my said former and the present Essay in particular, ought to be *studied*, if they shall answer the just expectations of the diligent Reader, and afford him that instruction which is contained in their Doctrines and Examples.

§ 2. But before I proceed to the particulars of the said Method itself, I beg leave to point to *two faults*, which I have discovered in the general method of studying musical Books, viz: *first*, that they are studied *not methodical enough*; and *secondly*, that Students do *not dwell a sufficient time upon every particular* of the Book.

§ 3. The *first* of the said faults is committed when a theoretical work is studied merely according to the order in which it is written.

That it is good and necessary to peruse a Treatise first in the order in which it is written, I endeavour to shew in § 6; but that this is not the only order in which it should be studied, will as I hope follow from what I say in § 7, *& seq.* For, a theoretical work ought to be written systematically, so that its contents become properly connected, and may be easily comprehended and examined in that connection. There must consequently be often things mentioned or explained in one Chapter, which ought to be made practical use of in connection with those of another Chapter; and this renders a methodical *selection* of the contents of a work necessary for that *particular study*, which the practical use of them requires.

As an Example of what I have said in this section, I beg leave to mention my Opera V, entitled *the first Beginning of the Piano Forte*. This work, which I also mention in Chap. I, § 7, contains first the Rudiments of the Art of playing on Keyed Instruments, in a systematical Order; and then a series of practical Lessons and Sonatinas. The former or theoretical part therefore may be compared to a Treatise; and the latter or practical part, shews in what methodical manner the former may be studied, and applied to the practice of playing. That studying the theoretical part of the work in question, without such a methodical selection as the practical part requires, would not make a person a Player, will as I think require no demonstration; but that if the work was only consisting of its practical part,

without

without the theoretical, it would not be calculated to give players a complete knowledge
of the Rudiment of that art, is equally evident.   This example therefore ſhews, how in-
ſufficient it is to ſtudy theoretical works merely in the order in which they are written; and
that if they were written in ſuch Leſſons as their doctrines ſhould be ſtudied and tried in
practice, they could not be ſyſtematical Treatiſes.   The latter alſo appears from *Hiller's*
Guide to Singing, (Anweiſung Qum Geſange, Leipzig 1774,) which is a very excellent
theoretical and practical work, written in Leſſons, but no regular or ſyſtematical Treatiſe.

§ 4.   The *ſecond* Fault mentioned in § 2, ariſes from a Students expecting of a book
powers which no Author can give it; I mean the powers of rendering him perfect in the
theory and practice of what the book teaches, if he but reads it till he perfectly comprehends every thing it contains.   According to the ſaid expectation therefore a muſical Treatiſe is laid aſide as *done* with, and perhaps condemned as not being ſufficient for the ſtudy
of what it teaches, when its Reader is but juſt prepared to *begin* ſtudying it in that methodical manner, which I have mentioned in § 3; or is at leaſt hurried through, as faſt as it
can be comprehended, without that patient perſeverance which is required for learning to
bring its Doctrines into practice.

But how is it poſſible to learn from a Book, even from the cleareſt and moſt inſtructive
one, any Science, and particularly that of Muſic, ſo faſt as from a ſkilful Maſter?   For the
Book cannot lay its Rules and Practices before the Student ſo as he wants them; but it lies
open before him by whole chapters, and frequently offers to him firſt, what according to
his capacity he wants laſt.   A Book can alſo not directly tell the Student, what he miſun-
derſtands, or what faults he makes in his practices; but it ſuffers him to proceed, right or
wrong, as he does it.   Theſe and more diſadvantages are not met with under a ſkilful in-
ſtruction by Mouth; and yet it is well known that a conſiderable time is required under
the tuition of the greateſt Maſter, to make the moſt able Student any ways proficient in
muſical Compoſition.   It is therefore natural, that by the above Method of ſtudying, the
moſt attentive Perſon finds little improvement from the Study of muſical Treatiſes.

§ 5.   The *Method* now, which I preſume to propoſe is: that the Study and Practice of
Harmony and Compoſition ſhould be divided into the following *two principal parts*, viz:
firſt the *general ſtudy* of a whole Treatiſe, in the order in which it is written; ſecondly,
the *particular ſtudy and practice* of the three chief branches of the Art of Compoſition, viz:
Simple Counterpoint, Double Counterpoint and Imitation, and Whole Pieces.

§ 6.   The ſaid *general ſtudy* of a whole Treatiſe requires: the reading and conſidering
of it in the order in which it is written; and an attention to the Nature of its Doctrines
and Examples, and to the Connection in which the one ſtands with the other.   It muſt be
continued till the Reader has a clear general Idea of the whole, and of the nature and uſe
of what is contained in the work; and is therefore the foundation of the whole.

§ 7.   The *particular Study and Practic* pointed out in § 5, begins with Simple Counterpoint, of which I have treated in Chap. XIII, of my Eſſay on Harmony.

The

The practice of it requires a *previous Study* of all that belongs to the Scale; to Intervals; to the conftruction of Intervals one over the other, and their progreffion one after another; to Chords; and to the Signatures of Chords in Thorough Bafs. All thefe particulars therefore a Student may make himfelf acquainted with according to the firft Eight Chapters of my Effay on Harmony, by reading every doctrine they contain fo long and fo often, till he perfectly comprehends it, and till he can immediately recollect and explain the Examp s I have given to it; or better, till he can demonftrate it by Examples of his own invention.

After the faid previous ftudy, the *Practice* of fimple counterpoint begins, which comprehends: firft, the expreffing of a *given harmony* in a certain number of parts; fecondly, the *inventing of a regular harmony*, and expreffing it in any fixed number of parts.

§ 8. The *firft* fort of practices mentioned juft now, or that of expreffing a *given Harmony* in regular parts, muft be divided into the following branches, viz: firft, that of writing *Chords in clofe Harmony* to a figured bafs; and fecondly, that of writing *melodious parts in difperfed Harmony*, either to a figured Bafs and another given Melody, or to a figured Bafs alone.

1. To write *Chords* to a figured Bafs requires, befides the previous ftudy in § 7, an intimate acquaintance with the rules of Thorough Bafs, viz: firft, to which note of a well figured Bafs a Chord belongs, (fee my Effay on Harmony, Chap. VIII.); fecondly, how high or how low the chords may be fet. This latter depends partly upon the Rules I have given in Chap. III, § 5, of the faid Effay; and partly upon the confideration, how high or how low the Bafs, or a Principal melody to which the Chords fhall be an accompaniment, is fet.

The practice in queftion fhould begin with *four* regular parts; that is to fay, with Chords of three parts to the Bafs. A reafon why I recommend the beginning with four parts fee in my Effay on Harmony, Chap. XIII, § 4. The Chords muft be written in clofe harmony, or fo as they are played in a regular Thorough Bafs accompaniment. See them written in this manner in the Examples at Plate 7, of the quoted Effay. From four parts a Student muft proceed to *fewer*, and to *more* regular parts; but never fewer or more parts muft be intermixed promifcuoufly, or for want of the knowledge how to write in a fixed number of regular parts.

2. To write melodious parts in *difperfed harmony* ought to be begun with fetting firft two, and afterwards one or three regular middle parts to a Bafs and a given Melody; and afterwards it ought to be continued with fetting both, middle and upper parts, or only upper parts alone, to the fame Bafs and given Melody. In all thefe cafes the harmony muft be ftrictly regular according to the figures of the Bafs, as well as every part regular and melodious in itfelf.

In both the above practices the beginning muft be made with plain Baffes and fimple Harmonies, like as in the Examples to Chap. XIII, § 5, of my Effay on Harmony; and the Student muft progreffively advance towards figurative Melodies and complicate Harmonies. But never a fucceeding practice muft be begun, before the Student is fufficiently perfect in the preceding.

e   § 9. The

§ 9. The *fecond* fort of practices mentioned in § 6, is that of *inventing a regular harmony*. It may be begun and continued in the following progreffive order, viz: *firft* by figuring a given regular Bafs in different manners, and expreffing the different harmonies in parts, according to the methods fhewn in § 8, under No. 1 & 2; *fecondly*, by fetting different figured Baffes to a given upper part, fo as to make a regular harmony of two parts, or to be calculated for the addition of one or more parts, which may be added to the Bafs and given Melody according to the directions given in § 8, No. 2; *thirdly*, by inventing harmonious and melodious Periods, without any given Bafs or upper part. Thefe practices require a previous ftudy of Cadences, of Modulation, of Time, and of Rhythm; of which I have treated in my Effay on Harmony, Chap. IX, X, XI, XII.

§ 10. After all the above practices, and when the Student finds himfelf fufficiently fluent in each fort of them, he may indulge himfelf with attempting fhort Pieces of a certain eftablifhed Form and Character; fuch as Minuetts, Marches, or others of thofe I mention in Chap. XII, § 13, *& feq.* The reafon why I propofe the faid pieces, follows from § 12 of the fame Chapter; for, they affift him in inventing, which he wants, till he has practice and courage enough to invent without this or any other affiftance. But the more patiently he can ftill fubmit to that ftudy which I am now going to point out, and the lefs he diverts his attention from it, by compofing too foon, the greater muft be his fatisfaction at laft.

§ 11. The *fecond* great branch of the particular Study and Practice pointed out in § 5, is the ftudy of *Double Counterpoint* and *Imitation*; and its importance in compofition will as I truft follow, from what I have faid in my Effay on Harmony, Chap. XIV, § 1, near the end; and in the prefent Effay at Chap. V, § 1, and Chap. VIII, § 2. The progreffive order in which the different parts of the ftudy in queftion fhould be gone through, is as follows:

Firft, a Student may read the chapter of Double Counterpoint in my Effay on Harmony, fo long, till he perfectly underftands every Doctrine and Example it contains. Afterwards he muft practife writing Double Counterpoints in all Intervals, and in all forts of Imitations, as fhewn in the faid Chapter; and this practice he muft alfo continue till he is familiar with it.

Secondly, he may read the chapter of Imitation in the quoted Effay, with the fame attention as that of Double Counterpoint. And afterwards he fhould take Subjects of different Lengths and of different Qualities, from Sonatas and other pieces of great Compofers, but particularly from pieces which he is not much acquainted with; and to thofe he fhould try to make Imitations, yet without regard to putting them in fuch connection as in a formal piece. The faid imitations he fhould then compare with thofe of the Authors of the different fubjects, to fee whether he had the fame or other fancies than they, and what forts of the beft Imitations he has perhaps not hit upon.

§ 12. The final ftudy and practice of all that relates to fimple and double Counterpoint, and the preparatory one to that of writing whole pieces, is united in the *analyzing* of all

forts

forts of mufical pieces. This very important branch of the ftudy of Compofition fhould not be neglected. For, on the one hand it teaches us how to difcover the perfections or imperfections of the compofitions of other Authors; and on the other hand it enables us to compofe fo, as to be able of accounting for every period or note we write ourfelves.

I have therefore taken particular pains to make the diligent Reader acquainted with the ftudy and practice in queftion, by analyzing various Examples, and for various purpofes. For in my Effay on Harmony, Chap. XIII, § 6, 9, and 11, I have fhewn how to analyze the Harmony of fimple Counterpoint; in § 22, of the fame Chapter—Harmony in regard to the Fundamental Bafs; in the whole of Chap. XIV—Double Counterpoints; and in the prefent Effay every Example from Plate I. to Plate XLIX. fome more and fome lefs, according to the different occafions, as the Text will explain.

As another Example for the purpofe in queftion I beg leave to mention my *Symphony* with *analytical explanations*, Op. VII, which as it would have taken up too much room in the prefent Effay, I have publifhed feparately as an introductory piece to it. The particulars explained by the analyfis, are: the Subjects and Imitations; the Modulations; the Counterpoint Inverfions; and the Rhythmical Order contained in that Symphony. And though I know, that in point of fancy, and humourous elaboration, the piece in queftion ftands far behind the Symphonies of *Haydn*, and other great compofers; yet I prefume to think it calculated to exemplify *fimple regularity*, and the various manners in which longer or fhorter *fubjects may be treated*. Thefe I have found to be important objects for a young Compofer; and I do not doubt that a perfon who is once perfect in them, will find it eafy to proceed to more bold and fanciful pieces. More refpecting this Symphony fee in Chap. I, § 11, and Chap. VI, § 30.

§ 13. The *third* or laft great branch of the particular Study and Practice pointed out in § 5, is that of writing *complete pieces*. It requires a *previous ftudy* of the following particulars, viz: firft a *general ftudy* of the whole prefent Effay, according to the direction given in § 6; fecondly the *particular* ftudy of Chap. I, and of that Chapter to which a piece to be compofed belongs, alfo of thofe Chapters of my Effay on Harmony, which have not yet been much attended to, viz: that of Time, Rhythm, Variation, Fancy, and the antient Ecclefiaftical Modes.

After the faid previous ftudy, the Student fhould fix upon a *fhort and fimple form* of that fort of pieces which he intends to practife firft or moft; that is to fay: upon a Sonatina or fhort Sonata, rather than upon a Symphony for an Orcheftra or a Concerto; upon a fhort fimple Fugue or Canon, rather than upon an elaborate Double Fugue or Canon; and upon a fimple Air, rather than upon a Bravura Song or a Chorus.

Of the piece he has thus fixed upon he muft make a *previous Plan*, according to all the particulars pointed out in Chap. I. of this Effay; and to affift himfelf in inventing, as well as to compofe from the firft attempt nothing but pieces that are fpeaking and interefting, he may plan it as one of the pieces defcribed in Chap. XII, § 13, *& feq.* or after any other piece which he particularly admires. According to that Plan he may then elaborate the Piece. But he fhould never adhere fo clofely to the form or character of a piece which he

has

has chofen for a pattern, as merely to copy or counterfeit the fame, and not freely and ingenioufly to invent in imitation of it. For the former would deferve cenfure, when the latter has been always thought honourable.

From fhort and fimple pieces a Student may gradually advance to *longer* and more *complicate* ones, till he finds himfelf able to attempt any piece he choofes.

§ 13. The above is the Method I prefume to propofe for a proper and methodical ftudy of mufical Treatifes in general, and of my Effay on Harmony and Compofition in particular. Should it at firft fight appear tedious and troublefome, I beg leave to obferve: *firft*, that I hope the diligent Reader will not find it fo when he tries it with proper attention, becaufe one ftudy and practice leads progreffively into the other, and facilitates the fame; and *fecondly*, that I do not doubt but the certainty of purfuing a method of ftudying which cannot finally difappoint his expectation of improvement, will make him regardlefs of that real trouble, which the perfeverance of attending to it may coft him.

To the faid confiderations I beg leave ftill to add: that though I have taken pains to write my two Effays in queftion as plain and intelligible as I poffibly could, yet I know how difficult it is for any perfon to make fuch a *Beginning* in the ftudy of Harmony, as to lay a fure foundation in it. If therefore a diligent Student can have the affiftance of a fkilful Mafter, he fhould not refufe it himfelf in the ftudy of fimple counterpoint, being the firft and fundamental ftudy pointed out in § 7; and afterwards he may try how much he can help himfelf without a Mafter.

§ 14. I conclude this Introduction with remarking: that though I have in § 4, fhewn fome difadvantages which the moft attentive Student meets with in the ftudy of mufical Treatifes; and though I muft confefs, that ftudying a treatife under the guidance of an able Mafter, cannot but fave much time and trouble: yet that I prefume, good Treatifes are the only means by which a ftudent can obtain a compleat and clear Idea of all that belongs to Compofition, or by which he can recollect in a fyftematical order what he has learnt in another order from a Mafter.

According to the above confideration therefore I may flatter myfelf, that if the prefent Effay fhall not be found undeferving the approbation of the difcerning Reader, it will be ufeful, not only for *learning* compofition, but alfo as a companion to thofe who have already made fome progrefs in that art.

AN ESSAY

AN

ESSAY

ON PRACTICAL

MUSICAL COMPOSITION.

CHAPTER I. OF THE PLAN FOR A PIECE TO BE COMPOSED.

I. *Of the Plan in General.*

§ 1. COMPOSING a piece of Mufic, requires, like executing any other piece of art. or fcience, a previous confideration of its intended *nature* and *quality ;* of the *purpofes* for which it fhall ferve; and of the *means* by which it can be made to anfwer its intended nature and purpofes, in the moft proper manner. According to the faid confideration a previous calculation of its outlines and *general* charaćteriftics muft not only be made, but in writing the piece itfelf, unremitted attention muft be paid to render every *particular* of the piece conformable to the general idea of it. And this is what I call forming a *Plan* of the piece; and executing it accordingly.

II. *Particulars in the faid Plan for a Mufical Piece.*

§ 2. In regard to the *nature* of a mufical piece, there muft be confidered : *what fort* of a piece it fhall be, whether an opera, a concerto, a fymphony, a fonata, or whatever elfe it may be ; and in regard to its *quality :* whether it fhall be long and grand, or fhort and fimple ; for an orcheftra or not. Of the former, or the different *forts* of pieces I fhall fpeak in all the fucceeding Chapters of this work. I therefore proceed here immediately to their *qualities* as follows :

A. LENGTH AND DISPOSITION OF A PIECE.

§ 3. Though fome charaćteriftic dance tunes muft be compofed according to a certain prefcribed *length*, yet in general a compofer is at liberty to make his pieces as long as he

B

thinks

thinks proper. But even in the latter cafe it muſt be previouſly conſidered, firſt how long the piece to be compoſed may be *in the whole,* and ſecondly what proportional length may be introduced in its *component parts.*

In the *whole,* a piece may be either of a common length, *i. e.* as long as ſimilar pieces generally are; or longer, or ſhorter, than uſual.

And in its *component parts* a piece may conſiſt of one or more movements; and every movement of one or more ſections.

§ 4. According to the ſaid length of a piece, its *diſpoſition* muſt be made, and it muſt be previouſly conſidered and determined upon: firſt, *how long* the piece ſhall be in the whole; ſecondly, *how many movements* there will be proper in it, and what relation and proportion one ſhall bear to the other; thirdly, how many *ſections* there ſhall be in every movement, and what connection there ſhall be between them; fourthly, what *ſubjects, periods,* and *paſſages,* will be moſt proper for the length and intended character of every particular movement and ſection.

More of the length of every particular ſort of pieces, ſee in their reſpective Chapters.

B. MODULATION OF A PIECE.

§ 5. There are two particulars to be obſerved in regard to the object in queſtion, viz: firſt the modulation of *every movement;* ſecondly the relation of key and mode between ſeveral *movements in connection.*

§ 6. Reſpecting the *firſt* of the ſaid particulars, every movement is conſidered as a piece by itſelf, and has three principal objects in its modulation, viz: firſt the *ſetting out;* ſecondly the *elaboration;* thirdly the *return* of the modulation. Theſe I ſhall endeavour to explain in regard to the different lengths of pieces.

§ 7. In *ſhort pieces,* where there is no room for a particular elaboration, the ſaid three objects are not always diſtinguiſhed, becauſe the piece either remains entirely in one and the ſame key, or it conſiſts only of a *ſetting out* from the key to one of its related keys, and a *return* from thence to the original key. This I will exemplify by referring to my Op. V, entitled *The firſt Beginning on the Piano Forte,* &c. the pieces of which I ſhall divide into nine different claſſes, as it appears under the following numbers.

1, In all the twelve *Leſſons* from page 15, to page 24 of the ſaid work, ſee *Preludes* of one ſection, which begin, remain, and end, in the ſame key; and the ſame in the *Moderato* of Leſſon III.

2, Pieces of two ſhort ſections, which both begin and end in the principal key, ſee in Leſſon 1, 2, 4, 5, and 7; and two alternate pieces, each of two ſections of the ſame quality, are frequently met with, as minuets or cotillions, but they ought to be ſet with much judgment if they ſhall not become tireſome in effect.

3, In the *Allegretto* page 37 and 38, ſee the firſt ſection begin and end in the ſame key as before; the ſecond ſection alſo begins in the ſame key, but the firſt period ends with the half cadence on the dominante, on which it afterwards dwells for another whole period, and then makes a concluſion by repeating the firſt ſection, in the key again.

4, In the *Adagio,* page 34, the firſt ſection is the ſame as above; but the ſecond ſection begins with the leading chord, on which it dwells through four bars, and then concludes like the laſt piece (page 38).

5, Pieces

5, Pieces in which the firſt ſection ends with the leading chord, and the ſecond ſection begins with the ſame chord, but ends in the key again, ſee in *Leſſon* 6, 9, 11, and the *Moderato* page 32. The accidental ſharps or naturals in the two latter ones, make no difference in this explanation. (See my *Eſſay on Har.* Chap. X, § 5.)

6, In the pieces page 27, 30, 31, 33, and 35, ſee the firſt ſection end in the key; and the ſecond ſection begin in the ſame key, but make a digreſſion to the fifth of the ſcale, and afterwards conclude in the key again.

7, A piece in which the firſt ſection alſo ends in the key, but the ſecond begins in the fifth, and ends in the key, is the *Moderato* in *Leſſon* 8.

8, Pieces in which the firſt ſection ends with the leading chord, and the ſecond begins with the ſame chord as chord of a key note, but ends in the key, ſee in the *Menuetto* page 22, and *Allegretto* page 24.

9, In the pieces page 28 and 29, ſee the firſt ſection end in the fifth of the ſcale, and the ſecond begin in the ſame ſubſtituted key, but end as before.

N. B. In all the above caſes the piece conſiſted of a *ſetting out* from the key, and a *return* to the key. In thoſe at Nos. 1, 2, 3, 4, 6, and 7, where each ſection ends in the key, the ſetting out is from the beginning to the middle of each ſection, and the return from thence to the end of the ſection, which makes every ſection like a piece by itſelf. But in the Moderato, No. 5, the *ſetting out* is from the beginning to the end of the firſt ſection, and the *return* begins after a ſhort *elaboration* at the middle of the ſecond ſection.

The ſame as with theſe ſhort pieces it is with thoſe of any length. For they conſiſt of nothing but the deſcribed ſetting out, elaboration, and return, and are only prolonged in the different manners I ſhall ſhew below. (See § 9, & ſeq.) Extraordinary caſes naturally make an exception.

§ 8. But though the piece ſhall be *ſhort*, the ſetting out need not always be to a nearly related key, as in all the examples of the laſt §; it may be to a key that is more or leſs *foreign* to the original one. This has a good effect in *characteriſtic* pieces; or alſo in thoſe, which are like a *ſubject* for more elaboration in pieces of ſome length.

1, An example of the former ſee in my above work Opera V, page 36, where the firſt ſection begins in *major*, and the ſetting out ends the firſt ſection with a concluſion in the fifth, ſuſpended by the *minor* ſixth, which makes the *minor* of the principal key to be expected; but the ſecond ſection begins in the third of the principal key, *minor*, and after a little elaboration the regular return to the key is introduced and makes the concluſion.

At that place I muſt alſo take notice of the ſhort *Adagio* which follows at page 37. This is nothing but a tranſitory period, which conſequently need not return to the key, from which it ſet out.

N. B. The ſame muſt be underſtood of other ſhort movements in the courſe of long pieces, which do not ſet out and end in the ſame key and mode.

2, An example of the latter ſort, or a piece calculated for more elaboration, ſee at Plate I. of this work, No. 1. It is the laſt preſto of the quintett I have written but not yet publiſhed; in this the fourth and fifth bar of the firſt, and the twelfth and thirteenth of the ſecond ſection, ought to be taken notice of. A ſimilar piece is the laſt preſto in *Haydn's* Sonata V, Opera 14; and is remarkable for the ſtrange but fine concluſion, both of the firſt and ſecond ſection. Both theſe pieces are afterwards varied, viz: the firſt with a ſucceeding piece alternately; and the ſecond by itſelf.

§ 9.

§ 9. When pieces shall be *longer* than those of two short sections I have explained above, they may be planned in two different manners, viz : first by making them of *more* than two *short sections* ; and secondly, by making them of one, two, or more, *long sections.*

N. B. By *Piece* is here still understood, every *movement,* which begins and ends like a piece by itself.

§ 10. Those of *more* than two *short sections*, may be set as follows, viz : of *three* short sections : first, so that all three set out and end in the principal key ; secondly, so that the first and second sections both end in the fifth of the scale, and the third section in the key ; thirdly, so that the first section ends in the key, the second in its fifth, and the third in the key again. Also in more varieties of modulation which follow from what has been said above.

Of *four* short sections, pieces may also be set so, that every section begins and ends in the principal key, of which sort I know a beautiful minuet for dancing ; but more generally the four sections are divided into twice two, or two alternate pieces of two sections each : such as a march and trio ; a minuet and trio ; or as the first movement in *Sonatina* 1, 2, 4, and 5, of my above-mentioned Opera V. These may stand, either in the same, or in a related key and mode, as will appear from those works of good composers where they have been introduced.

Of *five* or more short sections, are in general those pieces called *Rondos.* In these the first section begins and ends in the principal key ; the second section begins either in the same key and modulates to the fifth, or begins in the fifth at once and ends with the leading chord of the principal key ; the third section is nothing else but a repetition of the first ; the fourth section begins and ends in another related key ; and the fifth, is a repetition of the first again. Pieces of this sort which consist but of the three first sections, and without separating the second from the third, are those at page 27, 30, 31, 33, 35, and 37, in my *Opera* V, to which I have referred above, in § 7. But the principal part, or subject of Rondos, need not always be of one section only ; it may also be of two sections, like the last presto in my *Symphony*, Opera VII. Of this sort see a Rondo in *Vanhall*'s two sonatas for two performers Opera XXXII, the last piece, which consists of a subject of two sections, followed by alternate pieces of two sections, and a transitory section to each of them, so that the whole consists of twenty-two sections, in the following manner, viz : first the subject, being two sections ; followed by two sections in the fourth of the scale, and a transitory one, (makes 5 ;) secondly, the subject, and three sections in the principal key *minore*, (makes 10 ;) thirdly, the subject, and three sections in the fifth of the scale, (makes 15 ;) fourthly, the subject, and three sections in the sixth of the scale *minore*, (makes 20 ;) lastly the subject two sections, (makes 22.) The sections between the subjects also touch on their nearest related keys, in such a manner, that the whole is a beautiful series of natural modulations, and far from becoming tedious by its number of sections.

As a piece or movement of *seven* sections, which all stand in one and the same key and mode, I mention the first part of my *Shipwreck*, Opera VI. It is no Rondo, but a Moderato of one long section, which has been reduced to smaller ones, by the interspersion of two other short pieces, of two sections each. How short pieces of one or two sections may be prolonged by *variation*, I have sufficiently shewn in my Essay on Har. Chap. XVI.

§ 11. Pieces or movements of *one* or *two long sections*, require a setting out and a return, like those of the preceding description, and are only different from them in the elaboration. This I will endeavour to shew, by going over the whole plan of modulation in an elaborate movement.

1, In its *outlines*, a long movement is generally divided into *two sections*. The first, when the piece is in major, ends in the fifth of the scale, and the second, in the key; but when the piece is in minor, the first section generally ends in the third of the scale, and the second in the key. (See my Essay on Har. Chap. X, § 9.) These two sections are either separated by a *double bar* or *repeat*, or not distinguished by any particular mark; which latter commonly is the case in concertos or those pieces which would become too long by a repetition. But though pieces are not calculated for a repetition, the above distinction of two sections is required in them, if they shall create an expectation at the beginning, and give a satisfaction at the end; without which they cannot be truly entertaining. (Of those that are divided into *more* elaborate sections, see § 12.)

2, In regard to *other particulars*, the said two sections admit, besides a regular setting out, and a return, *three sorts of elaboration*, all of which may be distributed in the following manner, viz:

Each *section*, may be divided into two *subsections*; which in the whole makes *four* subsections.

The *first* subsection must contain the setting out from the key towards its fifth in major, or third in minor; and it may end with the chord of the key note or its fifth, but the latter is better. The *second* subsection comprehends a first sort of elaboration, consisting of a more natural modulation than that of the third subsection; it may be confined to the fifth or third of the key only, or also touch on some related, or even non-related keys if only no formal digression is made to any key but the said fifth in major, or third in minor. The *third* subsection or beginning of the second section, comprehends a second sort of elaboration, consisting of digressions to all those keys and modes which shall be introduced besides that of the fifth (or third;) and being the place for those abrupt modulations, or enharmonic changes, which the piece admits or requires. The *fourth* subsection contains the return to the key, with a third sort of elaboration, similar to that of the first subsection.

All the above I will endeavour to demonstrate, according to the first Allegro of my *Analyzed Symphony* Op. VII, viz:

First subsection: The piece begins with two subjects in the key, which make a period of eight bars. The subjects are repeated, the second one with an extension, and end with the chord of the Dominante; from bar 9 to 24. *Second* subsection: the said first sort of Elaboration, which there begins, remains, and ends, in the fifth of the key; from bar 25 to 80. *Third* subsection: the said second sort of Elaboration, containing three digressions which are pointed out in the analysis of the piece itself; from bar 1, after the Repeat, to bar 56. *Fourth* subsection: the return to the key, with a short previous digression to its fourth, by the third sort of Elaboration mentioned above; from bar 57 to 128.

The above is the plan of modulation, which will be found attended to in most sonatas, symphonies, and concertos, as well as elaborate airs and chorusses, of all great Composers, because it is the most reasonable one, and the most adapted to the nature of our attention, and our feeling, hitherto known. But it may be *varied* almost to the infinite. For, the different sections and subsections of a piece may be of any reasonable variety of length, and the said sorts of modulation and elaboration may be diversified without end,

as

as it alfo appears from the compofition of great Compofers, and will require no demonftration.

§ 12. From the above plan of modulation are in fome meafure *excepted ;* firft pieces which contain *three, four,* or *more* long fections ; fecondly Rondos; and thirdly Fugues.

Of the *firft* fort is the firft movement in *Haydn's* third fonata Op. LXXV, which confifts of five fections. But upon examination it will be found, that it depends on the fame plan, which I have mentioned § 10, refpecting pieces of more than two fhort fections.

The *fecond* fort, or Rondos, may be divided into *proper* and *improper* ones. The *former* are thofe, in which the firft fection always returns in the principal key, either in its original form, or varied like as in the example I give in Chap. II, § 9, under *Bach's* Sonatas with varied reprizes. (See Plate V ;) and the *latter,* thofe in which the fubject or firft fection alfo appears in keys to which a digreffion may be made. A beautiful example of this fort fee at Plate I, No. 2. It is taken from *Eman. Bach's* firft fet of three Sonatas with Accompaniments, *Leipzig* 1776; and I have added to it an explanation of the courfe of its modulation. A lefs elaborate piece of the fame fort is a *Tempo di Gavotta* in my Sonata IV, Op. II.

Of the modulation of *Fugues,* fee Chap. VI, § 24.

§ 13. In regard to the *fecond* particular mentioned at § 5, I muft now fhew the required relation of key and mode, between the feveral *movements* of a piece.

The greateft relation of key and mode naturally is : when all the different movements of a piece ftand in *one and the fame* key and mode, like as in my *Analyzed Symphony,* Op. VI. But in pieces of this fort, a good *variety* of the *forms* of the different movements is required, as otherwife they become tedious, on account of the continual famenefs of key and mode that is felt in them.

More ufeful therefore, than the faid relation, is that : where a good *variety* of key and mode is united with a proper relation. This may be done as follows : in pieces of *two* movements, the firft may be in minor and the laft in major, which produces a fpirited finifh. The firft movement in major, and the fecond in minor, produces in general a melancholy effect.

In pieces of *three* and *more* movements, the firft and laft fhould be fet in the fame *key,* to preferve the impreffion of one and the fame piece, but they may be different in *mode,* the fame as in thofe of *two* movements. And the one or more movements between the firft and laft, may be fet in any variety of related keys and modes ; which a judicious fancy can fuggeft. Fine examples of pieces of *four* movements are moft of *Haydn's* Symphonies. And as one of *more than four* movements I mention my *Shipwreck* Op. VI, which confifts of *nine* movements, related to each other in the following manner, viz : The firft is in D major ; the fecond, alfo in D major ; the third, in A minor ; the fourth, in D minor ; the fifth, in D major ; the fixth, in G minor ; the feventh, in G major ; the eighth, in D major ; and the ninth, likewife in D major.

C. CHARACTER OF A PIECE.

§ 14. A piece may be compofed, either in a certain *prefcribed* character, or its character may be *optional.* But in both cafes it ought to have fome *general* character, which receives its fhades and lights from *particular* characteriftics.

Of

Of the *former* fort, or of a prefcribed character, are: *George Benda's* Ariadne of Naxos; *Eman. Bach's* fonata which reprefents a converfation between a Melancholicus and a Sanguinicus; *Haydn's* feven words of Chrift; *Clementi's* La Chaffe; and, if I may be permitted to add it, my *Shipwreck*, mentioned § 13. Alfo characterific Overtures; and all thofe Vocal pieces, in which the mufic properly expreffes the words.

Of the *latter* fort, or of an optional character, are all well compofed fonatas, fymphonies, concertos, or thofe pieces of any other defcription over which no certain character is pointed out.

§ 15. The *means*, by which prefcribed as well as other characterifics may be brought into a mufical piece, are: Time, Rhythm, Subjects, Modulation, Imitation, Variation, the nature and management of Voices or Inftruments, and any thing elfe which can produce ufeful varieties. For, each of thefe particulars is in fome meafure calculated to produce ftrong characterifics of various forts, by itfelf; and in their combinations, particularly when words are fet to mufic, they may be rendered expreffive, not only of any thing that is conceivable by Sound or Motion, but even of many paffions of the foul.

In *what manner* the faid means muft be ufed for producing characterific expreffions, the intended limits of this work will not permit me to venture upon. But fome ufeful hints may be found in my Effay on Har. Chap. XII, (of Rhythm,) and in Chap. XVI, (of Variation) § 7, with the Examples Plate XXXVI, No. 2; which, with an attentive ftudy of the works of great compofers, will fufficiently affift an ingenious ftudent, to help himfelf in moft cafes, by his own confideration.

But I muft endeavour to fhew, *what characterifics*, of thofe that might be expreffed, are proper or improper to be brought into a mufical piece, viz: Proper to be expreffed, can only be fuch characterifics, which a Poet might fet a ftrefs upon, if he was to write a poem on the thought or fentiment to be expreffed in mufic; and improper: all thofe which, if the Poet was to fet a particular ftrefs upon them, would be cenfurable in the poem. All mere by-thoughts, or trifling circumftances, are therefore not to be expreffed at all, or at leaft not fo much as the principal thoughts of a fentiment; and the worft would be, to exprefs mean or indelicate things.

How eafily a lively imagination may be led too far in this refpect, appears from fome compofitions of great *Handel* himfelf, particularly from a chorus in Ifrael in Egypt, where he carefully expreffes the fwarming of flies, and the crawling of other infects, which I mention merely as a caution to young compofers, and fhould not have taken notice of it, had not other authors done it before me.

§ 16. With particular regard to the *optional* characterifics of a piece, there muft be confidered what degree of Gravenefs or Vivacity, or what other general characterifics a piece to be compofed ought properly to have; and the Movement and Meafure, Subjects, Air, and Harmony of the piece, muft be calculated accordingly, fo that it may admit of imitations and other elaborations fuitable to the intended character.

When a piece confifts of *two or more movements*, a previous calculation muft be made of the variety as well, as the relation of character between thofe movements, as I have partly fhewn in § 13; fo that one general character may be found in the whole, and yet particular characterifics in every movement, to fet each other off by a judicious variety.

And in a *collection* of fonatas, or other pieces of one fort, there ought likewife to be fuch a relation between the different pieces, that they are fomething fimilar in length,

style

ftyle and form, but various in Character and Elaboration; and it is beft if they ftand in
fuch a relation of key and mode, that they may be played in the order they ftand, without a tranfitory interlude, as fome players would neglect the faid interludes, and others
not be fuccefsful in the extempore invention of them.

All the above will be found attended to in the works of good compofers, except the
laft, (the relation of key and mode between the different fonatas of one collection) which
fome neglect.

D.   THE INSTRUMENTS OR VOICES FOR WHICH A PIECE IS TO BE COMPOSED.

§ 17. The two particulars which muft be attended to in planning a piece, refpecting
the one or more inftruments or voices for which it is to be fet, are: firft, that it may be
practicable in its principal as well as other parts; fecondly, that its refpective inftruments
or voices may be ufed *to advantage*.

This requires a proper knowledge of their nature, and treatment, according to which
not only the *fubjects* of the piece, but in many cafes alfo its *key* muft be judicioufly chofen. Refpecting Subjects fee Chap. III, § 12; and that the key muft alfo be confidered,
both on account of the nature of certain inftruments, and of their temperament, needs no
demonftration.

More belonging to the object in queftion follows from Chap. II, III, and XI.

E.   THE NUMBER OF PARTS, PARTICULAR PERFORMERS, &c.

§ 18. As fome paffages are calculated more for a folo, others for a duo, trio, &c. it is
neceffary to have the *number of parts* in view, for which a piece fhall be compofed, and
to make the previous difpofition accordingly; which will require no further demonftration.

§ 19. If a piece fhall be compofed for a certain particular *performer* or fort of performers, attention muft be paid to their ability or their capacity. For, fome fingers have a
greater or leffer compafs or ftrength of voice than others of the fame clafs, or a greater or
leffer perfection in certain paffages: this muft be attended to if a piece is exprefsly compofed for them. In the fame manner, pieces for keyed inftruments may be calculated for
one who can reach farther than players in general; or for one who can not reach fo much
as an octave. Of the latter fort are my pieces for *The firft Beginning*, Opera V, in which
no more than a fixth is required to be reached throughout.

§ 20. The particular *place*, or *occafion*, for which a piece may be intended, is the laft
I fhall point out for the purpofe in queftion; in regard to which there muft be confidered: firft, or in general, whether it fhall be for the Church, the Chamber, the Theatre,
or an open Field, of which I fhall fpeak in Chap. XII; fecondly, or in particular, whether it is to be for general ufe, or for fome extraordinary purpofe or occafion, and what
particular qualities or characteriftics are required in each of the faid cafes.

§ 21. That a proper attention to all the above particulars, is ufeful and neceffary in
making the plan for a piece to be compofed, if it fhall deferve to be called a piece of art,
and have an intended effect, will I hope be allowed; I therefore only add, that making
fuch

fuch a previous plan, cannot but facilitate the elaboration of the piece itfelf, and infure its effect, which alfo will require no demonftration.

CHAPTER II. OF SONATAS.

§ 1. *Sonatas, Symphonies,* and *Concertos,* are in fo far *one like the other,* that they may be fet of the fame length, and confift of the fame number of connected Movements, of one, two, or more fections each; and alfo that they muft be compofed according to the General Plan, and all the Particulars pointed out in Chapter I.

But they are *different,* in regard to their Nature, and to the Purpofes for which they are ufed. This is moft diftinguifhable in their characteriftic form, and lefs fo, in thofe forms, where the one becomes fimilar to the other.

The above I fhall endeavour to fhew and exemplify in the prefent, and the two following Chapters.

I. *Of Sonatas in General.*

§ 2. A *Sonata* is: a piece, chiefly calculated for *one performer* to *each part;* and may be compared in Inftrumental Mufic, to what an *Air* is in Vocal Mufic.

Its *characteriftics* therefore are: a finer fort of Subjects, and a higher finifhed, or more delicate, and embellifhed Elaboration, than what would be proper for Symphonies, or Tuttis in Concertos. It ought to be melodious in every part, yet, as *Emanuel Bach* fays, without confining its melodies to what the human voice can execute; and richly harmonious in the combination of its parts, without betraying an anxiety for ftrange, or learned modulation.

§ 3. Sonatas may be fet of different lengths, and confift of one, two, three, or more Movements;—for one Solo inftrument only;—for one or more Principal inftruments, with Accompaniments;—or for two, or more Concerting inftruments, without any accompaniment. And in all the faid forms they may be, either characteriftic, or free; as I fhall fhew in the courfe of this Chapter.

§ 4. In regard to the proper *length* of Sonatas, there can be given no other general rule, than: that they may be fet as *long,* as they can be expected to engage and entertain our attention; or as *fhort,* as they can be made without becoming infignificant. For, one fort of fubjects and elaborations will entertain a long while; when by others, a great deal of intereft may be brought into a narrow compafs of length. It is therefore beft for a young compofer, to take the length of fome good Sonata for a pattern, till he is able to make judicious difpofitions of his own.

§ 5. The *Number of Movements* proper for Sonatas, is alfo optional, and depends upon the fancy and good judgment of the compofer. For, though in general moft fonatas are found confifting of two, or three movements, yet they may alfo confift of four or more movements, according to the plan fhewn in Chap. I, § 12 and 13.

      The

The *Number of Sections* that may be contained in every Movement of a Sonata, follows from what I have faid in Chap. I, § 9, *& feq*.

The proper *Modulation* of every movement, and the relation between the different movements, follows from Chap. I, § 5, *& feq*. In regard to the latter, I muft mention four cafes of abrupt changes of the key from one movement to another, which are found in *Haydn*'s Sonatas Op. 75. The firft is in Sonata I, where the firft movement is in C major, and the fecond in A major. This change is allowable, according to the rules of abrupt modulation by omiffion, in my Effay on Harmony, Chap. X, § 13; for C is the key, and the triad of A the leading chord to a related key; but A is retained, and made a fubftituted key. The fecond cafe is in the fame Sonata, where the fecond movement ends in A major, and the third one begins in C major, which, as it is too great a fkip in harmony, ought not to be imitated by young compofers. The third and fourth cafe is in Sonata III, where the firft movement is in E flat major, the fecond in B (or C flat) major, and the third in E flat major again. Both thefe changes of the key are very good, according to the rules mentioned juft now.

II. *Of the different Sorts of Sonatas in particular.*

A. OF SONATAS FOR ONE SOLO INSTRUMENT ONLY.

§ 6. In § 3, I have mentioned three claffes of fonatas, of which that in queftion is the firft.

§ 7. A fonata for one folo inftrument only, is a *Solo* in the ftricteft fenfe. It may be written either for keyed, or other inftruments.

The particular rules for this fort of fonatas are: firft, they muft contain fo *complete a harmony*, that neither the want of an additional part is felt, nor that it can be eafy to add to it any interefting accompaniment, without fpoiling the effect of the original part; fecondly, they ought to be more particularly *calculated for the nature of their refpective inftrument*, than what can be expected in pieces for more than one inftrument.

§ 8. Of the Solos for Keyed Inftruments, thofe for the *Organ* deferve the firft rank. They may be calculated for one fet of keys only; or for two or three fets of keys without Pedals; or for Manuals and Pedals. As I fhall fpeak of Organ Pieces in Chap. XI, § 12, *& feq*. I muft refer the Reader to that place.

§ 9. Next in rank are Solos for *ftringed keyed Inftruments*; of which the *Piano Forte*, the *Harpfichord*, and the *Clavichord* make the three principal claffes. The two former ones are fufficiently known in this country; but of the laft, which is ftill much efteemed in Germany, I muft give the following fhort defcription; viz: The Clavichord refembles in fhape the common oblong Piano Forte, but is more fimple, becaufe it is made to found not with hammers or quilled jacks, but with a thin piece of brafs, upon which the ftring comes to reft like as upon a fmall bridge. Its found is not nearly fo ftrong as that of a Piano Forte, but very good; and it has fome good qualities which are not found in the Piano Forte.

The Solos which may be written for the inftruments in queftion, are called either *Solos*, or according to their nature: Sonatas, Suites, Leffons, Divertiments, Capriccios, Fancies, Inventions,

Inventions, Rondos, &c. To write them according to the rules given in § 7, requires, both an intimate acquaintance with all the rules of Harmony, and with the nature and treatment of Keyed Instruments in general, as well as the particular nature of that Keyed Instrument for which they are calculated to be.

If they shall be *easy*: care must be taken that they do not become insignificant; or only easy in some places and difficult in the others. And if they shall be *difficult*: the difficulty must not arise from a mere awkwardness of their passages, as is the case in many difficult Sonatas, which might have been very easy without losing in effect, had their passages been properly managed. But it is best if the composer is at liberty to write without particular regard to difficulty or facility; for in that case the piece will be more natural than under the above restrictions.

To give the Reader a more complete idea of what may be called good pieces for Keyed Instruments, than what can be formed from a mere description of them, I will point out a few capital works for his examination, viz:

1, *Handel*'s Lessons, or Suites pour la Clavecin. Part I, and II; which are sufficiently known.

2, *Emanuel Bach*'s *Probestüke*, or Examples to his Essay on the proper manner of playing the Clavichord. Berlin 1759, second edition 1780, which go progressively through simple and complicated, single and double passages.

3, The same Author's *Six Sonatas with varied Reprises* (mit veranderten Reprisen;) Berlin 1760; which have been printed here entitled: *Sei Sonate*— dal Signore *C. P. E. Bach*. (Walsh.) They are remarkable for shewing the way to a particular sort of elaboration, by varying the returns and imitations of the subject, which Bach has done in a masterly manner. As an imitation of them I presume to lay before the Reader my *Rondo* at Plate V, *& seq.*

4, and 5, *Haydn*'s three Sonatas Op. 58, and three ditto Op. 75. Both these works, though they are set with very interesting Accompaniments, contain the finest Solo passages, and deserve to be studied.

6, *Kozeluch*'s three grand Sonatas, called Op. 14, or 17; which are remarkable for some brilliant spreading passages, peculiar to that Author, as well, as for the other real merit found in them.

7, *Clementi*'s Musical Characteristics, Op. 19. A work, which consists of Preludes and Cadences, in the style of Haydn, Mozard, Kozeluch, Sterkel, Vanhall, and Clementi; in which it gives the choicest specimens, not only of the manner of the said Authors, but also of proper and brilliant passages for the Piano Forte.

8, The same Author's three Sonatas Op. 27; which though they are set with an Accompaniment, may be used as Solos, and are remarkable for those passages, in which longer and shorter rhythmical cæsures meet one under the other, so as not to begin and end at the same time.

9, *Dussek*'s three Sonatas dedicated to *Clementi*; in which grandeur and fullness are skilfully united with taste and delicate expression.

As the above works are sufficient to exemplify what may be called good music for Keyed Instruments, I forbear mentioning more, for fear of appearing prejudiced against the Authors of so many other valuable works which I should after all be obliged to leave unnoticed.

§ 10. Next to Keyed Instruments, the *Harp*, and particularly the *Pedal Harp*, is one of the best calculated for Solos; and the sweetness of its tone in some measure compensates for its being of a more limited use than the former.   That

That Solos of the defcription in queftion may be fet for almoft any inftrument, can be proved by two of *Sebaftian Bach's* works, the one being Solos for a *Violin*, and the other for the *Violoncello* ; both without any accompaniment, and both fuch mafterly compofitions, that hardly any thing finer can be imagined.

The requifites for the Solos mentioned in this §, will follow from what I have faid in the former.

SONATAS FOR ONE OR MORE PRINCIPAL INSTRUMENTS, WITH SOME OTHERS AS ACCOMPANIMENTS.

§ 11. There is a great difference between the *principal* part or parts of a piece, and thofe called *accompaniments ;* and even the latter muft be divided into *neceffary* and *voluntary*, or *obligato* and *ad libitum* ones.

§ 12. When a Sonata is compofed fo, that one or two, or more inftruments, are diftinguifhed above the reft, it is for fo many *principal* inftruments ; and the others are *accompaniments.*

According to this definition Sonatas may be compofed for a *Piano Forte*, with Violin and Violoncello accompaniments ; or for a *Violin* or *Violoncello*, with a Piano Forte accompaniment ; or for *any one* inftrument, with a fimilar one, or with different ones, as accompaniments.

And in the fame manner as for one, they may alfo be fet for *two* or *more fimilar* or *different* principal inftruments, with others as accompaniments.

This can produce a great variety of Solos, Duos, Trios, and Quatuors, *with accompaniments.* But I do not remember to have feen any other pieces of this fort but *Solos*, or fimple *Sonatas*, with accompaniments.

§ 13. In regard to the *accompaniments* mentioned in § 11, I begin with the confideration of thofe called neceffary or *obligato* ones. They are thofe which cannot be omitted without rendering the harmony or effect of the piece imperfect.

Accompaniments of this fort may be fet to a piece in two different manners, viz : firft, fo that the principal part and the accompaniment take the chief melody *by turns*, and form a fort of concertante ; fecondly, fo that the accompaniment ferves only as a bafs or other *filling part*, to fupport the principal ones.

Of the former fort are the accompaniments to *Haydn's* Sonatas Opera 58 ; and *Pleyel's* grand Sonatas Op. 31, and of the latter are the thorough bafs accompaniments to *Corelli's* Violin Solos. Accompaniments called *voluntary*, or *ad libitum* ones, are thofe, which make an agreeable addition to the piece, but do not render it imperfect when omitted. Examples of this fort are *Clementi's* Sonatas Op. 27.

In regard to all the faid accompaniments, there ought to be expreffed in the title of the work, whether they are obligato, or *ad libitum* ; fo that a perfon who fees the work only advertifed or in a catalogue, may be able to form an idea of it. But this rule has hitherto been very little attended to ; and I know fonatas, which the Title fays to be for the Piano Forte, with an *accompaniment* for a Violin, but the Violin begins with a *Solo*, and the Piano Forte only has an accompaniment paffage to it.

C. SONATAS FOR TWO OR MORE PRINCIPAL INSTRUMENTS, WITHOUT ACCOMPANIMENTS.

§ 14. Under this denomination come regular or proper Duos, Trios, Quatuors, Quintetts, &c.

§ 15. A *Duo* or *Duett* of this description, is a piece for *two* concerting instruments, without accompaniment. It must not only contain as complete an harmony throughout, as has been required for Solos without accompaniments, (§ 7;) but the two parts should also be constantly imitating each other, or at least the one have as good a share in the harmony and the passages as the other.

It may be set, either for two performers on *one* Keyed Instrument, such as the Organ or the Piano Forte; or for *two similar* instruments, such as two Violins or two Violoncellos; or for *two* instruments of a *different* nature, such as a Violin and Hautboy; or a Violin and Violoncello. And in all three cases it may consist either of two regular parts or melodies only; or of passages which contain a harmony of three and four parts. See my Essay on Harmony, Chap. XIII, § 14, 15. I shall endeavour to speak of the pieces in question in the following order:

1, Duetts for two Performers on *one* Keyed Instrument may be set for three or four hands. Of the former sort is *Haefsler's* grand Sonata for three hands, published by Wornum; and my Fugue at Plate XVIII, which also may be considered as a *trio* on one instrument; and of the latter sort *Duffek's* grand overture for two performers; and similar fine works by *Kozeluch*, *Clementi*, and other composers. These duetts for four hands may also be set as *Quatuors* on one instrument, when each hand has an obligato part different from the others; of which sort, I have not yet seen a good example. The particular rule for pieces of all these descriptions is, that the parts must be distributed according to what I have said in my Essay on Harmony, Chap. III, § 2; and so, that neither the bass be too noisy for the upper parts, nor the parts of the first and second performer be in each other's way.

2, Duetts for *two keyed instruments* are the most respectable sort of the second class; or of those for similar instruments: but as it is seldom that two such instruments can be found in the same *room*, as well as the same *pitch of tune*, there have been but few attempts made to write them. But two excellent Fugues of this description are in *Seb. Bach's* Art of the Fugue, which might be played on the two sets of keys of one Organ. This great Author has also written Concertos for two, three, and even four Keyed Instruments. Duetts for two *Violins* or two *Flutes*, or two *Hautboys*, &c. are more frequent. But in regard to these Duetts, I must mention a fault which is very frequently committed, viz: that of repeating a passage with the mere change of primo for secondo, or *vice versa*. This change in similar instruments such as the above-mentioned, has no other effect than a mere repetition without a change of the parts; and consequently is no proper variety for the duetts in question. But for those of the following class it produces a variety in the effect. The third class of Duetts are those, for two *different* instruments. In regard to these, one of the principal considerations is: to choose such instruments as may have a good effect together.

Another consideration is: that if a Duett is set for a *Bass* and a *Treble* Instrument, and intended to be also executed by two Basses or two Trebles, the harmony must be calculated accordingly. If therefore a Duett for a Violin and Violoncello shall be also calculated

lated for *two* Violins or *two* Violoncellos, care muſt be taken, that it produces no irregular *intermixture*, or no diſallowed *inverſion* of the parts when contracted on two ſimilar inſtruments.

§ 16. *Trios* of the deſcription in queſtion, are: pieces for *three* concerting Inſtruments, without accompaniment.

They may be written either for *one* performer on an Organ with two ſets of Manual and one ſet of Pedal Keys; or for *two* performers on one or two ſets of Keys of an Organ; as I ſhall ſhew in Chap. XI, § 18; alſo for *three* performers on three ſimilar or different inſtruments.

N. B. When I have mentioned a trio on *one* Keyed Inſtrument, it will be naturally underſtood, that the parts muſt be ſet ſo clearly diſtinct, that they may have an effect, as if they were played on *three* different Inſtruments. See my Fugue at Plate XVIII.

How trios may be written ſo, that they conſiſt but of three regular Parts or Melodies, or of paſſages which contain four, five, or more parts of a harmony, I have ſhewn in my Eſſay on Harmony, Chap. XIII, § 14, 15.

According to the latter explanations pieces may be called trios, that conſiſt of a Piano Forte part, and a concerting Violin and Violoncello part. Some of the beſt of this ſort are by *Mozard*, *Haydn*, and *Pleyel*; and inſtead of the Violin, a Clarinet or Flute has alſo been uſed.

When the ſecond of the two alternate pieces is called a Trio, ſuch as a Minuet and Trio, a March and Trio, &c. the denomination relates to thoſe pieces in antient Compoſitions, where the trio has been ſet in *three parts* to diſtinguiſh it from the firſt piece; but in modern compoſition that diſtinction is generally not attended to, and the name trio only remains to the ſecond of the ſaid ſort of pieces.

§ 17. *Quatuors* or *Quartetts* of the deſcription in queſtion are: pieces for *four* concerting Inſtruments, without accompaniment.

They may be ſet for four ſimilar or different Inſtruments; and conſiſt either of four regular parts or melodies only, or of paſſages which include a harmony of five and more parts; and in all the varieties which follow from what I have ſaid in § 15, and 16.

Some of the beſt Examples are *Mozard's* Quartetts for a Piano Forte, a Violin, a Viola, and a Violoncello; *Haydn's* ſeveral ſets for divers Inſtruments, particularly his one ſet, which contains the fineſt ſimple and double Fugues; alſo *Pleyel's* ſeveral ſets.

§ 18. *Quintetts* of the deſcription in queſtion, are pieces for *five* concerting Inſtruments, without accompaniment.

All that need be obſerved reſpecting them, follows from what I have ſaid in § 17.

§ 19. In regard to *Sextetts*, *Septetts*, and *Octetts*, I alſo need add no more than that the firſt are for *ſix*, the ſecond for *ſeven*, and the third for *eight* concerting Inſtruments.

III. *Of Sonatinas.*

§ 20. The word *Sonatina* is a diminutive of *Sonata*, and denotes ſmaller pieces than what generally are called Sonatas.

They may conſiſt of *one* or *two* Movements; but not well of more, as that would render them longer than Sonatinas are commonly found. Of the former ſort *George Benda*

Benda has given fome good fpecimens in his Mifcellaneous pieces. A principal rule for them is: that they muft not found like pieces taken out of their connection with others, but have a perfectly fatisfactory beginning and conclufion. Several Minuets, or Andantes, out of *Haydn's* Symphonies, make very good Sonatinas of this fort, when adapted for the Piano Forte.

Of the latter fort, or of two Movements, are my Six Sonatinas, Op. IV, and the fame number in my Op. V. In regard to both thefe fets of Sonatinas I beg leave to obferve, that I prefume them to be ufeful for the ftudy of imitation as well as the treatment of different fubjects. The laft in Opera V, confifts of three Movements, of which I have fpoken in Chap. I, § 8, No. I.

§ 21.   All that I have obferved above, refpecting Sonatas, may alfo be underftood of Sonatinas, with the only difference: that, as they are fhorter pieces than Sonatas, they cannot properly contain fuch long, grand, and elaborate paffages as the latter.

§ 22.   That all forts of Sonatas and Sonatinas may be calculated to exprefs certain prefcribed *characteriftics*, follows from what I have faid in Chap. I, § 14, 15.

─────────────

CHAPTER III.   OF SYMPHONIES.

§ 1.   A *Symphony* is : a piece calculated to be performed by *more than one Performer* to each part ; and may be compared in Inftrumental Mufic, to what a *Chorus* is in Vocal Mufic.

According to this defcription the nature of Symphonies requires : a fimpler fort of *Subjects,* and a more grand and manly *Elaboration,* than what would be proper for the finer fort of Sonatas.

I.   *Of Symphonies in General.*

§ 2.   From what I have faid above, it follows : that Symphonies in general require to be fet for, and performed by an *Orcheftra.* But as thofe written for an Orcheftra may be arranged for fewer Inftruments, or even for one Keyed Inftrument only, it follows : that they may be alfo originally compofed in the latter forms, if only proper attention is paid to their general character as defcribed in § 1.

In regard to their *particular character,* Symphonies may be either characteriftic or free.

A.   OF CHARACTERISTIC SYMPHONIES.

§ 3.   By characteriftic Symphonies I mean thofe, which are to exprefs a certain *prefcribed* character ; and the faid character may be expreffed either in general only, or both in general and with regard to particular characteriftics, as I fhall now endeavour to fhew.

§ 4.

§ 4. One of the moſt characteriſtic pieces I know, is *George Benda*'s Ariadne of Naxos, mentioned at Chap. I, § 14; being a Duodrama of one Act, written and compoſed ſo, that the two acting perſons ſpeak, (not ſing) their parts as uſual, and that the Muſic expreſſes at the intervals of every period, and ſometimes at ſhorter ſtops, the character of the ſentiment. It is one of the moſt expreſſive pieces of compoſition, and univerſally admired in Germany, ſo that it has been arranged for a Keyed Inſtrument; and I wiſh that it might at leaſt in this latter form be publiſhed in this country. The *general* character of it is the ſerious or rather tragic hiſtory, of Theſeus's leaving Ariadne on the Iſle of Naxos; and every *particular* characteriſtic, by which it is poetically embelliſhed, is expreſſed in the Muſic.

After the above I beg leave to mention again my *Shipwreck*, Op. VI, as a Symphony calculated to expreſs throughout a preſcribed *general* character, with its *particular* characteriſtics.

§ 5. A ſecond claſs is formed by thoſe Symphonies, which are calculated to expreſs a *preſcribed* general character, but without pointing out its particular characteriſtics, or the places where they are to appear.

Beautiful examples of this ſort are *Haydn*'s Seven words of Chriſt on the Croſs, as publiſhed in ſeven Movements, of which the laſt, the Earthquake, is particularly expreſſive.

§ 6. The laſt claſs of characteriſtic Symphonies comprehends thoſe, calculated to expreſs a preſcribed *general* character, without pointing it out in their title, or without regard to preſcribed *particular* characteriſtics. And of this ſort are all proper *Overtures*.

An *Overture* is a piece calculated to open or precede a muſical or other Action or Solemnity. If it ſhall precede an Opera, Oratorio, or another theatrical Piece, it ought not to be ſo long as to keep the audience in a long ſuſpenſe; except when this ſhould be required; but the more it contains of the general character of its reſpective piece, and the more it ſerves to prepare the hearer for the ſame, the better it is.

Moſt antient Overtures are found conſiſting of *two* Movements, viz: the firſt a *Grave* or ſomething ſolemn; and the ſecond a *Fugue* in the character of the piece. But modern Compoſers ſeldom bind themſelves to that form; and the Fugues in particular are quite neglected.

When ſome of *Haydn*'s or other Authors' Grand Symphonies are called Overtures, it is, becauſe they are calculated to open a grand Concert. But as they allude to no particular Hiſtory or Action, there can be no other characteriſtic expected in them, than that of a Solemnity of Movement and Modulation, and a variety of predominating paſſages on the principal Inſtruments contained in the Orcheſtra, for which purpoſe they are excellent.

B. OF FREE SYMPHONIES.

§ 7. Under this denomination I comprehend all thoſe Symphonies which have *no preſcribed* Character; though I have ſaid before that every Muſical Piece ought to have *ſome* general character. (Chap. I, § 14.)

They may be uſed either to precede a Concert or Theatrical Piece like an Overture, or to fill up ſome intervals between the ſaid pieces; or alſo on any other occaſion.

§ 8. They may be written of any reaſonable *Length*, like Sonatas, (ſee Chap. II, § 4,) and conſiſt of the ſame Number and Variety of *Movements* as Sonatas, from which they

they differ chiefly in the particulars mentioned at § 1 and 2.   But *Haydn's* Symphonies generally confift of *four* Movements, viz: an Allegro ; an Adagio ; a Menuetto ; and a Prefto ; or fome other Movement fimilar to thefe.   In moft of his latter Symphonies that Author alfo begins with a fhort Adagio before the firft Allegro, which ferves to prepare the hearers for the piece to which it is an introduction, and heightens the effect of its beginning ; and in one, (No. XII,) he introduces an Allegretto inftead of the Adagio.

N. B.   Here, and in fome other parts of this Chapter, I refer to *Haydn's* twelve Symphonies lately publifhed by Mr. *Salomon.*

That any other Number as well as judicious Variety of Movements, than thofe mentioned above, may be introduced in a Symphony, follows from what I have faid in Chap. I, refpecting the Plan of a Piece, in general as well, as in all its particulars.

§ 9.   The *Harmony* and the *Paffages* of the Symphonies in queftion, muft, according to § 1, be more *grand* and *bold*, than fublime or embellifhed with graces.   And though predominant melodious paffages may be given to the different Inftruments, or even Variations be introduced in the flow Movement; yet they fhould always be fo fimple, that more than one performer of moderate capacity, can properly execute them at once, and never refemble a Solo in a Concerto.

§ 10.   In regard to *Modulation*, the Symphonies in queftion muft be conformable to the Plan pointed out in Chap. I, § 5—13 ; and to § 1 of the prefent Chapter.

II.   *Of Symphonies for an Orcheftra.*

§ 11.   When a Symphony is to be written for an Orcheftra, there ought to be confidered : firft, the conftruction of its *Subjects*; fecondly, the diftribution of its *Harmony* between the different Inftruments.

§ 12.   If a Symphony for an Orcheftra fhall not be imperfect, its principal *Subjects* ought to be of fuch a nature, that all Inftruments can *execute* them, or at leaft *join* in them in the principal Key.   If this rule is not attended to, a Symphony cannot anfwer the purpofe of employing the whole Orcheftra to advantage ; and *Haydn* will be found very particular in attending to this rule, for the fubjects of moft of his beft Symphonies are not only calculated for the Horn and Trumpet, but even for the Kettle Drums, of which the beginning of No. I, of the twelve mentioned at § 8, may ferve for an Example.

In this particular the firft Allegro of my Analyzed Symphony, Op. VII, is deficient, for its firft Subject can neither be executed entirely, nor be well accompanied by eafy and natural founds of the Trumpet and Horn ; the faid piece is therefore better calculated for the form in which I have publifhed it, than for the ufe of a grand Orcheftra.

§ 13.   The *diftribution* of the *Harmony* between the different Inftruments employed in a Symphony, is alfo an object of importance in compofing it, for the leaft inattention or unfkilfulnefs in that refpect may fpoil the beft harmony.   It is therefore neceffary to obferve : that the harmony of a Symphony muft confift throughout of at leaft *four regular parts*, except in extraordinary cafes, where any of the parts may reft a fhort time ; and that, in general, the faid four parts muft be given to the four *principal Inftruments*, the firft Violin, the fecond Violin, the Viola or Tenor, and the Violoncello or Bafs. For the faid Inftruments the four parts of the harmony muft confequently be calculated in fo far, that they lie within their compafs as well, as are practicable on them for players of a moderate capacity. How exceptions may be made from this general diftribution of harmony will appear at the end of this §, and in § 14.

The other Inftruments of the Orcheftra may be brought in as follows :

1, In *Unifons*, or paffages where all inftruments play the fame melody, though in different Octaves. Here the firft and fecond Flute, Hautboy, or Clarinet, may go in the Unifon or in the higher or lower Octave, with the firft and fecond Violin; the firft Baffoon with the Tenor, and the fecond Baffoon with the Bafs; and if the paffage is calculated for Horns and Trumpets they may be introduced in that Octave where they can ferve beft, or elfe they muft have refts.

2, In *Tuttis*, or paffages where all inftruments come in, but not with the fame melodies as above, the diftribution may be made in two different ways, viz : firft like as in Unifon Paffages, which I have fhewn juft now ; fecondly, fo, that fome or all Wind Inftruments, take the harmony like as in Chords of Thorough Bafs, confequently without playing all the Notes of the principal parts ; in which cafe they may have either *holding* notes, or notes interfperfed with *refts*.

3, In *Solos*, by which I underftand thofe paffages where one or a couple of inftruments have a predominant melody, though not of fuch a nature as Solos in a Concerto, (fee § 9,) the harmony may be diftributed in many different manners, of which I fhall fhew the following ones, viz : firft, if the Solo is for one or two of the four *principal* Inftruments (Violins, Tenor, and Bafs,) the other principal inftruments may accompany it fo as not to overpower the Solo, and one or more *wind* inftruments may join in the accompaniment fo as to take the principal notes of the harmony, but Piano, that the Solo be not obfcured. Secondly, if the Solo is for one or two *treble Wind Inftruments* (Hautboys, Flutes, Clarinets, or fometimes the Trumpet) the Violins may play the principal notes either holding, or with intermixed refts, or pizzicato, and the Viola or Bafs join in the fame manner, or differently from the Violins; the other Wind Inftruments may according to circumftances either have refts or join in the accompaniment. Thirdly, if the Solo is for one or two *Bafs Wind Inftruments* (Baffoons, Trombonos, or in fome meafure Horns,) it may be accompanied by the four principal inftruments, fo that the Bafs and Tenor do not overpower the Solo parts ; and if required treble Wind Inftruments may join in the Accompaniment.

In all the above cafes one of the principal Inftruments may alfo have refts, and the harmony confift but of three regular parts, as will require no demonftration.

§ 14. When I have faid at the beginning of § 13, that the harmony of a Symphony fhould confift at leaft of *four* regular parts ; it is natural, that harmonies of *five* and *more* real parts, fhould alfo be allowable in Symphonies as well as in Concertos or other Vocal and Inftrumental Pieces. I fhall therefore now endeavour to make fome remarks on the faid greater number of parts.

In *five* real parts, the principal Inftruments may be : two Violins, two Tenors, and a Bafs, which take the principal parts of the harmony in the fame manner as in four parts ; and all the obfervations made in § 13, under *Unifons*, *Tuttis*, and *Solos*, are alfo applicable to five parts, if two Tenors are taken inftead of one.

To fet *more than five* real parts throughout a Symphony, is uncommon, and may only ferve for extraordinary purpofes, as five is plenty for our ear to attend to. But for the said extraordinary purposes, six, seven, or eight real parts, may *occasionally* be introduced, in a Symphony of only *four* parts.

§ 15. As I have in this Chapter frequently mentioned *real parts* of a harmony, I must here observe that not all parts of a *score* are real parts of a Harmony. For though a score may consist of twelve or more parts, yet the said parts may only contain a Harmony of three, four, or five *real* parts, and all the others are but mere *duplicate* parts.

By *real* parts therefore I understand those, which are essential in the harmony of the piece ; and by *duplicate* ones, those, which are only drawn from the real parts, either by doubling them in the Unison or Octave, or by selecting from them the principal notes of the harmony, in the different manners shewn at § 13, No. 2, and 3.

Respecting this distinction, between the parts of a harmony, *Kirnberger* mentions a Score by *Scheibe* which consists of *nineteen* parts, and yet contains but a harmony of *three* parts. (See his Kunst des reinen Satzes, Part II, page 39.)

As the limits of this Essay will not allow me to give Examples of all I have said in the present Chapter, I must instead of them refer the diligent reader to an attentive hearing of the Symphonies of good Composers, particularly those of *Haydn*, and to the study of their Scores, if he can meet with any of them.

III. *Of Symphonies for one, or only a few Instruments.*

§ 16. In § 2 I have said, that as Symphonies composed for an Orchestra, may be arranged for fewer Instruments, or even for one Keyed Instrument only, they may be also originally composed in the latter form, if only proper attention is paid to their general character as described in § 1. But it must be observed, that though in writing Symphonies for one or only a few Instruments, a composer is more at liberty in the choice and construction of their Subjects, and has less to consider in regard to the distribution of the Harmony, than in writing them for an Orchestra ; yet he is deprived of the principal means of rendering them grand and more like Symphonies than Sonatas, by not having to employ in them the powerful and various effects that can be produced by an Orchestra. If therefore the Symphonies in question shall not be too much like Sonatas, it is required to give them more *plain*, but also more *grand* and *bold* Harmonies and Passages, than what would be proper for Sonatas according to Chap. II.

§ 17. Under the above limitation Symphonies may be written in all the forms of Sonatas described in the said Chapter, viz : for one Solo Instrument only ; for one or more Principal Instruments, with Accompaniments; or for two or more Concerting Instruments without Accompaniments.

From this it follows : that Solos, Duos, Trios, Quartetts, Quintetts, &c. may be set in the style or character of a Symphony as well as a Sonata, if their author is able and disposed to distinguish the two Characters; but that if no particular attention is paid to the true Characteristics of a Sonata or a Symphony, all the said pieces for one or a few Instruments may resemble both. But in the latter case I would rather call them what they are in outward appearance, I mean Sonatas.

Some good Symphonies for a Keyed Instrument only, have been written by *Emanuel Bach, George Benda,* and *Schobert ;* and the best collection I know, as arranged for the

Piano

Piano Forte, a Violin, and a Violoncello, is that of *Haydn's* Twelve Symphonies, mentioned in § 8.

CHAPTER IV.   OF CONCERTOS.

§ 1. A *Concerto* is a grand Inftrumental Piece, chiefly calculated to fhew the abilities of a Player on a certain principal Inftrument. It confifts of *Tuttis*, in which it refembles a Symphony, and of *Solos* that are like the principal paffages of a grand Sonata; and confequently may be confidered as a Compound of Symphony and Sonata.

I. *Of Concertos in General.*

§ 2. A Concerto may be written, for one, two, or more *Principal Inftruments*, with the accompaniment of an *Orcheftra ;* or for the faid *principal* inftruments, with the accompaniment of a *few* inftruments only ; or for *two* or *more Keyed* Inftruments without any accompaniment.

The particulars which muft be confidered in all the faid forms of a Concerto, are: firft, its *Length* and *Character;* fecondly, the Number and Nature of its *Movements;* thirdly, the *Fancy Cadences* which may be introduced in them.

A. LENGTH AND CHARACTER OF CONCERTOS.

§ 3. The proper *Length* of a Concerto depends upon the fame general rule I have given refpecting the length of Sonatas, in Chap. II, § 4. For it may be fet as *long* as it can be expected to engage and entertain our attention ; or as *fhort* as it can be made without becoming infignificant. And though *Quantz* in his excellent Treatife on the art of playing the German Flute, (Anweifung die Flöte zu fpielen,) Artic. XVIII, thinks a Concerto fhould properly laft about a quarter of an hour, viz : the firft Movement about five ; the fecond, five or fix; and the third three or four Minutes; yet I have obferved in the quoted place, that much depends upon the nature of Subjects, and the forts of Elaboration, and that confequently no certain length can be fixed in general for Concertos as well as Sonatas and Symphonies.

§ 4. The *Character* of a Concerto may, like that of a Sonata or Symphony, be either *prefcribed*, or *optional*. For, though I do not recollect having heard of any *characteriftic* Concertos, fimilar to characteriftic Sonatas or Symphonies ; yet what can prevent a great Compofer to write the former as well as the latter if he choofes it ? For, would *Emanuel Bach* not have been able to write a Concerto, to exprefs a Converfation between a Melancholicus and a Sanguinicus, as well as his celebrated sonata of that Character ? And might not fuch characteriftic Concertos be expected to entertain more than thofe of the common fort ? But in general they are of an *optional* Character, that is to fay, calculated to exprefs nothing particular, but a grandeur of Harmony in their Tuttis, and brilliant paffages in

their

their Solos; and in that quality they can anfwer no other purpofes, but fhewing the hearer how the Compofer could fet them, and the principal Performer execute them.

B.   NUMBER AND NATURE OF THE MOVEMENTS IN CONCERTOS.

§ 5.   Though any judicious Number as well as Variety of Movements may be intro-duced in Concertos, as well as in Sonatas or Symphonies, and the Concertos of *Handel, Corelli, Geminiani,* Dr. *Arne,* and *Stanley,* are found confifting of various and different Numbers and forts of Movements; yet modern Concertos in general confift of *three* Movements, viz: a *lively,* a *flow,* and another *lively* one.   And as a perfon who is able to compofe a Concerto properly of *three* movements, will alfo be able to write one according to any other judicious plan, I think it fufficient if I go through the particulars which muft be confidered in the faid *three* movements.

§ 6.   The *firft* movement is generally an *Allegro.*   The two Sections or four Subfections of which it confifts, according to the general plan of a piece fhewn in Chap. I, § 11, are managed as follows:

The *firft Subfection* is a *Tutti,* calculated to exhibit the number and fort of inftruments that fhall be ufed in the Concerto; and to imprefs on the ear of the hearer, the Key and Mode, the principal Subjects, and the Character of the Movement.   It confequently fhould be in the Key, with the fort of Modulation fhewn in Chap. I, § 11.   And nothing fhould be introduced in it, but Subjects or Paffages, which are to be elaborated in the courfe of the movement.   Some authors make this Tutti longer, and others fhorter; but commonly its length is about one third, or fourth, of the whole firft Section.   It ends, either with a perfect cadence in the Key; or better, with the half cadence on its Domi-nante, according to my Effay on Harmony, Chap. X, § 7.

The *fecond Subfection* begins with, and chiefly confifts of, a *Solo,* calculated to fhew the powers of the principal inftrument, and the abilities of the principal performer.   The faid beginning may be with the Subject or Subjects, without any variation; or with a ju-dicious variation or imitation of the fame.   This Solo is occafionally relieved by fhort Tuttis, to keep up the grandeur of the piece; and when it has got its proper length, which is about twice or three times that of the firft Tutti, a conclufion is made, commonly with a Tutti, in the Fifth, or (in minor,) in the Third of the Key, by which the firft *Section* is completed.   The proper Modulation for this part of the movement, fee alfo at Chap. I, § 11.

The *third Subfection* is fimilar to the fecond, in confifting of a *Solo* relieved by fhort *Tuttis;* but it is different from it in the fort of Modulation and Elaboration it admits of, or requires.   See alfo Chap. I, § 11.   It may be a little fhorter than the fecond Subfec-tion, and muft end with a half cadence on the Fifth of the principal Key.

The *fourth Subfection* again contains a *Solo,* which generally begins with the Subject in the principal Key, and continues with the fort of Modulation and Elaboration fhewn at Chap. I, § 11, till it is about fo long as the third Subfection; when it proceeds to a grand Cadence on the Key note, of which I fhall fpeak in § 10; and after this cadence a fhort Tutti is added as a *Coda,* to make a complete and formal conclufion of the firft *Move-ment.*

§ 7.   The *fecond* Movement is generally an *Adagio,* or other flow movement.   It may confift of two *long* Sections, planned fimilar to thofe of the firft movement; or of two

G.   *fhort ſhort* Sections, with *variations;* or be ſet in the form of a proper or improper *Rondo,* without, or with variations of the Subjects; or in any other well calculated form. In all the ſaid forms it may alſo contain, a *fancy cadence,* like the firſt movement ; or, in the laſt caſe, tranſitory fancy paſſages, to lead in the returning ſubject; and *Solos* and *Tuttis* may be judiciouſly intermixed in it, like as in the firſt Movement.

§ 8. The *third* Movement uſes to be of the *quicker,* or *quickeſt* ſort again. It may be ſet in any of the different forms mentioned in § 7; if only proper attention is paid to all the particulars, pointed out in § 2, and through the whole of Chap. I.

§ 9. In all three or more movements, the *Solos* may be accompanied with any one, two, or more ſuitable inſtruments, and with more inſtruments in one, or fewer in another place; according to the nature of the paſſages, and the purpoſes of the compoſer. And though the Solos of one and the ſame Movement muſt bear a good *proportion* to each other, yet their Length and Diſpoſition ſhould alſo be calculated to produce a fanciful *variety,* which is one of the beſt qualities of a good compoſition.

C. THE FANCY CADENCES.

§ 10. The grand Cadence towards the end of the firſt movement, which I have mentioned in § 6, is commonly ſet with a Pauſe over the leading note, and it is uſual to introduce a *Fancy* between the chord of the ſixth and fourth, which ſuſpends the leading chord on that note, and the leading chord itſelf. In regard to the ſaid fancy, I have given three Rules in my *Eſſay on Harmony,* Chap. XVII, § 13; the firſt of which I will endeavour to expreſs here a little clearer, and the ſecond and third I ſhall repeat for the convenience of the reader.

Rule I, (altered.) The whole can properly conſiſt of no other *harmony,* than what may be introduced as a continued cadence or an Organ Point, between the ſuſpending chord, (or chord of the ſixth and fourth,) and the leading chord, on the leading note.

For, the ſuſpending chord creates a deſire to hear its reſolution in the leading chord. This ſuſpenſion therefore may be *continued,* by letting the harmony go ſeveral unexpected but regular ways, in the ſame manner, as the reſolution of the Eſſential Seventh may be ſuſpended; (ſee Eſſay on Harmony, Chap. VI, § 6;) but the whole muſt remain *one continued* cadence, like an Organ Point, and no ſatisfactory concluſion muſt be made in it, before the ſuſpended final reſolution.

Yet the following *liberties* are allowable in the cadence in queſtion, viz : *firſt,* the Baſs note need not be continued, as in a real Organ Point, if only the harmony is of ſuch a nature as to admit the ſame note, when ſuppoſed under it ; *ſecondly,* the harmony may take even ſuch turns, as to oblige the ſuppoſed holding note to quit its ſtation for a few chords. But this laſt muſt be done with great diſcretion, and under the limitations of what I have ſaid in explanation of the rule in queſtion.

Rule II. No other *paſſages* muſt be introduced in a fancy cadence, than what are conformable to the Style, Movement, and Meaſure, of the piece in which it is made ; though without confining it to one fixed *movement* or *meaſure,* which would be againſt the following rule.

Rule III. The more *novelty, richneſs of modulation,* and *variety,* a fancy cadence contains without treſpaſſing againſt the two foregoing rules, or without making it too long, the better it is.

§ 11.

§ 11. Conformable to the above rules are all the written cadences of great authors as well, as the extemporary ones of good and ſtrict players.

Two fine examples of written cadences ſee at Plate X and XI. They are tranſcribed from *Clementi*'s Muſical Characteriſtics, Op. 19, mentioned at Chap. II, § 9, and will be found ſtrictly conformable to the above rules in § 10. The *firſt*, (that at Plate X,) is of the firſt ſort, mentioned under the *liberties* allowable according to Rule I. For, the firſt Baſs Note might have been continued throughout, as in an Organ Point, though it has not been continued. To prove this, I have analyzed the harmony the cadence contains, by thorough Baſs Figures. The *ſecond*, (that at Plate XI,) is of the ſecond ſort, mentioned in the ſame place. For, the harmony does not admit of the continuation of the firſt baſs note through the whole cadence, and yet the whole is felt as one continued cadence throughout, according to Rule I, § 10. I have alſo analyzed the fine courſe of harmonies contained in this example, by thorough baſs figures; and as I had room for it, ſubjoined to it another line with the *fundamental* baſs of every chord, according to the principles of my Eſſay on Harmony.

But though authors like *Haydn, Mozard, Kozeluch,* and *Clementi,* may take the laſt ſort of liberties, I would adviſe young Compoſers or Players, not to venture beyond the above firſt example, till they have a ſufficient command over all the rules of harmony. And all thoſe who have no real knowledge of harmony and compoſition, ſhould not attempt writing or extemporiſing any fancy cadences at all. For, nothing can more torment a muſical ear, or more ſpoil the effect of a concerto, and more expoſe an author or player, than a bad fancy cadence.

That the cadences in queſtion may be introduced in all three movements of a Concerto, I have already ſaid above; yet they ſhould not be uſed too often.

Of *double Cadences,* ſee § 13.

II. *Of Concertos in regard to the Principal and other Inſtruments, for which they are ſet.*

A. OF THOSE FOR ONE PRINCIPAL INSTRUMENT.

§ 12. If a concerto is compoſed for one principal inſtrument only, it may be called a *Simple Concerto,* in diſtinction from Double Concertos. The particulars which muſt be obſerved in ſimple concertos are as follows :

Firſt. They muſt be planned and conſtructed, according to all that has been ſaid in the foregoing part of this Chapter.

Secondly. The Solos muſt be particularly calculated for the principal Inſtrument of the Concerto. Of which ſee Chap. I, § 17.

Thirdly. The number as well as nature of the inſtruments for accompaniments muſt be properly conſidered.

That a Concerto may be written with accompaniments for only a few inſtruments, or for a ſmaller or grander Orcheſtra, I have already mentioned in § 2.

The ſmalleſt number of accompaniments generally uſed for a Concerto on the Piano Forte is: two Violins, a Tenor, and a Baſs; though *Chriſtian Bach* has even omitted the Tenor in a ſet dedicated to Her Majeſty. To theſe may be added Flutes or Hautboys, and Horns, or all the inſtruments of a grand Orcheſtra, as circumſtances permit or require it.

Other

Other confiderations, refpecting the Nature and Combination of inftruments, which relate particularly to Concertos for a Bow, or Wind-Inftrument, fee in Chap. XI, § 2, & feq.

All thefe particulars will be found attended to in the Concertos of good Compofers.

B.   THOSE FOR TWO OR MORE PRINCIPAL INSTRUMENTS.

§ 13.   According to the number of principal inftruments a Concerto may be called a *double, triple,* or *quadruple,* one.   But it is more cuftomary to fay : a Concerto for *two Violins,* or for *three Hautboys,* or for *two Hautboys* and *two Baffoons,* &c. as alfo a *Concertante.* And the following are the particulars which ought to be obferved in all forts of them :

Firft.   The whole muft be planned and elaborated according to what has been faid from § 1 to § 11, in this Chapter.

Secondly.   The Solos muft be particularly calculated for the principal Inftruments, and accompanied with fuch inftruments as are moft fuitable to them.   See Chap. XI, § 2, & feq.

Thirdly.   The Subjects muft be of fuch a nature, that every principal inftrument can imitate them ; though they may fometimes be imitated by each inftrument in a different manner, or in a manner peculiar to that inftrument.

Fourthly.   All principal inftruments fhould be equally employed in the Solos ; but every one according to its particular nature.   Yet fometimes the one, and then another may reft, if a judicious compofer finds occafion for it.

Fifthly.   If there fhall be fancy cadences introduced in them, they ought always to be previoufly written and ftudied, fo that every principal inftrument can appear to advantage in them.

A fine *triple* Concerto is the well known one by *Fifher,* originally compofed for three Hautboys, and now ufed for an Hautboy, a Violin and Violoncello.

Fine *Concertantes,* which conftitute a medium between Symphonies and Concertos, are thofe by *Pleyel.*

§ 14.   The antients have alfo written *Concerti Groffi,* or Concertos in which all or moft parts have been principal, or concerting.   But as they muft have been too laborious to compofe, and too intricate for the generality of hearers, to perceive all the beauties they contain, they are become out of fafhion.

C.   CONCERTOS FOR ONE OR MORE SOLO INSTRUMENTS, WITHOUT ANY ACCOMPANIMENTS.

§ 15.   As I have, in § 1, confidered a Concerto as a piece in which the properties of a Symphony and a Sonata are united ; and both thefe pieces may, as I have alfo fhewn before, be written for one or two folo inftruments, without any accompaniment, it follows, that Concertos may be written in the fame manner.   But as one of the principal characteriftics of Concertos is Grandeur, and as it is more neceffary to diftinguifh in them the fullnefs of Tuttis, from the nicety of Solos, than in a Symphony, or in a Sonata, it alfo follows : that they cannot be properly written for any other Solo Inftrument, but the *Organ,* or two or more *Piano Fortes.*

The *Organ* naturally is beft for the purpofe in queftion, particularly one with two or more fets of *Manual,* and a good fet of *Pedal* Keys.   For on fuch an inftrument, the

grandeft

grandeft Tuttis may not only be executed, but alfo the fineft Solos, imitative of particular inftruments, either on one of the Manuals, or even on the Pedals, as we have feen *Vogler*, and *Haefsler*, do fome years ago.

That *Sebaftian Bach* has written Concertos for two, three, or even four Keyed Inftruments, which I fuppofe to be without accompaniments, I have mentioned in Chap. II, § 18, No. II.

CHAPTER V. OF FUGUES IN GENERAL.

§ 1. A *Fugue* is a piece, in which one or more fubjects are imitated according to fome particular rules, which I fhall fhew in this, and the two following Chapters. It admits, and requires, a clofer combination of the arts of harmony, imitation, and double counterpoint, than any other piece of compofition; and therefore writing a good Fugue is not only the fureft proof of a compofer's being a perfect harmonift, but the knowledge of it alfo enables a compofer to write any other fort of mufical pieces more original, and with more ingenious inventions, than what he would be able to do without fuch a knowledge.

The principal work treating of Fugues hitherto known, is that by *Marpurg*, entitled: *Abhandlung von der Fuge*, Berlin 1753, two volumes in quarto; tranflated into the French 1756, entitled *Traité de la Fugue*. But though the truly great merit of that work has perhaps never been difputed, yet I know from my own experience as well, as from the teftimony of my friends, that it is very difficult to learn to write Fugues by it, becaufe it does not reduce the art in queftion to fuch fimple, general, rules, without exceptions, as there are required in any art or fcience, for laying a fure foundation upon them, or fetting out from them. This I have endeavoured to do, as much as lay in my power. And it fhall be my higheft ambition to find, that the diligent reader, who ftudies this Effay according to the Rules laid down in the Introduction, has been enabled by it to form a clear idea of the doctrine of Fugues.

§ 2. All Fugues may be brought under the two general denominations, of *periodical*, and *canonical* ones. The former, which I fhall treat of in the prefent, and the two following Chapters, are commonly called *Fugues* only; and the latter, as will be explained in Chap. VIII. and IX, are called *Canons*.

A Fugue according to the above definition, is a piece, in which but a certain *Period*, ftrain, or phrafe, is imitated according to its rules; and a Canon, that, in which the *whole* beginning melody is imitated throughout; as I have faid in my Effay on Harmony, Chapter XV, § 8, 9.

§ 3. *Sulzer* or *Kirnberger* fuppofes, and Dr. *Burney* and Dr. *Forkel* whom I have taken the liberty of confulting about it, allow, that Fugues had their rife, in the *Antiphones* of the antient Church, where a prieft or choir fung a fhort fentence, and the congregation or another choir fung an anfwer to it. But both, the quere and the anfwer, were fung in a fimple melody or unifon, without a counterpoint to them. From the nature of the faid Antiphones, from the nature of the antient Ecclefiaftical Modes in which they were fung,

and

and from their improvements by the gradual introduction of fimple and double counter-point, follow all the principal rules on which Fugues ftill depend.

N. B.   A feries of very judicious remarks on this fubject, fee in *Dr. Burney's* Hiftory of Mufic, Vol. II, page 466, & *feq.*

§ 4.   Refpecting the nature of the faid Antiphones, it was natural, that if the begin-ning and the anfwering perfon or party fhould feem to agree in the object of their devo-tion, the latter muft *imitate* the former.   This is what we ftill obferve between the Subject and the Anfwer in Fugues.

§ 5.   The nature of the antient Ecclefiaftical Modes, in which the Antiphones in quef-tion were fung, required, that if the firft melody was in the *authentic* mode of a certain key, the imitating one muft be in the *plagal* mode of the fame key; or *vice verfa.*   This produced an agreeable variety by the tranfpofition, without making an alteration in the melody, and laid the foundation to Fugues *in the fifth.*   See § 13; and Chap. VI, § 8, 9, 10.

§ 6.   By the above-mentioned Improvements of Mufic it was invented, to employ both parts at once, by giving them the beginning and anfwering melody repeatedly, alter-nately, and with a *counterpoint* to it.   This was the origin of our prefent Fugues in *two parts.*

And from two parts the antients gradually proceeded to *three,* and *four* parts, in which the fubject and anfwer were alternately imitated in the three following manners, viz: firft, fo, that every part became *equally interefted* in the harmony; fecondly, that the fubject and anfwer returned in the different parts, at every opportunity, and *without a fixed rhythmical order;* and thirdly, that *no full* (or fatisfactory) *conclufion* was made in all the parts at once, before the real end of the piece.   Thefe particulars were calculated to re-prefent an equal eagernefs in every part, to affift in the folemnity of the devotion as much as poffible, to repeat or imitate the principal thought as often as poffible, and not to let it be given up till they were all apparently fatisfied with hearing and repeating it.

Thus *real Fugues* of three, four, and more parts were completed.   And though many improvements have ftill been made in them, by introducing the modern diatonic chro-matic enharmonic Scale, and all the harmonies and melodies it affords, and by not con-fining Fugues to the Church and the limited paffages of Vocal Performers only, but by cultivating it with all the unconfined melodies, which can be produced by good Inftru-ments: yet the knowledge of the above fimple and natural courfe of their invention, fpreads fuch a light over that fort of mufical pieces, that it facilitates the ftudy of them, and teaches us, to compofe Fugues according to their true and original nature, without confining ourfelves to the antient limitations, under which they were written in former ages.

§ 7.   The Fugues hitherto known may be divided, into proper, or improper; ftrict, or free; fimple, or double ones; Fugues in the Fifth, or in fome other interval; in equal, reverfe, or any other imitation; and in two, or more parts.   According to all thefe par-ticulars I fhall endeavour to give a defcription of them, in the following part of this Chapter.

I. *Of proper or improper Fugues.*

§ 8. A *proper* Fugue is that, in which all the principal characteriſtics of a Fugue are found ; and one that is deficient in ſome of the ſaid characteriſtics is called an *improper* Fugue. But by the latter I do not mean Fugues which contain any impropriety of harmony or compoſition, as that would render them undeſerving of ſtanding in the liſt of regular pieces at all.

Proper Fugues therefore are : thoſe ſix by *Handel*, publiſhed for the Organ by Walſh ; alſo twenty-four Fugues by *Sebaſtian Bach*, which I intend to publiſh analyzed if I find ſufficient encouragement for it ; and all ſimilar Fugues for an Orcheſtra or not.

Improper Fugues, but yet the moſt excellent pieces of compoſition, are many of the Choruſes and other pieces of *Handel*, who, as one of the greateſt Fugue writers in the world, has thereby ſhewn, how the knowledge of writing Fugues may give dignity to free pieces, ſee § 1. *Sebaſtian Bach* alſo has written a whole collection of improper Fugues, in two parts, for a Keyed Inſtrument, entitled : Inventions, which deſerve to be known and ſtudied.

II. *Of ſtrict or free Fugues.*

§ 9. When a proper Fugue is ſet ſo, that no liberties are taken in its firſt anſwer, and that it conſiſts throughout of nothing but the Subject and its Anſwers, with ſuch connective paſſages as are related to the Subject or its Counterpoint, it is called a *ſtrict* Fugue ; but when liberties are taken in the firſt Anſwer, or when the whole is ſet with more freedom than the ſtrict rules allow, it is a *free* Fugue. *Strict* therefore are all thoſe I give in the Plates of this Work ; and *free*, but ſet with the moſt judicious freedom, ſome in *Handel*'s Oratorios as well as Concertos.

§ 10. A Fugue which depends but on *One* Subject, is called a *Simple* Fugue.
One depending on *Two* Subjects, is called a *double* Fugue.
-    -   -   - *three*   -   -   *triple* ———.
-    -   -   - *four*   -   -   *quadruple*—.
But often the word *double* Fugue only is uſed, to indicate *more than one* Subject ; in the ſame manner as double, triple, and quadruple Counterpoints are commonly comprehended under the general denomination of *double* Counterpoints.

A Fugue of *five* Subjects is called a *quintuple* ; and one of *ſix* Subjects a *ſextuple* one. Of more ſubjects I do not recollect having ſeen Fugues ; and indeed it requires a great acquaintance with the art of the Fugue, to be able to perceive and comprehend every ſubject and imitation in a *quadruple* Fugue only, ſo that ſtrict Fugues of more than four ſubjects ſerve more for examples of the great abilities of their Authors, than for an extraordinary entertainment to moſt hearers.

Of all theſe Fugues I ſhall ſpeak in Chap. VII.

III. *Fugues in regard to the Interval in which the Anſwer is made.*

§ 11. As the Subjects of free pieces may, according to circumſtances, be imitated in the Uniſon, or any other Interval ; ſo the Subject of a Fugue may alſo be anſwered, in
the

the *Unison* or *Octave;* in the *Fifth,* or *Fourth;* in the *Third,* or *Sixth;* and in the *Seventh,* or *Second.*

§ 12. But according to what I have said in § 4, the answer must be *like* the subject, and this not only in melody, but also in character; and it must also produce an agreeable musical *variety.* It is therefore necessary to shew in which Interval these two qualities can be united best; and also, what ought to be observed respecting Fugues with answers in the other intervals.

§ 13. In Fugues in the *fifth,* or inverted the *fourth,* the answer appears in a key different from that of the subject, which produces an agreeable musical *variety;* and yet, if the answer is made according to the rules I shall give in Chap. VI, § 6, *& seq.* no real digression is made from the key and mode of the subject, nor any striking deviation from its melody, which renders the answer perfectly or sufficiently *like* the subject. These Fugues, therefore, have the said two qualities more than those in other intervals; and as they are by far preferable to the latter, we find that great Fugue Writers have used them most, and hardly paid any attention to Fugues in other intervals.

A Fugue in the *fifth* is that, in which the scale of the Fifth answers that of the Key Note, or *vice versa,* according to the rules I shall give in Chap. VI, § 6, *& seq.*

An apparent Fugue in the *fourth* therefore is: when the subject is in the scale of the Dominante, and the answer in the scale of the Key, a fourth higher than the subject; but I say, this is only an apparent Fugue in the fourth, as it is nothing else but an inversion of that in the fifth.

Real Fugues in the *fourth* would be those, in which the scale of the Key was answered by that of the Fourth. But as in these Fugues the perfect Fourth of the Key cannot be properly answered by that of the Fourth; and also: as I have said in my Essay on Harmony, Chap. X, § 9, that the key of the fourth is the best to be introduced immediately before the Return to the key, consequently near the end, and not at the first setting out from the key : whole Fugues in the fourth will not easily be found. However, after the first Section, a reply may be made in the fourth as well, as in the third, or sixth of the key.

§ 14. Next to Fugues in the fifth, those in the *Octave* may be ranked. For they answer still the purpose of producing a reply *like* the subject, as well as some *difference* between the subject and answer. Yet as the subject and answer appear in the *same key,* the said similitude is too great, and the difference too little; this sort of Fugues therefore have also not been much regarded by good Fugue Writers. Some examples of them however are found in the works of *Handel,* viz: the thirteenth Chorus in Israel in Egypt, Part I, being a vocal fugue in C minor $\frac{3}{2}$, where all the parts enter into the Octave; also the second movement in his second Grand Concerto, being an allegro, common time, and an improper Fugue both in the Octave, and the Unison. The particular *rule* for Fugues in the Octave is: write them in all respects like Fugues in the Fifth, and only make the answer an Octave, or double Octave, higher or lower than the subject, and without regard to the division of the Octave required in Fugues in the Fifth.

Fugues in the *Unison* are entirely like those in the Octave. But as there is not the least difference between the Subject and the Answer, except that which may arise from the different voices or instruments by which the Fugue is performed, this sort of Fugues are less useful than those in the Octave, and fewer examples of them are found in the works of

good

good Authors.   Imitations in the Unifon, in a fort of improper Fugue, fee in *Handel's* Mef-fiah, the fourth and fifth Chorus.

§ 15. Fugues in the *Third* may be written when the Subject is in *Minor;* and Fugues in the *Sixth,* when the Subject is in *Major.*   But it is with them the fame as with a counter-point inverfion in the Tenth, for, they anfwer with major to minor, and minor to major; and in thofe cafes, where the anfwer can be made as mere tranfpofition in the *fame key,* there is no fufficient variety between the fubject and anfwer.   A whole Fugue, therefore, in the Third or Sixth, can have no good effect.   But for the purpofe of expreffing two different characters, *e. g.* a fpirited and a depreffed mind, as finging a Fugue together, thefe two forts of Fugues might perhaps be ufed with a good effect.   That replies in the third or fixth may be made in a Fugue, occafionally, and after the firft Section will require no demonftration.

Dr. Burney remarks refpecting the Fugues in queftion, that they furnifh Imitations, but no Anfwers to the Subject; which diftinction is ufeful, to make ftudents attentive to the rules of a real anfwer.   See his General Hiftory of Mufic, Vol. II, Art. Fugue, in the Index.

§ 16. Whole Fugues in the *Seventh* or in the *Second* cannot be good, as thefe intervals are diffonances to the Key Note; for the faid diffonancy is not only felt in the interval it-felf, but would be perceptible in its whole Scale, if an Anfwer was made in it.

Yet for curiofity's fake, or to produce extraordinary effects, thefe Fugues might be fet; and in any elaborate Fugue, occafional imitations of the Subject in the fecond or feventh may be introduced with proper judgment, as well as thofe in the other intervals.

V. *Of Fugues in regard to the different Sorts of Imitation.*

§ 17. A Subject may be imitated by the Anfwer, in *equal* or *reverfe* motion; with notes of the *fame length,* or by *augmentation* or *diminution;* and in its *original form,* or *varied.*   Each fort of thefe imitations conftitutes a particular fort of Fugues, when ufed by itfelf; but fome, or all of them may occafionally be introduced together in one and the fame Fugue.

Fugues in *equal motion,* are all thofe I give in the prefent work, and in general moft Fugues that are met with.   But occafional reverfions are introduced in my third and fourth one analyzed at Chap. VI, § 31.

Fugues in *reverfe motion* are found in *Sebaftian Bach's* Art of the Fugue, viz : reverfe anfwers from the beginning to the end in the fame Fugue, at No. V, of the faid work; reverfions as well as inverfions of a whole preceding Fugue, at No. XIII, and at No. XV; alfo at No. XXII, which is a Fugue for two keyed inftruments, and the reverfed inverfion of No. XXI.   A fine double Fugue which begins in reverfe motion, though it contains alfo anfwers in equal motion, fee in *Handel's* Ifrael in Egypt, Part I, the 8th Chorus, " Ifrael was glad," &c.

Fugues with anfwers of notes of the *fame length* are again all thofe I give in the prefent work; and an occafional augmentation, as well as diminution, fee in my fecond one ana-lyzed at Chap. VI, § 31.

I

Fugues

Fugues with anfwers by *augmentation* or *diminution* throughout, are found in *Sebaftian Bach*'s Art of the Fugue, viz : No. VI, called *alla Francefe;* and No. VII, expreffly called per augment. & dimin.   Both are the moft fublime pieces imaginable.

Fugues with *varied* anfwers are alfo found in the above moft valuable work by *Sebaftian Bach*.   For the principal Subject, which has been ufed there in no lefs than twenty-three periodical and canonical Fugues, is not only varied from Fugue to Fugue, as I have done the fubject of my four Fugues in this work, but alfo in one and the fame Fugue.

Sufficient Examples of all the above forts of Fugues, I hope, will be found under *The Anfwer*, at Chap. VI, § 6, *& feq.*

VI.   *Of Fugues in two, three, four, and more Parts.*

§ 18.   A Fugue may, like a double Counterpoint, confift either of *real* parts alone, or one or more *additional* parts may be fet to it as accompaniments, or filling parts.   But in fpeaking of a Fugue of two, three, four, or more parts, the *real* parts, or parts which contain the *Fugue*, are in general meant only *;* and if it is otherwife, it ought to be ex-preffed.

§ 19.   Of *real parts only*, confift in general all proper Fugues for the Organ or other Keyed Inftruments without Accompaniments ; Examples of which will be given in the two following Chapters.   Alfo thofe in fome of *Haydn*'s Quartettos ; in *Barfanti*'s fix An-tiphones in five and fix parts ; and in thofe of *Handel*'s Chorufes where the Inftruments only double the vocal parts in the Unifon or Octave.

§ 20.   *Additional parts*, may be fet to a Fugue, either as a fupporting Bafs only, which may fometimes go in the unifon or lower octave with the loweft part of the Fugue, and fometimes take its own feparate notes ; or as a fingle middle or upper part ; or alfo as Bafs and other parts at once.   In all thefe cafes, they may either be drawn from the har-mony of the Fugue, the fame as I have fhewn refpecting the wind Inftruments in Sym-phonies ; fee Chap. III, § 13, *& feq.* ; or as feparate obligato melodies.   The moft inge-nious varieties of which are alfo found in *Handel*'s works ; particularly a double Fugue in *Jephtha*, on the words, " Chemofh no more we will adore," which even begins with a bafs accompaniment to the firft fubject.

CHAPTER VI.   OF SIMPLE FUGUES.

§ 1.   As I have given an explanation of the *word* Simple Fugue in Chap. V, § 10, I may immediately proceed to fhew the *Particulars* of it, and the *Rules* that muft be obferved in regard to each particular.

I. *Particulars*

I. *Particulars of a Simple Fugue.*

§ 2. *Marpurg* in his Treatife on Fugues, mentioned at Chap. V, § 1, points out five particulars of a Fugue, to which I venture to add a fixth and feventh, which he alfo treats of, but as fubordinate to the third.　They are as follows:

1, The Subject; 2, the Anfwer; 3, the Order of the Replies; 4, the Counter Harmony; 5, the Intermediate Harmony; 6, the different Sections; 7, the Modulation.

A.　OF THE SUBJECT.

§ 3.　The *Subject* of a Fugue, is a fhort melody, with which it begins, and on the imitation of which it depends.

Though almoft any fhort melodious paffage may ferve for a fubject to a Fugue, yet fome are better for Fugues *in general* than others, and fome muft be calculated for a *particular fort* of Fugue; all of which ought to be confidered in making the plan for the Fugue.

§ 4.　The particulars that muft be confidered in regard to fubjects for Fugues *in general* are; firft, their Length; fecondly, their Contents; thirdly, their Beginning and Ending.

1, The *Length* of a Subject is fo far optional, that it may confift of two, three, four, or more bars; but the rule for its length is: that it muft be *no longer*, than what the hearer can eafily remember it; or *no fhorter*, than to contain fomething interefting.　That a *long* Fugue will admit of a more long, and a *fhort* one require a more fhort fubject, is naturally underftood.

2, The *Contents* of a fubject muft be confidered in regard to Melody, Compafs, and its qualification for Imitation.　Its *Melody* fhould be fimple, and energetic.　For the more fimple it is, the more room it leaves for agreeable melodies in the other parts; and the more energetic, the more ftrength and dignity it gives a Fugue.　How fimple a Subject may be without rendering a Fugue trivial, *Handel* has fhewn in two mafterly Fugues, the one in his feventh Grand Concerto; the fecond Movement, Allegro; and the other in Jephthah, upon the words, " Chemofh no more we will adore."　And particularly energetic are his Subjects of the Fugues, " And through his Stripes we are healed," in *Meffiah*; and " Hallelujah," with the fine Counter Subject, " We will rejoice," in *Jofeph*, befides many others.　All thofe embellifhed figurative paffages therefore, which are calculated more for melodious fweetnefs, than a manly progreffion, are, generally fpeaking, improper for Subjects of a Fugue.

In regard to *Compafs*, a Subject fhould, in general, not exceed an Octave.　This is neceffary in Vocal Fugues, for enabling the Singer to execute it in more than one Interval; and in Fugues of three or four parts for a Keyed Inftrument, to leave each part room for moving without croffing the others, and to enable the performer to reach them conveniently.　But in Fugues for *different inftruments*, where the melody of every part remains diftinguifhable, though the parts run one into the other; or in Fugues of *two parts* for a Keyed Inftrument, the compafs of the Subject need not be limited to an Octave, and may extend farther.　That excellent Fugues may be written on Subjects which do not exceed the compafs of a Third, or Fourth, will appear from the works of many good Fugue Writers.

The

The qualification of a fubject for *Imitation* fhould alfo be previoufly confidered, befides its other contents. For the more it is calculated to be anfwered, or replied to, at various Diftances, in various forts of Imitation, and by Detached Pieces, the better it is.

3, The *Beginning* and *Ending* of a Subject muft be confidered with refpect to two particulars, viz: the *Interval* with which it begins or ends, and the *time of the meafure* on which it begins or ends.

Refpecting the *Interval*, it is good to *begin* the Subject with fuch an interval, or fuch two or three intervals, as will immediately determine the Key and Mode of the Fugue. A beginning on the *Key Note*, or its Octave, is therefore one of the beft, for the Anfwer replies to it with the Fifth, and the Fugue can obtain moft of its antient characteriftics. Examples fee at Plate XII, Nos. 1, 2, 3, 4, 5. But it may alfo begin on the *Fifth*, to which the Anfwer replies with the Key Note, if only the Key Note and its third are introduced foon after the Fifth, to determine the Key and Mode. Examples fee at Plate XII, Nos. 6, 7, 8. And if it begins with the *Third*, the Anfwer replies with the Third of the Dominante, according to the rules in § 6, *& feq.* If the beginning fhall be with the *Fourth* or another interval of the fcale, care muft be taken to introduce the moft characteriftic intervals, the Octave, Fifth, and Third, foon after it. And the general rule refpecting the *Ending* of the fubject is : that it fhould end with an interval, *after* which the Anfwer may be immediately introduced, or *with* which the Anfwer may begin, without a fault in the harmony or modulation. This is eafy to obferve when the compofer is at liberty to choofe or invent the Subject ; but if a Fugue fhall be made on a given fubject, or on the plain fong of an Hymn or Pfalm, and the End of the Subject is not reconcileable to the Beginning of the Anfwer, it is allowed to add a few tranfitory or conciliatory notes to the former before the latter begins. Yet the faid addition to the fubject fhould be either an imitation of a part of the fubject, or the beginning of a melody which fhall be continued in the Counter Harmony, and not a mere flourifh like as in Rondos. See the addition to the Subject of my Fugue for three hands, No. IV, at Plate XVIII, which is the fhort counterpoint that has been afterwards introduced to the Subject, and fhews that the tranfitory paffages in queftion may be ufed, even where the anfwer might have appeared without them.

The *time of the meafure* on which the Subject may *begin*, is optional; for it may begin on any accented or unaccented time of the meafure. But in general it fhould *end* on the accented time, except in thofe vocal Fugues, where an unaccented fyllable renders a conclufion on the unaccented time neceffary.

§ 5. In regard to the fubjects for a *particular fort* of fimple Fugues, mentioned in § 3, there muft be confidered : whether the Fugue fhall be for Voices, or for Inftruments, or for both ; and for what fort of voices or inftruments it fhall be written.

N. B. That all the above previous confiderations are ufeful, and neceffary in the choice or invention of a Subject for a Fugue, is evident. For, without fuch confiderations, it is a mere chance, to hit upon a Subject calculated for all the varieties, which a compofer may wifh to introduce in his Fugue ; and if he is not acquainted with the whole nature of his fubject before he begins the Fugue, he is in danger, to be either too fparing or too profufe, with the varieties the fubject offers, and confequently unable to continue and conclude the Fugue, in the manner in which it was begun, if he will not make it longer or fhorter than he intended, and not lofe time and labour in compofing it twice.

B. OF THE ANSWER.

§ 6. By the Anſwer of a Fugue is underſtood: a *Reply to the Subject*, according to the general Idea of a Fugue given in Chap. V, § 3, 4, 5. But though I have in the ſaid Chapter mentioned Fugues in all Intervals, I ſhall here ſpeak of thoſe in the Fifth only, as being the moſt proper and moſt cultivated ſort of Fugues.

§ 7. Nothing has hitherto been more perplexing in the ſtudy of Fugues, than the doctrine of the object in queſtion; and yet it is reducible to two very ſimple *general rules*, if we attend to what I have ſaid reſpecting the origin of Fugues in Chap. V, § 3; viz:

Rule I. Every Interval of the Subject muſt be replied to by the Anſwer according to the *degrees of the diatonic ſcale*, both with regard to the *length of notes*, and to the progreſſions by *tones and ſemitones.*

N. B. The *firſt note* of the Anſwer or of any ſucceeding Reply is allowed to be made longer, or ſhorter than the firſt note of the Subject, if the Anſwer cannot well begin in its intended place without taking that liberty.

Rule II. The Scale of the Fifth, in which the Anſwer is to be made, muſt appear as an *upper part of the Scale of the Key Note*, and not as a *ſubſtituted Scale of the Fifth.*

Theſe Rules I ſhall endeavour to explain and exemplify in the three following Sections.

§ 8. According to Rule II, the ſcale of the Key Note muſt be conſidered, as divided into *two parts*, viz: the *lower*, which goes from the Key Note to the Fifth; and the *higher*, which goes from the Fifth to the Octave of the Key Note, as thus:

Lower part: 1, 2, 3, 4, 5; higher part: 5, 6, 7, 8.

The former is the *authentic*, and the latter, the *plagal* ſcale of the Key, according to the doctrine of the Antient Eccleſiaſtical Modes, in my Eſſay on Harmony, Chap. XVIII. How each of them can be extended to its Octave, and farther, I ſhall ſhew in § 10.

§ 9. The ſaid higher and lower part of the Scale muſt anſwer each other ſo, that when the Subject is in the *lower* part, the Anſwer muſt be in the *higher*; and *vice verſa.* Conſequently the Subject may be in the latter as well, as in the former.

But as the lower part conſiſts of *five*, and the higher only of *four* degrees of the diatonic Octave, it is neceſſary to anſwer *two* degrees of the former with *one* degree of the latter; and *vice verſa.* In regard to which the following *particular rules* muſt be obſerved, viz:

Rule I. In general, the *fourth* and *fifth* degree of the lower, or authentic part of the diatonic Octave, are both anſwered with the *fourth* degree of the higher, or plagal part; according to the following repreſentation of the intervals:

Higher part of the Octave   5   6   7   8   Anſwer } or *vice verſa.*
Lower part   -   -   1   2   3 4 5   Subject }

Here it appears: that the Key Note (1), is anſwered with the Dominante (5); the ſecond of the key, with the ſecond of the Dominante (6); the third of the key, with the third of the Dominante (7); and both the fourth and fifth of the key, with the fourth of the Dominante (8).

An example, in which the Subject goes only from the Key Note to its fourth, and which conſequently requires no alteration in the anſwer, ſee at Plate XII, No. 1; and two others, in which both the fourth and the fifth of the key are anſwered with the fourth of the Dominante,

K   minante,

minante, at No. 2, and 3. The laſt is the ſubject and anſwer of my four Fugues, at Plate XIV, *& ſeq.*

In this manner all the particulars mentioned in the two general rules of § 7, can be obſerved. For, when the ſubject begins, leaps or modulates to, or ends, on the fifth of the *key*, the anſwer ought not to proceed to the fifth of the *dominante*, as that would carry the modulation out of the principal key; the anſwer therefore muſt always reply to that interval with the fourth of the dominante, as octave of the key; even in thoſe caſes which come under the following rule.

Rule II. In all caſes, where a melodious progreſſion makes the *third* of the Key appear as *ſixth* of the Dominante, the firſt and ſecond degree of the lower part of the diatonic Octave are both anſwered with the firſt degree of the higher part, as thus:

Higher part of the Octave	5	6	7	8		Anſwer	
Lower part		1.2	3	4	5	Subject	or *vice verſa.*

At Plate XII, No. 4, ſee an example to this Rule, it is from a Fugue by *Albrechtsberger*, and the ſecond note after the dot in the fourth bar, is that, which muſt be conſidered as ſixth of the dominante, and anſwered accordingly; which occaſions the alteration in the whole latter part of the anſwer.

At No. 5, ſee a Subject, which I ſuppoſe to be by *Emanuel Bach*, becauſe he laid it before my Brother at Hamburgh to extemporize upon, at a public trial of ſkill for a place, as it is the cuſtom in Germany. The anſwer is ſtrict, according to the above firſt, and this ſecond rule; but the firſt note in the ſecond bar of the anſwer might have been the fifth of the dominante, (A,) according to the rules in § 11. The notes joined together by dots are thoſe belonging to Rule I, and the four laſt ones thoſe belonging to Rule II, of this Section.

§ 10. As the Subject for a Fugue is not always confined to one half of the diatonic Octave, like as in the examples to the above § 9, I ſhall now ſhew, how the authentic and plagal ſcale of the key muſt be anſwered, when extended to a *full Octave*, or farther. See the following repreſentation of their intervals:

	A Fourth.	A Fifth.	A Fourth.	
Plagal Scale, or Scale of the Dominante,	5, 6, 7, 8,	9, 10, 11, 12,	13, 14, 15,	&c.
Authentic Scale, or Scale of the Key,	1, 2, 3, 4, 5,	6, 7, 8,	9, 10, 11, 12,	
	A Fifth.	A Fourth.	A Fifth.	

Here it appears: firſt, that the Octave of the Key is divided into a *fifth*, and its inverſion the Fourth; when the Octave of the Dominante is divided into a *fourth*, and its inverſion the Fifth: ſecondly, that the *five* degrees of the former muſt, in general, anſwer the Four degrees of the latter; and the *four* degrees of the former, the Five degrees of the latter, or *vice verſa*; according to which the two rules in § 9 muſt be underſtood as thus:

Rule I. In general, the fourth and fifth of the Key are both anſwered with the fourth of the Dominante, being the octave of the Key; and the ſeventh and octave of the Dominante, (11 and 12 of the Key) with the Octave of the Key, as fourth of the Dominante; and the other intervals as the above table ſhews.

Rule

Rule II. In all thofe cafes where a melodious progreffion is made from the *fixth* of the Key, either upwards or downwards that interval is anfwered with the *fixth* of the Dominante, and the whole ftrain to which it belongs is alfo anfwered without regard to the above Rule I.

See the following examples :

Plate XII, No. 5, by *Sebaftian Bach*. The firft bar is anfwered according to Rule I, and all the reft according to Rule II, as the figures fhew. .

No. 7, is the celebrated fubject which the *King of Pruffia* laid before Sebaftian Bach to extemporize upon, with its anfwer by the latter. The three firft notes are anfwered according to the above firft, and the reft according to the fecond rule.

No. 8, is the fubject on which the fame Author has written his inimitable work, " Die Kunft der Fuge," (Art of the Fugue;) the whole is anfwered according to Rule I. But a liberty is found in the note before laft of the Anfwer, being B flat, which fhould be B natural.

No. 9, is the fubject of *Handel's* fifth Fugue, in the well known collection, by which I have proved the Syftem of Harmony, upon which my Effay on Harmony is founded. The fecond, third, and fourth note, are anfwered according to the above Rule II, and all the reft according to Rule I. A liberty muft alfo be taken notice of, being the Sharp by the laft note of the anfwer.

No. 10, from the fame collection by *Handel*. The firft fix notes are anfwered according to Rule I, and the reft according to Rule II.

No. 11, alfo from the fame collection. The two firft notes only are anfwered according to the firft rule, and the reft according to the fecond.

No. 12, is by *Albrechtsberger*. The three firft notes are anfwered according to Rule I, and the reft according to Rule II.

No. 13, is by the fame Author. The firft note only is anfwered according to Rule I, and all the reft according to Rule II.

§ 11. In the three preceding Sections I have treated of anfwers, in which the divifion of the Octave ought to be obferved, according to its authentic and plagal fcale, (fee § 8;) in the prefent now I add two rules, refpecting cafes, in which the faid divifion of the Octave need *not* be attended to. They are as follows :

Rule I. When the Subject is in the Scale of the *Key*, and does not end on, or leap or modulate to, the *Fifth*, the Anfwer may be made in the fcale of the Dominante, exactly with the fame intervals, and without regard to the divifion of the Octave pointed out in § 8, 9, and 10.

Rule II. When the fubject is in the Scale of the *Dominante*, and does not end on, or leap or modulate to, the *Key* (or its Octave,) the anfwer may be made in the fcale of the Key, without regard to the faid divifion of the Octave.

Examples fee as follows :

Plate XIII, No. 1, by *Handel*, which begins, remains, and ends, in the Key, and confequently the anfwer is made according to the above Rule I.

No. 2, by *Sebaftian Bach*, which begins, and remains in the Key, but ends on its Third. It is alfo anfwered according to Rule I.

No. 3, from a Fugue in two parts by *Marpurg*. It begins, and remains in the Key, entirely, except the laft note of the fubject, which is the Fifth of the Key. The whole therefore is anfwered according to Rule I, except the laft note, which is anfwered according to Rule I, § 10.

No. 4,

No. 4, another example by *Sebaſtian Bach*, ſimilar to No. 1 and 2, which I give on account of the originality of the Subject.

§ 12.   I now proceed to the anſwers to *chromatic* and *enharmonic* ſubjects.

N. B. An explanation of what is underſtood by the terms diatonic, chromatic, and enharmonic, in modern muſic, ſee in my Eſſay on Harmony, Chap. I, § 9, *& ſeq.*

1, The rules which muſt be obſerved in anſwers to *chromatic* ſubjects are as follows:

Rule I. Diveſt the ſubject of thoſe accidental ſharps, flats, or naturals, which produce the chromatic intervals, and ſet a regular anſwer to the diatonic ſubject thus appearing.

Rule II. Reſtore the former ſharps, flats, or naturals, in the Subject, and add the ſame to their reſpective notes in the Anſwer, which completes the Anſwer.

Rule III. Should the ſaid Accidents not be properly admiſſible in the anſwer, when made according to the rules in § 9 and 10, the anſwer muſt be made according to thoſe in § 11.

Examples of Chromatic Subjects and Anſwers have already appeared at Plate XII, No. 7, and 9; and the beginning of a Fugue in a ſublime chromatic Sonata for the Piano Forte, by *Sebaſtian Bach*, ſee at Plate XIII, No. 5. And a whole chromatic Fugue ſee at Plate XXI, being that of ſix ſubjects by *Hachmeiſter*.

2, With the anſwer to *enharmonic* ſubjects it is the ſame as with that to chromatic ones. But particular attention muſt be paid to the Interval on which the enharmonic change takes place.   For ſhould the ſaid change not be proper if the anſwer is made according to the rules in § 9 and 10, the anſwer muſt be made according to thoſe in § 11.

An example of a regular enharmonic anſwer ſee in the Fugue by *Stoelzel*, at Plate XXIV.

§ 13.   The above, I hope, will be found ſufficient, to give the diligent reader a perfect idea, of all that is material in ſetting a proper anſwer to the ſubject of a Fugue.   I therefore need to add no more, but that many ſubjects may be regularly anſwered in two or more different manners, as I have already hinted reſpecting the anſwer at No. 5, Plate XII. (See the end of § 9;) and examples of two different anſwers which *Sebaſtian Bach* has ſet to the reverſed ſubject, given before, at Plate XII, No. 8, each in a ſeparate Fugue of his celebrated *Art of the Fugue*, ſee at Plate XIII, No. 6, and 7.   At No. 6, ſee the whole, except the four laſt notes, anſwered according to Rule I, § 10; and the four laſt notes only according to Rule II, § 9.   At No. 7, the two firſt notes alone are anſwered according to the ſaid Rule I, and all the reſt according to the ſaid Rule II.

If a ſtudent therefore wiſhes to become acquainted with all the caſes, in which the one or another ſort of anſwer has been thought beſt, by the antient ſtrict Fugue Writers, he ſhould collect ſubjects from as many good Fugues as he can meet with, and firſt ſet a regular anſwer to them according to what I have ſaid and exemplified above, but afterwards compare his anſwers with thoſe of the different authors by whom the Fugues are ; this, I preſume, will not only make him more acquainted with the rules I have given, than merely ſtudying them, but alſo lead him to many obſervations, which if they were written here would more perplex than inſtruct him.

That great Fugue Writers will ſometimes take an extraordinary liberty, has already appeared at Plate XII, No. 8, and 9, N. B. and at Plate XIII, No. 7, N. B. ; in all which places accidental ſharps, flats, or naturals, have been introduced contrary to the firſt general rule at § 7.   And a particular inſtance of that ſort is found in the Anſwer of *Handel's* Fugue, in the Overture to Muzio Scævola, ſee Plate XIII, No. 8, where the third note, at N. B. in the Anſwer, has a ſharp, contrary to the ſtrict rule, and yet that liberty has been admired by *Geminiani*, the ſtricteſt obſerver of rules at thoſe times.   See Memoirs of the
Life

Life of *Handel*, London 1760, in a note to page 44, (Dodfley). But young Compofers fhould never imitate great authors in their *deviating* from the ftrict rule, before they are able to *obferve* it fluently and almoft habitually like them.

That both, the Subject and the Anfwer, may in the courfe of the Fugue be introduced *varied* I have mentioned before, (at Chap. V, § 17,) and two examples taken from *Sebaftian Bach*'s Art of the Fugue, fee at Plate XIII, No. 9, and 10.

That at No. 9, is a variation of No. 6, in the fame Fugue; and that at No. 10, a variation of No. 7, in the fame Fugue.

§ 14. All the above, (except what has been faid juft now refpecting variations of the fubject,) muft be obferved at leaft in the *firft Section* of the Fugue, (fee § 22). If in the other Sections a particular Modulation or Imitation require fome more liberties in the Subject or Anfwer, they are allowable; but they muft be introduced fparingly, and with proper judgment.

C.   OF THE ORDER OF THE REPLIES.

§ 15. By a *Reply* I underftand here: every repetition of the Subject, after its firft appearance in one part of the harmony; either as Subject, or as Anfwer. And by the *Order of Replies:* firft, in what order both the Subject and Anfwer may be at firft *introduced;* fecondly, in what order and fhape, and at what diftance, they may afterwards *return*.

§ 16. The rules, refpecting the order in which the Subject and Anfwer may be at firft *introduced*, are as follows.

Rule I. The different parts of the harmony of which the Fugue confifts, fhould for the firft time take the Subject and Anfwer *alternately*, or like one, two, or more *couple of parts*. The application of this rule to Fugues of two, or more parts, is as follows:

1, In Fugues of *two* parts, either of the parts may begin the Fugue with the *Subject*, and the other part follows with the Anfwer. But both, the Subject and Anfwer, cannot be properly introduced in immediate fucceffion, in one and the fame part; nor the fubject alone in both parts, before the anfwer has been made to it.

2, In Fugues of *four, fix*, or *eight* parts: the firft, third, fifth, and feventh part, take the Subject; and the fecond, fourth, fixth, and eighth part, the Anfwer. *Or vice verfa.* But the beginning is always made with the *Subject*, and in general it is fucceeded by the Anfwer: then the Subject appears again, and is fucceeded by an Anfwer; and thus the Subject and Anfwer appear *by turns*, from two parts to two parts, till all the parts have regularly entered.

Introducing therefore the Subject, in two or more parts of the harmony, before the Anfwer has appeared, is a liberty, which *Handel* and other great Fugue Writers fometimes have taken for particular reafons; but young compofers fhould ftrictly adhere to the above rule, till they have acquired fome perfection in compofing Fugues.

3, In Fugues of three, five, or a greater number of *odd* parts: the *even* number of parts contained in them, muft take the Subject and Anfwer, alternately, and in the fame manner as pointed out under No. 2, juft now; and the remaining *odd* part may, according to circumftances, take either the Subject or the Anfwer.

N. B. The odd part may be, either the firft, or third, or fifth, or feventh part; or the fecond, or fourth, or fixth part, may be introduced as an odd part between two others.

Rule II.   *Any part* of the harmony may *begin* the Fugue, and the other parts may come in, in the following order :

1, In *clofe* fucceffion, as thus :

a, when the *higheft* part begins, the others fucceed in regular order downwards.

b, when the *loweft* part begins, the others fucceed in regular order upwards.

c, when a *middle* part begins, the others fucceed regularly both up and downwards.

N. B.   This clofe fucceffion is the beft, becaufe it keeps the parts together, and produces no difagreeable vacancy between the parts as they appear.

2, In a more *diftant* fucceffion, when the above clofe order cannot be conveniently attended to, that in which but *one part* is fkipped at a time, is the only fucceffion tolerable, befides the clofe one.

According to the above rules and explanations, therefore, all the good and tolerable Orders of Replies in Fugues of two, three, and four parts, are as the following Tables fhew, where 1, denotes the firft, or higheft part of the harmony; 2, the next part downwards; 3, the third part from above, and fo forth.

a, In Fugues of *two* parts: (fee No. 1, under Rule I.)

b, In Fugues of three parts :

$$\left.\begin{array}{l}\text{Subject 1, anfwer 2, fubject or anfwer 3.}\\ \text{Subject 2, anfwer 3, fubject or anfwer 1.}\\ \text{Subject 2, anfwer 1, fubject or anfwer 3.}\\ \text{Subject 3, anfwer 2, fubject or anfwer 1.}\end{array}\right\}\text{good.}$$

c, In Fugues of four parts :

$$\left.\begin{array}{l}\text{Subject 1, anfwer 2, fubject 3, anfwer 4.}\\ \text{Subject 4, anfwer 3, fubject 2, anfwer 1.}\\ \text{Subject 2, anfwer 3, fubject 4, anfwer 1.}\\ \text{Subject 3, anfwer 2, fubject 1, anfwer 4.}\end{array}\right\}\text{good.}$$
$$\left.\begin{array}{l}\text{Subject 3, anfwer 4, fubject 1, anfwer 2.}\\ \text{Subject 2, anfwer 1, fubject 4, anfwer 3.}\end{array}\right\}\text{tolerable.}$$

The order of replies in Fugues of *more* than four parts will require no farther demonftration, as it follows from the above tables, and from what I have faid before.

Though great compofers have alfo, but feldom, taken the liberty of fkipping *two* parts in the order of introducing the different parts of a Fugue, by beginning with the Subject in the firft part, and letting the anfwer immediately appear in the fourth part, before the fecond and third have appeared ; yet this can only be done for particular purpofes, and requires great judgment, if the diftance between the parts fhall not be felt as too great.

§ 17.   I proceed now to fhew : in what *order* and *fhape*, and at what *diftance*, the fubject and anfwer may *return* in the different Sections of a Fugue, after their firft introduction according to § 16.

N. B.   Refpecting the term *Sections*, fee § 22.

1, The *order* of the replies in the fucceeding fections depends on the following rules :

Rule I.   The order of any fucceeding fection ought not to be perfectly like that which immediately precedes it.

Rule II.   A fucceeding fection ought not to begin with the fubject or anfwer in that part, where the fame has been heard immediately before.

Rule III.   After the firſt Section of the Fugue, the Subject and Anſwer need not always be introduced according to Rule I and II, § 16, but either of them may appear *more than once*, in immediate ſucceſſion, though not in the ſame part; and even the Anſwer may *begin* a new *Section*.   For, the term Anſwer need not always be taken in its ſtricteſt ſenſe, and that of Plagal Subject might be ſubſtituted for it, according to what I have ſaid in § 8.

Rule IV.   In all replies, both the Subject and Anſwer ought as much as poſſible to begin in a *conſpicuous* manner.   For this purpoſe it is required: either to let that part, in which a reply ſhall take place, have ſome Reſts before the reply; or to let the firſt note of the reply begin with a Leap.   N. B.   A liberty, reſpecting the prolonging or ſhortening of the firſt note of the Reply, has been mentioned at N. B. under the firſt general rule in § 7.

2, The *Shape* or form, in which the ſubject and anſwer may appear after the firſt ſection of the Fugue, requires the obſervation of the two following rules:

Rule I.   When the ſubject and anſwer have been ſufficiently impreſſed on the ear of the hearer, in their original form, they need not always return in one and the ſame ſhape; but they may alſo be introduced *reverſed*, by *augmentation* or *diminution*, or *even varied*. Of all theſe ſorts of replies there will be found examples in my four Fugues at Plate XIV, *& ſeq*.   And the beginning of a moſt ſublime Fugue, both with reverſe, and augmented or diminiſhed replies, ſee at Plate XIV, No. 1, it is by *Sebaſtian Bach*, in his Art of the Fugue.   Examples of two varied replies I have given before, at Plate XIII, No. 9, 10.

Rule II.   The ſubject and anſwer need not always return at full length, but may be introduced by *detached pieces*; or the latter part may be *ſhortened*, or *altered* a little when a particular imitation requires it.   Of theſe replies examples will alſo be found in my ſaid four Fugues.

3, The *Diſtance* at which the ſubject and anſwer may follow each other, comprehends: firſt, the reply at *full diſtance*; ſecondly, its various *reſtrictions*.

By a reply at *full diſtance* I underſtand that, where the Anſwer begins *after*, or *with* the laſt note of the Subject; and *vice verſa*.   At this diſtance the Subject and Anſwer ſhould follow each other through the whole firſt Section of the Fugue, or at leaſt the firſt time, as otherwiſe the hearer would be uncertain about the length, and the ending of the Subject. That in ſome caſes a few conciliatory notes may, or muſt be added to the Subject, before the firſt Anſwer appears, I have ſaid in § 4, under the *ending* of the ſubject.

And by a *reſtriction* of the Subject and Anſwer, I underſtand: the introduction of the one, *before* the other is ended.   From this definition it follows; that, according to circum-ſtances, the different replies in a Fugue may be made under *various* reſtrictions; the ſame as the replies in a Canon may ſucceed the leading melody at various diſtances.   In an ela-borate Fugue therefore, it is generally expected, that ſome replies ſhould be made at leaſt under *two* different reſtrictions, viz: a *leſſer*, and a *greater* one.   The former is: when a ſucceeding Subject or Anſwer begins near the End of the preceding; and the latter: when the ſucceeding Subject or Anſwer enters, ſoon after the Beginning of the preceding one. Both theſe reſtrictions will be found in my Fugue 1 and 2, Plate XIV, XV; and ſeveral more in Fugue 3 and 4, Plate XVI, and XVIII.   As a greater reſtriction of the replies re-quires more acquaintance with the Subject than a leſſer, if the hearer ſhall be able to attend both to the preceding and ſucceeding Subject or Anſwer, it follows: that the former ſhould be ſpared till near the end of the Fugue, where the hearer is ſuppoſed to be ſuffi-ciently acquainted with the Subject; and that the latter may be introduced ſooner.   That by a perfect knowledge of the Art of Canons, a Subject may be expreſsly calculated for any intended reſtriction will require no demonſtration.   Both,

Both, at full diftance, and under the faid reftrictions, the Subject or Anfwer may be removed from the *accented* to the *unaccented* time of the meafure, or *vice verfa*. That is to fay: they may be introduced both *per arfin et thefin*; or at the lifting up, or letting down of the hand in beating time. Examples of this fort will alfo be found in my four Fugues at Plate XIV, *& feq.*; particularly one, in Fugue 2, third Section, where the reply appears on the laft quarter of the meafure *per arfin*, and proceeds by *fyncopation*. The above, I prefume, is the proper fenfe of the words *arfis* and *thefis*, (fee *Chambers's* Dictionary,) which I think neceffary to mention, as I have found fome Author (I think *Bevin*,) call thofe Canons *per arfin et thefin*, which, according to both my Effays, fhould be called *right* and *reverfe*, or alfo, in *contrary motion*.

D. OF THE COUNTER HARMONY.

§ 18. By the *Counter Harmony* in a Fugue I underftand: that harmony, which is fet as an *accompaniment* to the Subject or Anfwer. It might be called the Counterpoint, as at all events every part of it makes a fimple, if not a double Counterpoint to the Subject or Anfwer. But as we are, in general, accuftomed to ufe the term Counterpoint, more in regard to *two* relative parts only, than to *three* or *more* parts, I think it beft to preferve the above denomination of *Marpurg* in faying *Counter Harmony*.

§ 19. The faid harmony may confift, either of melodies *different* from the Subject or Anfwer; or *partly*, or *entirely*, of the Subject or Anfwer itfelf. The *former* is the cafe, in the firft Section of the Fugue, where the Counter Harmony begins in one part only, and increafes from part to part till the required number of parts is completed; and the *latter* is required in thofe Reftrictions of the Fugue, where the fucceeding Subject appears before the preceding is ended, or where Subject follows Subject in two or three parts, like as in a Canon, without any other parts to them.

In all the faid cafes the following rules muft be obferved:

Rule I. The *whole*, that is to fay the Subject and Counter Harmony together, muft be regular according to the rules of *Simple Counterpoint*, (fee my Effay on Harmony, Chap. XIII, § 3;) and Double Counterpoints contained in it can make no exception from this rule.

Rule II. Every part of the Counter Harmony muft be an *Obligato* melody, different from the Subject in notes and motion, but related to it in character.

E. OF THE INTERMEDIATE HARMONY.

§ 20. By the Harmony in queftion I underftand, that, which is introduced *between* a *preceding* and a *fucceeding* Subject or Anfwer. It ferves for two purpofes, viz. firft: to prolong the Fugues in an agreeable manner; and fecondly, to link the different Sections of the Fugue together, with lefs conftraint, than what would arife from too clofe an adherence to the Subject.

The Particulars which ought to be confidered in regard to the Intermediate Harmony in queftion, are its *Quantity*, and its *Quality*.

Refpecting the *firft*, or Quantity, it is true, that more or lefs intermediate harmony may be introduced in a Fugue, according to its intended leffer or greater ftrictnefs; but if it fhall be a proper Fugue, it ought to contain no more of it, than what we can attend to,

without

without lofing, as it were, fight of the Subject. And it is alfo natural, that the Intermediate Harmony of one Section of the Fugue, fhould not be unproportional to that of the other Sections.

And in regard to the *fecond* particular, or Quality, it is a rule : that the intermediate Harmony ought not to appear as a *Difcontinuation* of the Subject and Counter Harmony, but as a Continuation or Prolongation of the fame.

The beft Intermediate Harmony therefore is that, which arifes from a judicious Imitation of fome part or parts of the Subject as well as the firft Counter Harmony ; and it may be prolonged, by introducing in it repeated beginnings of the Subject, which, as it keeps the hearer in conftant expectation of the whole Subject, renders the Fugue more interefting than otherwife. See my fourth Fugue, at Plate XVIII.

But improper for a Fugue, are thofe intermediate paffages, which appear more like interfperfed pieces of a Symphony, than as belonging to the Subject, and arifing from its Imitation.

F. OF THE DIFFERENT SECTIONS OF A FUGUE.

§ 22. By a *Section* of a Fugue I underftand : a *connected introduction* of the Subject and Anfwer, in its *different parts;* with the Intermediate Harmony that belongs to it. It is what *Marpurg* calls " Durchführung," or, The leading of the Subject through the different parts of the harmony. It differs from what is called a Section in other pieces of compofition, in not admitting of a conclufive Cadence in all parts, except at the end of the Fugue, (fee Chap. V, § 6.)

§ 23. The different Sections of a Fugue may be *complete,* or *incomplete; diftinct,* or *indiftinct.*

A *complete* Section is that, where the Subject appears in every part of the harmony, like as in the firft and fecond Section of all my four Fugues, at Plate XIV, *& feq.*

An *incomplete* Section confequently is that, where the Subject appears not in all parts of the harmony. Of this fort are the third and fourth Section of my third Fugue, Plate XVI, when the thirds or fixths, added to the fubject, are not confidered as a fubject.

A *diftinct* Section is that, where the replies in connection may be eafily difcovered, like as in all the fections of my four Fugues, mentioned before.

An *indiftinct* Section therefore is that, in which the replies in connection cannot be eafily difcovered; or fuch a part of a Fugue in which no regard has been paid to the connecting of replies. The former are often found in the mafterly Fugues of *Handel,* and *Sebaftian Bach;* and the latter betray no knowledge of their compofer, except in cafes where the irregularity depends upon a well-fuggefted regular plan.

A Fugue may confift of as many fections, as the order of replies pointed out in § 15, *& feq.* may be varied. But a proper Fugue confifts in general of no lefs than *three,* and no more than *fix* or *feven* fections ; as in the former cafe it would contain too little variety, and in the latter, become too long and tirefome.

G. OF THE MODULATION OF A FUGUE.

§ 24. Of the object in queftion I fhall endeavour to fpeak firft *in general,* fecondly in regard to the different *Sections* of the Fugue, and thirdly in regard to the *Cadences* which may be introduced.

1, The plan of Modulation *in general*, which muft be obferved in a Fugue, follows from what I have faid in Chap. I, refpecting the Modulation of all Mufical Pieces, for: at the *beginning* the Key and Mode muft be well expreffed; about the *middle* all forts of digreffions may take place, though with proper judgment; and towards the *end*, the Key and Mode muft be perfectly eftablifhed again, fo as to make a fatisfactory conclufion in it.

2, But in regard to the different *Sections*, the Modulation of a Fugue may be as follows:

In a Fugue of *three* Sections: the *firft* Section muft remain in the Key and Mode. For this reafon, the divifion of the Scale, as pointed out in § 8, 9, and 10, is particularly neceffary in thofe Fugues, where the fubject begins, ends, or has a diftinct cæfure, on the fifth. However, if no conclufion or cæfure takes place on the Fifth, or no particular ftrefs is put upon it by a *holding* note or *leap*, it may be anfwered by its fifth as fecond of the Key, according to what has been faid in § 11. The *fecond* Section may either *remain* in the Key and Mode, and only fome variety of the harmony may be produced by the different Imitations and Inverfions for which the Fugue is calculated; or fome *digreffion* may be introduced in it, by letting the Subject appear in a related Key and Mode, or in two related Keys and Modes. The *third* Section muft be in the Key again, though it may alfo begin in the Key of its Fourth, and then make a full conclufion in the Key, according to what has been faid above, under No. 1.

In a Fugue of *more than three* Sections, the Modulation of the firft and laft Section muft be the fame as in thofe of three Sections. But according to the number of Sections there may be more digreffions introduced in the intermediate Sections, than in Fugues of three Sections, if only the Order in which every fubftituted Key and Mode may appear, is properly attended to.   (See Effay on Harmony, Chap. X, § 9.)

3, Refpecting the *Cadences*, which fhall be made in a Fugue, it is a general rule: that *no perfect Cadence* muft be made in *all parts* at once, except at the End of the Fugue. The reafon for this rule appears from the defcription I have made of the origin of Fugues in Chap. V, § 3, 4, 5, 6. See alfo § 22 of this Chapter. The different Sections of a Fugue, therefore, muft not conclude like as in Sonatas, Symphonies, or Concertos, where a perfect Cadence ought to be made in all parts; but the Cadences with which the periods or fections end, muft be *interrupted*, either by letting a new Subject begin in one part, when a conclufion is made in another; or by introducing a Diffonance to the note on which the Cadence is made; and the latter is required in thofe cafes, where only fome intermediate harmony fhall fucceed the Cadence.

However, the laft, or ending Cadence of the Fugue, may be made as conclufive and formal as the length of the Fugue will permit. It may therefore be announced, and prepared, by an *Organ Point*; or even a *Fancy Cadence* may be made towards the end of the Fugue, if it is done according to the character of the Fugue, and with paffages that are related to the Subject, or to the Counter Subjects, and to the Intermediate Harmony. An Example of a conclufion preceded by an *Organ Point*, in which nothing but imitations of the Subject and Counter-point are ufed, fee in Fugue III, at Plate XVIII, near the end; and an example of a *Fancy Cadence* near the conclufion, which alfo is related to the character and the paffages of the Fugue, in Fugue IV, at Plate XX.

More, refpecting the Modulation of Fugues, fee in § 30, *& feq.*

II. *Conftruction*

II. *Conftruction of a whole Simple Fugue.*

§ 25. I now proceed to make the application of all I have faid above, to the conftruction of *whole Simple Fugues*, which I fhall endeavour to do, firft with regard to the *Sections*, and fecondly with regard to the *Parts* of which they confift.

A. CONSTRUCTION OF A FUGUE WITH REGARD TO ITS SECTIONS.

§ 26. As according to § 23, a proper Fugue feldom confifts of lefs than *three* Sections, I fhall explain its Conftruction firft with regard to *three*, and fecondly with regard to *more than three* Sections.

1, A Fugue of *three* Sections may be conftructed as follows.

Firft Section. The Fugue begins with the *Subject*, in any of the parts of which it is to confift; the anfwer appears immediately after the laft note of the Subject, or with the laft note; and the other parts, if any, follow with the Subject and Anfwer, one after another, according to the Order of the Replies pointed out in § 15, 16, 17, either at the fame Full Diftance, or after a fhort Intermediate Harmony.

N. B. This Intermediate Harmony may be immediately introduced between the firft Anfwer and fecond Subject, or between the fecond Subject and its Anfwer, or only after the introduction of the Subject and Anfwer in all parts, fo as to prolong and conclude the firft Section; and in thofe extraordinary cafes where the Subject ends with a note, immediately after which the Anfwer cannot properly appear, a fhort tranfitory paffage may even take place between the firft Subject and its Anfwer, to connect them properly. See § 4, No. 3. Another Liberty refpecting the *firft note* of the Anfwer, which may alfo be allowed to a returning Subject, fee under the firft general rule in § 7. Every preceding part may either be *continued* as a Counter Harmony to the fucceeding ones; or that part which fhall take the Subject or Anfwer again in the next Section, may *reft*, as foon as there is a proper Opportunity for it.

The Modulation of this Section ought to be in the Key and the Dominante only. The Section may end with a Cadence, on the Key Note, or on its Dominante, either immediately after the laft Anfwer, or after a proportionable Intermediate Harmony; but the faid Cadence muft be interrupted according to the remarks in § 24, No. 3.

Second Section. Either the Subject, or the Anfwer, returns in any part where it has not been laft, and if poffible in another Octave than where it was before in the fame part. The other parts follow with the Subject and Anfwer according to the Order of Replies in § 15, & feq. If the Cadence which ends the firft Section is made immediately after the laft Anfwer or Reply, an Intermediate Harmony may precede the firft Subject in this Section, or elfe it may be introduced between the different Replies, or at the end of this Section, the fame as in the firft Section.

The Modulation may either remain in the Key and its Dominante, according to § 24, No. 2, or the Subject and Anfwer may appear in a nearly related Key and Mode; or the Section may be divided between the two neareft related Keys, and thus appear like two Sections contracted into one.

The Diftance of the Replies is generally expected according to the leffer Reftriction, pointed out in § 17, No. 3, being Replies, which begin before the Subject is quite

ended;

ended; (fee the two Fugues at Plate XIV, XV;) but the fame diftance, or a greater one than that of the firft Section of the Fugue may alfo be chofen, if only it be done with proper knowledge and difcretion.

Both the Subject and Anfwer may in this Section appear in reverfe as well as right motion, by Augmentation or Diminution, entire or by detached Pieces, varied, and according to all the Arts of Imitation mentioned at § 17, No. 2.

The End of this Section may be made with a Cadence in one of the neareft related Keys, but it muft be interrupted, according to what has been faid in § 24, No. 3.

Third Section. The Order of the Replies may be made according to the rules given above, under Second Section. The Diftance of the Replies is generally expected according to the greater reftriction mentioned in § 17, No. 3, being replies nearly after the beginning of the fubject. The Modulation muft be in the Key again; or it may begin in the Key of the Fourth, and only the latter half of the Section may be in the principal Key, as has been faid in § 24, at No. 2. All forts of artificial Imitations may be continued in this Section, and even crowded more clofe together than before. Intermediate Harmonics may give this Section a length proportionable to the two former ones; and a full Conclufion may be made with a perfect Cadence according to § 24, No. 3.

2, A Fugue of *more than three* Sections, may be conftructed as follows:

The *firft* and *laft* Section ought to be like thofe of a Fugue of *three* Sections, as explained juft now.

The two, three, four, or more Sections *between* the *firft* and *laft*, muft fhare the intended variety of Replies, Modulation, and Imitation, in the following manner, viz: firft, that every Section becomes different from all the others: fecondly, that a regular and well connected courfe of Modulation appears through the whole; and thirdly, that the clofeft reftrictions of the Replies, and the moft intricate Imitations are referved for the latter part of the Fugue. This laft is required, for the purpofe of rendering the hearer firft fufficiently acquainted with the fubject, that he may be able to follow it in all its artificial Imitations, and not lofe the faid greateft beauties of a Fugue.

B. CONSTRUCTION OF A FUGUE WITH REGARD TO ITS PARTS.

§ 27. As a Fugue may confift of two, three, four, or more parts, I fhall endeavour to fhew firft their proper *diftance*; and fecondly, the *qualities* required in each part.

§ 28. Refpecting the *diftance* between the different parts of a Fugue there are two rules to be obferved, viz:

Rule I. The different parts muft not be *crowded* or run *one into the other*, fo that it becomes difficult to *diftinguifh* each part, or follow its melody.

This Rule is particularly neceffary in regard to Fugues for a Keyed Inftrument. For, the greateft beauties of the Fugue are loft if every part cannot be clearly diftinguifhed. See Page 31, near the bottom.

Rule II. The parts fhould not ftand at *too great* nor at too *unequal* a diftance one from another.

The former, or too great a diftance between two parts, creates a poverty of effect, becaufe the want of filling parts is perceived; and the latter, or too unequal a diftance between three, four, or more parts, would feparate one or two parts from the whole of the harmony, and render them either unequal to the others, or too confpicuous. Refpecting the proper diftribution of a harmony, fee my Effay on Harmony, Chap. III, § 2, *& feq.*

§ 29.

§ 29. The *qualities* required in the different parts of a Fugue are : firſt, that one part ſhould be properly *related* to the other ; and ſecondly, that all the parts ſhould be *equally intereſted* in the harmony and melody of the Fugue.

The ſaid *relation* between the different parts muſt be confidered : firſt, with regard to their acutenefs or gravenefs ; ſecondly, with regard to their being Vocal or Inſtrumental ; and (when Inſtrumental,) thirdly, with regard to the particular ſort of inſtruments for which they are intended.   In the firſt cafe, they may be either all treble, all alto, all tenor, or all baſs, Vocal or Inſtrumental parts ; or alſo be compofed of two or more ſorts, of the ſaid parts of a harmony.   In the ſecond cafe, they may be either Vocal alone, or Inſtrumental alone, or both Vocal and Inſtrumental.   And in the third cafe, they may be all for Inſtruments of a ſimilar kind, ſuch as ſtringed Bow Inſtruments, (Violins, Tenors, and Violoncellos ;) or for inſtruments different in nature.

What muſt be obſerved in regard to all the above confiderations will follow from what I ſhall ſay in Chap. XI, § 6, 7.

That all the parts of the Fugue muſt be *equally intereſted* in the harmony and melody of the Fugue, follows from Chap. V, § 3, & *ſeq.*   But here muſt be recollected what I have ſaid reſpecting *real*, or *additional* parts, in Chap. V, § 19, 20 ; for of the former I only ſpeak here.   That ſome of the parts may occafionally *reſt*, I alſo have ſaid before.

III. *Fugues analyzed according to the above Principles.*

§ 30. I now prefume to lay before the Reader, four Fugues, which I have written on *one and the ſame Subject,* to exemplify the rules I have laid down in the prefent Chapter ; and hope that their being on *one* Subject, will be found better for the purpofe in queſtion, than if they were on *different* Subjects, as the varieties of every one of them are in ſome meafure related to thofe of all the others ; from which it follows : that much more might have been done with the Subject, in every Fugue, than what I have done with it, had there been occafion for it.

The *Subject* is compofed of the two ſhort Subjects on which I have written the laſt Preſto in my *Analyzed Symphony,* Op. VII, the firſt by *augmentation,* and the ſecond by *diminution,* when compared to their original form in the ſaid Preſto.   By this Subject there-fore, I prefume to exemplify, how á Subject of a piece of free compofition may be pre-pared for a Subject to a Fugue ; or alfo : (if the Fugues are ſuppofed to be the original compofition,) how the Subject of a Fugue may be rendered proper, for writing a Sym-phony, or other piece of free compofition, upon it.   The ufe I have likewife made of the fame Subject, for Canons, as the ſtricteſt ſort of compofition, will appear in Chap. IX.

§ 31. To prevent crowding the examples in queſtion, with the ſaid analyfis, I ſhall make ufe of the following Characters in the Examples, viz :

1, The different *Sections* I ſimply mark with *numerical letters,* as thus : **I, II, III, IV, &c.** inſtead of ſaying the firſt, ſecond, third, or fourth Section.

2, The *Subject* I mark with a capital S, and the *Anſwer* with a capital A, to ſhew the difference between them.

3, The *Counter Harmony* I do not mark at all, except in thofe places of Fugue III and IV, where it is a double Counterpoint, and in that cafe I point it out by the ſmall letters *c p,* (counterpoint).

4, The

4, The *Intermediate Harmony* I mark with *inter.* to fhew how far a Subject or Anfwer goes.

5, The *Modulation* I only mark in thofe places, where a digreffion from the principal key is made, or a return to it, by fetting the *capital letter* of the Key in which the harmony is, with the word *major* or *minor* to it.

Firſt Fugue in queſtion.

§ 32. See Plate XIV, No. 2. This is a fimple but ſtrict Fugue in *two* parts. It confifts of three Sections, in which the Replies are made as thus: in the firſt Section at full diftance; in the fecond at a leffer diftance; and in the third at the leaft diftance   The Counter Harmony might have been ufed as double counterpoint, but I have avoided doing fo, for the purpofe of not making this a fort of double Fugue. The Intermediate Harmony is taken from the Subject, the firſt four notes of which are imitated in it by diminution; firſt in the higher part, and then in the lower part, towards the end of the firſt Section; in the fecond Section the fame imitation makes a Canon in the fifth above; and in the third Section again the fame, but reverfed, and as a Canon in the fourth above. The Modulation is quite natural, and remains in the Key and its Dominante. The Cadence which is made at the end of the firſt Section is interrupted by the Subject which begins the fecond Section, and the fame it is with the imperfect Cadence at the end of the fecond Section; but a formal conclufion is made at the end. Both parts are alfo equally interefted in the Fugue.

Second Fugue.

§ 33. See Plate XV, *Fuga* II, *a* 3. This is alfo a fimple, but a ſtrict Fugue in *three* parts. As it is an *inſtrumental* Fugue, there has been no occafion for having the compafs, or even the name of three *Vocal* parts, in view; for if it is only found confifting of three regular and obligato parts, it is fufficient in that refpect.

The *Subject* is exactly the fame as in the preceding Fugue, but it opens this Fugue in the loweft part, when in the former it appeared firſt in the higheft.

The *Counter Harmony*, which is different from that of Fugue I, might alfo have been ufed as a double counterpoint; but I have avoided ufing it fo, in order to leave the piece a *fimple* Fugue.

The *Intermediate* Harmony will be found throughout confifting of imitations of the Subject, though of no Canons like that in Fugue I.

The *Modulation* is again natural, and remains in the Key and its Dominante throughout the Fugue, though the fecond Intermediate Harmony and the Conclufion contain more free Modulations than the firſt Fugue.

This Fugue alfo confifts of *three Sections*. In the firſt, every reply is made at full diftance; in the fecond, a bar fooner; and in the third Section, the firſt reply is made two bars fooner, and the fecond three bars and a quarter fooner, than at firſt, which makes the latter reply to be *per arfin* and by fyncopation, when the Subject and all other replies are *per thefin*, and without fyncopation.

The *Conclufion* of this Fugue gives a fpecimen of introducing the Subject both by augmentation and diminution, to which nothing but imitations of the firſt Counter harmony and Intermediate harmony are continued.

No *Cadence* will alfo be found in it contrary to § 24, No. 3; and the parts are equally obligato, or interefted in the Fugue.

Third

Third Fugue.

§ 34. See Plate XVI, *Fuga* III, *a* 4. This is an elaborate Fugue with a double Counterpoint, on account of which it belongs to the firſt claſs of *double* Fugues, as I ſhall ſhew in the next Chapter. But as the order of Replies in it is conformable to the rules I have given in § 16 and 17 of this Chapter, I may analyze it in this place.

The principal *Subject* is the ſame as in the two preceding Fugues, though it appears in another ſort of Meaſure, and with Suſpenſions in the third and fourth bar. The *Counterpoint* appears ſoon after the beginning of the firſt Subject, for two reaſons, viz: firſt, to point out to the hearer, the triple time of the Fugue, which cannot be diſtinguiſhed in the firſt half of the Subject by itſelf; ſecondly, to keep up the life of the movement, which otherwiſe would be interrupted by the third bar of the Subject. See Eſſay on Harmony, Chapter XIII, § 3, Rule VI. That this Counterpoint is calculated for an inverſion in the Tenth as well as the Octave, will appear in the third and fourth Section of the Fugue where thirds have been added to the original parts which make the ſaid inverſion, according to Chap. XIV, § 16, of my Eſſay on Harmony.

As the principal object I had in view in writing this Fugue, was, to exemplify how much there can be done by ſtrictly adhering to a Subject, I have introduced in it but very little *Intermediate Harmony ;* and I am ſure, that if a Student has but once acquired a good perfection in treating a *Subject,* he will eaſily know or learn to help himſelf in regard to connective paſſages between one ſubject and another.

The whole conſiſts of ſix *Sections,* as follows :

Section I. The principal Subject begins in the *third* part of thoſe four which ſhall be introduced, and conſequently in a middle part, to make the Fugue begin different from the above firſt and ſecond Fugue. The Anſwer appears in the ſecond part ; the Subject again in the firſt, and another Anſwer in the fourth part. This is one of the beſt orders of replies pointed out under four parts in § 15, Rule II. The Counterpoint accompanies the Subject at every reply as pointed out by *c p,* and two other parts are added as Counter Harmony. The diſtance of the replies is here throughout ſo, that the ſucceeding Subject or Anſwer appears with the laſt note of the preceding one. The Intermediate Harmony between this and the following Section is two bars, becauſe the laſt bar of the laſt Anſwer has been altered, according to the liberties that are allowable when the Subject has been ſufficiently heard to be known.

Section II. The Subject begins in the *ſecond* part, according to the Rules given in § 26, and the Anſwer follows it in the firſt part, at a leſſer diſtance than before, and on the unaccented note ; the ſecond Subject appears in the fourth part, when the Anſwer is moſt ended, but on the accented note again, and its Anſwer follows in the third part, like the firſt Anſwer in this Section. The counterpoint again accompanies its Subject as before, but is broke off towards the end on account of the two Anſwers which render that alteration neceſſary. The intermediate harmony to this Section is three bars ; and as the Subject ſhall be introduced double, there has been no occaſion for a preceding reſt, to render the beginning of a new Section conſpicuous. The *Modulation* of the above two Sections has been in the Key and its Dominante ; but in the ſecond intermediate harmony it turns towards the Sixth of the Scale as the neareſt related minor, to the principal Key.

Section III. The Subject appears in the third and fourth part at once, and in thirds ; and the Counterpoint is in the two higheſt parts, in Sixths, as inverted Thirds. The *Modulation* is in the Sixth of the principal Key ; but in a ſhort intermediate harmony it turns

to

to the Third of the Principal Key. In this new Key the Subject appears again in Thirds, but inverted into Sixths, in the two higheſt parts; and the Counterpoint follows, in thirds in the two loweſt parts. The ſecond half of this Section therefore is the inverted order of replies of the firſt half. As both, the firſt and ſecond time, the Subject appears in the lower or authentic, and not in the higher or plagal part of its ſcale, this Section contains the Subject only as Subject, and not as Anſwer. In the two bars of the Intermediate Harmony which conclude this Section, the Modulation turns towards the minor of the principal Key.

Section IV. The Subject appears in the ſaid minor of the Key, both in Sixths, (as inverted thirds,) and *reverſed*, in the ſecond and third part; and the Counterpoint, alſo in ſixths, and reverſed, in the firſt and fourth part. The end of the Subject turns the Modulation to the fourth of the Key minor, as a related Key and Mode to the minor of the principal key. The Subject appears in the ſaid minor key, in the higheſt and loweſt part, alſo reverſed, but in thirds; and the Counterpoint reverſed and in thirds in the two middle parts. A very ſhort intermediate harmony turns the modulation to the principal key major again. The replies in this Section have been at the ſame diſtance as in the firſt; but no plagal Subject or Anſwer has been in this Section.

Section V. The Subject begins in the third part, and the Anſwer ſucceeds only two bars later, but *reverſed*, in the fourth part. The Counterpoint follows the Subject at its proper place, and in its original motion; but to the Anſwer the Counterpoint is not introduced in full, and only the thirds which might be added to the Counterpoint, appear in the higheſt part as marked by *c p*, which is the ſame as if the Counterpoint had been inverted in the tenth, and ſet an octave back again. (See Eſſay on Harmony, Chapter XIV, § 12.) The part next to this laſt Counterpoint is an imitation of the loweſt part in the 6th and 7th bar near the beginning, which makes varied ſixths to it, whilſt the Subject goes on in varied ſixths with the Anſwer. After an Intermediate Harmony of one bar the former half of this Section is introduced in another manner in the Fifth of the Principal Key, for the reverſed Anſwer begins in the ſecond part; its Counterpoint follows in the third part; the Subject then comes in, two bars after the Anſwer, in the firſt part; and its Counterpoint relieves the former, in the third part. The two upper and two loweſt parts unite then in ſixths again, as before in this Section, and one bar intermediate harmony turns the Modulation again to the principal key.

Section VI. The Subject begins in the third part; the Anſwer follows at one bar's diſtance in the firſt; their counterpoints accompany them as pointed out; and in the third bar of this Section the higheſt and loweſt part unite again in thirds, the ſame as the two middle parts. The Anſwer then begins again, and the Subject immediately follows at no more than half a bar's diſtance, *per arſin*, or on the unaccented note; the Counterpoint of the Anſwer therefore could not be introduced at this cloſe reſtriction of the Subject. A ſhort intermediate harmony leads to a Cadence with an Organ Point, in which the reverſed Subject appears again in thirds with an imitation of the Counterpoint, or the end of it in the fourth bar at the beginning of this Fugue. A *variation* of the Subject alſo is introduced in the two higheſt parts, which repeats a third lower when the baſs joins in it in contrary motion, and a formal concluſion takes place.

Fourth Fugue.

§ 35. See Plate XVIII, *Fuga IV, for three hands*. This alſo is an elaborate Fugue on the former Subject, which here appears in a third form, calculated to move with more

2   ſpirit

fpirit and freedom than in the three preceding Fugues. It is a regular *Trio* on one fet of Keys, to be performed by two perfons, the higheft part with the right hand alone, and the two lower parts with both hands.

I have introduced in it a fhort double counterpoint, to fhew that it is not always required to make the counterpoint as long, or nearly as long as the Subject; and the reverfion of this counterpoint is added, as a tranfitory paffage, to the Subject, before the firft Anfwer appears. Similar fhort additions to the Subject are fometimes required as conciliatory notes, when the end of the Subject is fo that the Anfwer cannot properly begin immediately after it, as I have faid in § 4, No. 3. But I know a perfon who, when the Subject ended with the fifth of the Key, would alfo end the Anfwer with the fifth of the Dominante, and then make ufe of a fimilar conciliatory paffage to lead the harmony back to the key, which is very improper, and contrary to the rules I have given in § 7, 8, 9, 10, and proved as generally eftablifhed, by examples from the works of the greateft compofers.

I need not explain this Fugue as minutely as the former, becaufe the diligent reader will fufficiently underftand moft particulars of it, according to what I have faid in § 34, and to the characters by which I have analyzed it in the Plates. I therefore only point out to the readers notice, the varieties of Replies which are again found in this Fugue when compared with the preceding ones; the different manners in which the Subject is announced in the fecond, third, and fifth Section, before it returns entire to begin a new Section; and the fancy Cadence towards the end of the Fugue.

I hope alfo that after what I have faid in the prefent §, and the above § 30, 31, 32, 33, and 34, the Fugues at Plate XXI and XXIV, will be fufficiently analyzed in the Plates, to be underftood. And fome particular remarks refpecting the Fugue at Plate XXI, will be made at § 10 in the next Chapter.

CHAPTER VII.   OF DOUBLE FUGUES.

§ 1. In Chap. V, § 10, I have given the definition of the term *double Fugue*, in its general and particular fenfe, and the general defcription of *double*, *triple*, and *quadruple* Fugues; I therefore need here only to fhew the Conftruction of each fort of the faid Fugues.

1. *Of Double Fugues, or Fugues of two Subjects.*

§ 2. There are *two forts* of double Fugues. The firft are *fimple* Fugues, with only a *double counterpoint*, as Counter Subject to the principal one; and the fecond, Fugues of two *independant* Subjects.

§ 3. The faid *firft* fort of double Fugues are in all refpects like *fimple* Fugues, except the Counter Harmony, which is not altered in every Section, or at every Reply, like as in fimple Fugues, but which contains a Counter Subject, calculated to accompany the principal Subject in all its appearances, and to be inverted with it. But the said principal, and counter subject, may occasionally appear one without the other; and consequently this sort of Fugues belong more properly to the class of *double*, than of *simple* Fugues.

§ 4. The Rules, which must be attended to in the first sort of Fugues in question, are as follows:

Rule I. The principal Subject, the Answer, the Order of the Replies, the intermediate Harmony, the different Sections, and the Modulation, must be regulated according to the Rules given in Chap. VI, § 2, & *seq.*; but the principal Subject must be calculated to admit of the intended Counter Subject, and make a regular Double Counterpoint with it.

Rule II. The Counterpoint may make its first appearance, either with the Principal Subject; or as a short transitory passage between it and the first Answer; or with the first Answer. An example of the first sort see in Fugue III, Plate XVI; one of the second sort in Fugue IV, Plate XVIII, where the transitory passage from the Subject to the first Answer is the reversed Counterpoint, which afterwards appears with every Subject or Answer; and an example of the third sort may be the same Fugue IV, if the said transitory passage is not attended to; and the first appearance of the Counterpoint considered as being with the Answer.

Rule III. The Counter Subject may be calculated, either for an inversion in one interval only, such as in the Octave, or Tenth, or Twelfth; or to be invertible in more than one interval, according to the rules of double Counterpoint given in my Essay on Harmony, Chap. XIV, § 9, 16, 21, and 25.

Examples of all that has been said above, are found in a great number of Fugues with a double Counterpoint by *Handel*; but the most remarkable work, in which Examples to the above Rule III are found, is *Sebastian Bach's* Art of the Fugue. In this latter work are Fugues with a Counterpoint in the Octave, the Tenth, and the Twelfth, most of which have been also imitated in other intervals.

See also the analysis of Fugue III, at Chap. VI, § 34.

§ 5. In regard to the *second* sort of *double* Fugues mentioned in § 2, being those, which consist of two Subjects *independant* of each other, the following Rule must be added, viz:

Rule. The two Subjects may be introduced and answered, each by itself, like as in two successive but connected simple Fugues; and the said Subjects must afterwards appear combined one with the other, like as in those Fugues explained at § 4.

In this last combination they may be introduced at various distances or restrictions; entire or by detached pieces; in equal or reverse imitation; by augmentation or diminution; and with all the varieties of inversion they are calculated for.

Examples of double Fugues of two *independant* Subjects, are found in many of *Handel's* works, of which I only point out the following ones, viz:

1, At Plate XXVI, No. 1, see the last movement of his Twelfth Grand Concerto, Allegro, common time. The first Subject see at a, and its Answer at the beginning of the fifth bar. This Subject is carried by itself through twenty-four bars, when the second Subject (at b,) appears as a Counterpoint to it, through eight bars. Afterwards the second Subject is used by itself; and at last both Subjects at once again.

2, At Plate XXVI, No. 2, see the beginning of a fine double Fugue in *Joseph*, mentioned before. At a, see the first, and at b, the second Subject. The particular nature

of

of this Fugue is : that the firſt Subjeƈt only returns in a majeſtic manner at a few places, and the ſecond is anſwered and imitated as a principal Subjeƈt throughout the Fugue.

3, At No. 3, a, and b, ſee the Subjeƈts of a double Fugue in *Iſrael in Egypt*; being that, mentioned at Chap. V, § 17. This Fugue is remarkable for being in the antient *Phrygian* mode, as deſcribed in my Eſſay on Harmony, Chap. XVIII, § 3. And the maſterly manner in which the two Subjeƈts are introduced together muſt alſo be taken notice of.

4, At No. 4, a, b, ſee the two Subjeƈts of a fine double Fugue, being in the ſame noble Oratorio with the former example, (Iſrael in Egypt.) It is in the antient *Dorian* mode, of which ſee alſo my Eſſay on Harmony, Chap. XVIII. This Fugue likewiſe ſhews, that in Vocal Fugues the firſt Anſwer may be made before the Subjeƈt is ended, becauſe the words ſhew how long the Subjeƈt is.

5, At No. 5, ſee the beginning of a double Fugue in *Jephtha*, being that, mentioned at Chap. VI, § 4, No. 2. The principal Subjeƈt at a, is upon the words, " Chemoſh no more we will adore ;" and the ſecond Subjeƈt appears in the fourth bar, at b. This Fugue is alſo remarkable, for beginning with an accompaniment of the Baſs. In the above claſs of double Fugues may be included two *alternate Fugues* which are contained in the ſeventh Chorus of *Handel's* Iſrael in Egypt, the firſt on the words, " He led them forth like ſheep," and the ſecond on, " He brought them out with ſilver and gold."

More examples of proper and improper double Fugues might be pointed out from the works of *Handel*, *Sebaſtian* and *Emanuel Bach*, *Graun*, *Corelli*, and other great Authors, but the above I hope, will be ſufficient.

II. *Of Triple Fugues, or Fugues of three Subjeƈts.*

§ 6. The Fugues in queſtion may confiſt of a Principal Subjeƈt, and two others as Occaſional ones, or Counterpoints to the principal Subjeƈt; or of three *independant* Subjeƈts. In the firſt caſe they reſemble the double Fugues deſcribed in § 3 and 4; and in the latter, thoſe of § 5.

§ 7. A triple Fugue of *one* principal Subjeƈt therefore, muſt be conſtruƈted according to all the rules of a Simple Fugue, given in Chap. VI; with the only difference, that the Counter Harmony, and the Intermediate Harmony contain alſo real Subjeƈts, when in ſimple Fugues they contain only paſſages related to the Subjeƈt.

A triple Fugue of *three* independant Subjeƈts, may be conſtruƈted in various manners, viz : firſt, ſo that every Subjeƈt is introduced and anſwered ſeparately, like as in ſimple Fugues; and that all three Subjeƈts are afterwards united, and introduced one with the other. Secondly ſo, that two Subjeƈts begin together, like as in the double Fugues at No. 2 and No. 5, § 5; and the third appears afterwards, like the ſecond one in the Example at No. 3, b. And in other manners, from which follow what I have ſaid above.

Examples of triple Fugues on one principal Subjeƈt, and two occaſional ones, I need not give, becauſe they are nearly the ſame as double Fugues of the ſame kind; I therefore immediately proceed to thoſe of three independant Subjeƈts.

1, At Plate XXVII, No. 1, a, b, c, ſee the three Subjeƈts of a fine triple Fugue by *Handel*, in Joſeph. The firſt, that at a, is in the antient *dorian* mode, like another example

ample by him given at § 5; and the chromatic Subject at b, with the graceful one at d, are so judicioufly ufed in various combinations with the firft Subject as well as with each other, that this Fugue deferves to be ftudied with great attention.

2, At No. 2, a, b, c, fee the three Subjects of that mafterly triple Fugue with which *Sebaftian Bach* has ended his " Art of the Fugue," and foon after which he died. The *firft* Subject, (at a) is part of that on which he has compofed all the twenty-three inimitable Fugues, and Canons in the form of Fugues, of the faid moft eftimable work, as given at Plate XII, No. 8. This Subject is worked upon as in a fimple Fugue through 114 bars. In the 115th bar the *fecond* Subject (at b) appears, Solo, like the beginning of a new Fugue, and is regularly anfwered and introduced in the four parts of the harmony, by itfelf, like the firft Subject, till the 148th bar, in which the firft and fecond Subject are combined; and with this combination of the two Subjects the Fugue is carried on till the 192d bar. In the faid bar the *third* Subject appears, which confifts of thofe notes called like the letters of that great Author's name B, A, C, H; it is alfo treated firft by itfelf, and then combined with imitations of the two firft Subjects, till the 231ft bar where the Fugue ends.

N. B. Refpecting the above letters B, A, C, H, it muft be underftood: that the Germans call B flat—B, and B natural—H. This diftinction feems to have arifen at thofe times, when B flat, as the firft accidental note, became to be allowed as a perfect fourth to F. For then the term B remained to the perfect fourth of F, and a new name was given to B natural, out of the alphabet, which according to the natural order of the letters fell upon H, the next after G. And to this cuftom of having the letter H in German notation, it is owing, that *Kirnberger* calls the interval $\frac{1}{7}$, (or $\frac{4}{7}$ to the double octave of $\frac{1}{7}$,) I, being the next letter to H. Refpecting the faid interval $\frac{4}{7}$ and its inverfion $\frac{7}{8}$ fee my Effay on Harmony, Chap. I, § 7. But the Englifh method of faying B flat and B natural, the fame as A flat and A natural, is much better than faying B and H, as above.

III. *Of Quadruple Fugues, or Fugues of Four Subjects.*

§ 8. A quadruple Fugue, may confift of *one* principal, and three occafional Subjects; or of *two* principal Subjects, and their double Counterpoints; or of *four* independant and equally interefted Subjects.

The faid *firft* fort, or thofe of one principal Subject, is quite fimilar to the Fugue of fix Subjects I give at Plate XXI. For if the two laft of the Subjects of that Fugue are not confidered as Subjects, the other four are a perfect fpecimen, of a whole Fugue of the defcription in queftion. I therefore need not give another example of that fort.

The faid *fecond* fort may be compofed, like a double Fugue of two independant Subjects, as explained in § 5; and in the combination of the two principal Subjects they may with their Counter Subjects produce real quadruple Counterpoints. But I do not recollect having feen a Fugue of this kind, and therefore have no example to give of it.

But an example of the faid *third* fort of quadruple Fugues is found in *Handel's* Alexander's Feaft, being the Chorus, " Let old Timotheus yield the prize." See the four independant Subjects on which it depends at Plate XXVII, No. 3, a, b, c, d, continued at Plate XXVIII. This mafterly piece is of the extraordinary nature, that the four Subjects are introduced one after the other, as four Solos in the different parts, without any other accompaniment than a thorough bafs, and that neither of them is regularly anfwered as in properFugues. But how ingenioufly the Subjects are afterwards combined, will appear at Plate XXVIII, No. 1, being no more than four bars out of the middle of the Fugue, and yet all four Subjects are contained in them. Many fine varieties of introducing thefe fub-jects at all diftances, and in divers combinations, will appear in the piece itfelf, which de-ferves to be ftudied with attention.

VI.   *Of Quintuple and Sextuple Fugues.*

§ 9. A *quintuple* Fugue naturally is that which confifts of *five*, and a *fextuple*, that which confifts of *fix* Subjects.

Though I have faid before, (at Chap. V, § 10,) that the Fugues in queftion are more calculated to fhew the great abilities of their authors, than to afford extraordinary enter-tainment to moft hearers ; yet there may be particular *purpofes* which can be anfwered by writing them, and a compofer may occafionally, or in the elaboration of a Fugue, which he at firft intended but for two or three Subjects, difcover more Subjects that can be com-bined with the others : in thefe cafes therefore a fkilful elaboration of a Fugue of five or fix Subjects cannot but create admiration in all thofe who are able to judge of it.

Both quintuple and fextuple Fugues may be written according to all the various plans that have appeared above, under double, triple, and quadruple ones, and according to many more ingenious plans which will be found in the numerous works of *Handel*, which will require no particular demonftration.

§ 10. An example of a *quintuple* Fugue I have not provided, but there will be no occafion for it, as I have a *fextuple* to lay before the Reader. See Plate XXI, XXII, and XXIII. It is by my late Uncle, *Charles Chriftopher Hachmeifter*, Organift at Hamburgh, who died about the year 1779, and by whom are alfo thofe fifty *variations* of a Minuet mentioned in my Effay on Harmony, Chap. XVI, § 6. This Fugue confifts of a principal Subject, and five others, calculated to be introduced as a Counterpoint, one to the other as well as to the principal Subject, at various diftances or reftrictions. I have analyzed it with the fame characters as the former Fugues, which fee explained at Chap. VI, § 31 ; and to which are added the Numbers 2, 3, 4, 5, 6, to point out the five fecondary Subjects.

Refpecting the faid Subjects, I muft remark : that the *fourth* one arifes from the reverfion of the latter half of the principal Subject ; and that the *fifth* one arifes from the latter part of the fecond, by drawing four crotchets together into two bound minims, or one femi-breve.

The Modulation, and the whole conftruction of this Fugue, will be found conforma-ble to the general and particular rules given in Chap. VI. I therefore need not enlarge upon it.

§ 11. Though I hope the above will be found fufficient to give the diligent Reader a proper idea of the different forts of Double Fugues, and all that is material in them, yet there is one material point ftill unexplained, being the *invention of the Subjects* for them ; and the knowledge of examining Subjects which fhall be ufed. This I fhall endeavour to fpeak of in the following Sections.

§ 12. To *invent Subjects*, that are calculated to be answered and imitated each by it-self, and to be combined at various restrictions, and in various forms, requires a proper attention to the following Rules, viz.:

Rule I. To a Subject which remains on *one* and the *same key or note*, a great variety of other Subjects may be introduced, the same as to a holding bass note in an Organ-Point; and equally the same as with a whole Subject, it is with any part of the Subject.

To the Subject at Plate XXVI, No. 5, a, therefore, a great number of various Subjects may be introduced, not only almost at any note, but also reversed, by diminution, and in all other sorts of imitation, because the greatest part of it remains on the same key or note.

Rule II. To a Subject which gradually *ascends* by diatonic or chromatic degrees, ano-ther may be introduced almost at every note which gradually *descends*; though the one proceed by a quicker sort of notes than the other.

According to this rule, therefore, a fixed, an ascending, and a descending passage, will in general be good for the three Subjects of a triple Fugue.

Rule III. As all the above motions (viz: the fixed, the ascending, and the descend-ing,) may be *varied* in many different, but uniform manners, it follows: that their varia-tions are in many instances as useful, as their original form.

In explanation of this Rule I must shew, what variations can be meant by it. They are as follows:

1, The division of a note into smaller ones, on the same key; which requires no Exam-ple.

2, The transposition of it to the Octave above or below, and back again; which also will require no example.

3, A gradual ascending or descending from it, to the second, third, or fourth, above or below, in a quicker sort of notes.

These are the variations of plain notes found in many Subjects of great Authors, and the gradual ascending or descending may remain, on the second, third or fourth of one note, and the other note be varied in the same manner; or the ascending notes may descend, and the descending ones ascend to the original note again.

An Example where a Subject is varied according to these observations, see at Plate XXVII, No. 3, b, from the second to the fourth bar.

Another variation of a similar nature see at Plate XXVII, No. 1, c, to the words " Tender Mercies," where all the notes may be considered like one F, or like F, A, F.

Rule IV. A *short* Subject of a *small compass*, may be introduced to most Subjects of a greater length and compass.

The reason of this rule is obvious. For a Subject of the description in question is like the variation of a long note according to the Rule III, and therefore it may be combined with most ascending, descending, or fixed passages, at most restrictions, though not in any interval. This appears in so many Fugues and other pieces of composition that it will re-quire no Example.

The above, I hope, will greatly facilitate the invention of proper Subjects for the Fugues in question. But as sometimes a Composer need not to invent, but has only to choose his Subjects, from passages of a piece or pieces already composed, I shall now endeavour to shew what ought to be observed in that respect.

§ 13. To *examine* two or more Subjects, for the purpose of discovering whether they are calculated for a double, triple, or quadruple Fugue or not, requires the observation of the following Rules, viz:

I

Rule

Rule I.　Confider the two or more Subjects you intend to bring into the fame Fugue according to the Rules given in § 12, to fee, firft, whether they are *different* in motion; and fecondly, if they are of fuch a difference, as is likely to *agree* together according to the faid Rules.

To acquire a certainty, and a perfection in the examination of Subjects according to this rule, it is good to collect the Subjects from as many double Fugues as poffible, and then to confider in which refpects they agree fo that they may be combined and inverted together; particularly, according to which of the Rules given in § 12, their reciprocal agreement may be accounted for.

Rule II.　If you have found as many Subjects as you want, which feem to be both different, and reconcileable together, you muft examine whether they are calculated for *more than one* combination, and fort of imitation, and of what fort thefe are.

This examination of two or more Subjects together, is of great utility in the ftudy of compofition.　For, it ferves not only for the purpofe of teaching us which Subjects are ufeful or not for our immediate wants; but it renders us more acquainted with the nature of Subjects, and with the varieties they are calculated to afford, than the mere ufe of thofe we may have the chance to invent or choofe without fuch examination.

In the above particulars, (I mean in the choice as well as the examination of Subjects for a certain purpofe,) *Handel* muft have been very great.　For all his works fhew, that whatever ufe he made of a Subject, it was always with the greateft knowledge, and yet with fuch a natural eafe, that his moft fcientific Fugues bear not the leaft fign of any want of entertaining variety.　That *Sebaftian Bach* was alfo great, and perhaps without a rival in the fame particulars, appears from the well known anecdote, how his fon *Emanuel* fhewed him one day a Subject for a Fugue, with the varieties he thought it would afford, afking if he thought there were more varieties contained in it.　The father then, as it is faid, looked at the Subject but a little while, and returned it, faying " *No more.*"　This fhort anfwer made the fon curious, to examine the Subject himfelf more minutely; but he found that his father had been perfectly right, for he could do no more with it than what his father faid.　Yet this muft naturally be underftood of thofe varieties which are material in the art of a ftrict Fugue; for in other refpects the Chapter of *Variation* in my Effay on Harmony will fhew that almoft any Subject may be varied almoft innumerable times.　And what makes *Haydn* fo great?　Is it not among his other mufical talents that of *choofing* proper Subjects, and making *proper ufe* of them?　The ftudy of thefe particulars therefore I beg leave ftrongly to recommend to my Readers, not only for the ufe of Fugues, of which I have treated in this Chapter, but in general, for all forts of mufical pieces, as I have taken pains to fhew by the Symphony from which the Subject of the above Fugues is taken, as well as by thefe Fugues.

§ 14.　Though I have mentioned in my Propofals, the analyfis of a *double, triple,* and *quadruple* Fugue, I hope the above chromatic *fextuple* one will be thought fufficient, inftead of the two latter ones, as I have already analyzed more than I promifed, in the preceding Chapter.　And as another compenfation I lay before my Readers the *enharmonic* Fugue at Plate XXIV, mentioned before at Chap. VI, § 12, which I have analyzed with the fame characters as the preceding Fugues, as explained at Chap. VI, § 31.

CHAPTER

CHAPTER VIII.   OF CANONS.

§ 1. A *Canon* is a piece, in which the *whole* beginning part or melody is imitated by the other parts. The exceptions from this general definition will appear under *finite* Canons, and Canons by augmentation. Respecting the term Canon, see Chap. V, § 2.

The melody which is to be imitated may be called the *Subject*, like as in Fugues; and every part which imitates the Subject, its *Reply*. These terms therefore I shall make use of in the present, and the following Chapter.

§ 2. The art of the Canon teaches the highest degree of mechanical contrivance in musical imitation, and deserves to be studied as well as Fugues and Double Counterpoint. For it is useful, not only in those cases where real Canons are to be written, but also in the invention of a Subject for a Fugue, which it enables us to construct so, as to be calculated for any intended Restriction; and it affords a great variety of practice and amusement, by making us acquainted with combinations of sounds, different from those in all other sorts of musical pieces.

A very good observation respecting the use of studying Canons, see in Dr. *Burney's* General History of Music, Volume II, page 508.

I shall endeavour to give a description of every thing belonging to Canons, first *in general*; secondly in regard to the different *sorts of imitation*; and thirdly in regard to the *number and quality of parts*.

I.   *Of Canons in General.*

§ 3. A Canon in general, may be *simple* or *double*; *resolved* or *unresolved*; *finite* or *infinite*; calculated for *one*, or *more sorts* of solutions.

§ 4. A *simple* Canon is that which depends but upon *one* Subject, though it consist of many parts.

Examples of simple Canons see: at Plate XXVIII, No. 3, Canon II and III. The first consists of four, and the second of two parts. Also that by *Marpurg* at Plate XXXV, the first line, which consists of nine parts. Besides several others in the Plates which I need not point out.

A *double* Canon in a general sense, is that, which contains *more than one* Subject; but in a particular sense a *double* Canon contains *two*, a *triple* Canon *three*, and a *quadruple* Canon *four* Subjects. The said two, three, or four Subjects of a Canon, must consist of melodies different from each other, or else it is no real double, triple or quadruple Canon. An example of a Canon of *two* Subjects see at Plate XXVIII, No. 3, Canon I; which consequently is a real *double* Canon. Real *triple* and *quadruple* Canons are found in *Kirnberger's* Kunst des reinen Satzes, Vol. II.

Mere apparent double Canons are those, in which the second, third, or fourth Subject arises but from a variation of the first Subject, either by reversion, or by bringing it into another sort of different form. See Plate XXIX, Canon IV, V. Such Canons are written in more than one line for the convenience of resolving them. But as the whole might be

drawn

drawn from the firſt Subject, if a ſufficient explanation was added to it, ſuch Canons cannot properly be called double ones.

To the claſs of double Canons may be added: *compound* Canons, by which I mean thoſe that contain *two* or more Canons in *one*.

Some excellent examples of this ſort ſee as follows: At Plate XXXIII, Canon I, by *Emanuel Bach*, which is of ſo extraordinary a nature, that at firſt it is a Canon by notes of *equal* length, and after a few notes it becomes a Canon by *diminution*, both before and after the Repeat.

At Plate XXXIV, Canon I, II, and III, by *Faſch*, are of a ſimilar nature, and have been written in imitation of the above one by *Bach*, as *Kirnberger* ſays, from whoſe above-mentioned work I have tranſcribed them.

§ 5. A *reſolved* Canon, as mentioned in § 3, is that, which either is written in parts and at full length, as it ſhall be performed, or which is perfectly explained by words or other known characters. But when a Canon is not written or explained in the ſaid manner, it is *unreſolved*. The latter, or unreſolved Canons, are alſo called *ænigmatical* ones.

Fully reſolved, or tranſcribed Canons therefore are Canon I, II, IV, and V, by *Bevin*, ſee Plate XL; alſo Canon II and III by Dr. *Burney* at Plate XXX and XXXI, and ſimilar others. Sufficiently explained by words and characters, I hope, will be found my Canons at Plate XXVIII and XXIX; and ſimilar other examples.

Not quite reſolved*or explained, are *Sebaſtian Bach*'s Canons VII, and VIII, at Plate XXXVI; where by the former it is not ſaid of how many *parts* it is to conſiſt, and where the replies are to begin; and by the latter it is alſo not pointed out where the replies are to begin. Such ſort of half explained and half ænigmatical Canons are frequently met with, and in the next Chapter, under Reſolution of Canons, I ſhall ſhew how the characters uſed in them are to be underſtood.

Quite ænigmatical is Dr. *Burney*'s Canon, No. 2, at Plate XXX. and *Bevin*'s No. 3, at Plate XL. when the ſolution is not added to each of them.

§ 6. A *finite* Canon, is that, which ends with a certain note of the Subject. It may be ſet ſo, as to end part after part, in the order and at the diſtance it began; like as Dr. *Burney*'s No. 3, Plate XXXI. Or ſome additional notes may be put to the Subject, and to thoſe replies which end before the laſt reply, to make the former as long as the laſt; as it is found in the ſmall notes of the quoted example; and as I ſhall explain in the next Chapter, under the Conſtruction of Canons.

But when a Canon is calculated ſo, that the Subject as well as every Reply may immediately proceed from the end to the beginning again, it is called an *infinite*, or perpetual Canon. Examples ſee at Plate XXVIII, No. 3, Canon I, and II; and ſimilar others in the ſucceeding Plates. Theſe Canons may end part after part, as they began; or all parts at once at any other place where the harmony will admit of it. A concluſion of the latter ſort ſee pointed out in Canon X, Plate XXX, by a pauſe over that note in the eighth bar where the Canon may end.

A particular claſs of infinite Canons are thoſe, called *per tonos*, or through all the keys. They are of two different ſorts, viz: firſt thoſe which proceed from key to key with ſuch intervals as the diatonic ſcale of the principal key produces; ſecondly, thoſe which make real digreſſions, from key to key, till they are gone through the whole circle of the twelve major or minor keys. Both ſorts may end in any key if required, or paſs through all and end in the principal key.

Of

Of the former fort is the Canon at No. 2, Plate XXVIII, and Canon III, at No. 3, of the fame plate. Alfo the fine Canon 9 in 1, by *Marpurg*, at Plate XXXV. And of the latter fort, two Canons by *Kirnberger*, at Plate XXXI, and XXXII.

§ 7. Moft Canons are calculated but for *one fort of folution*; that is to fay, for a certain fixed number of parts, and a prefcribed order, form, and variety, of replies. Of this fort are all the Canons by *Sebaflian Bach*, by *Bevin*, and others I give.

But fome Canons will admit of *more than one*, or *many* forts of folutions; and thefe, particularly the laft, are called *polymorphous*, or many Canons in one. Examples of the former fort, or Canons that will admit of *feveral* different folutions, fee at Plate XXVIII, No. 2, and 3. At No. 2, fee a Canon which may be replied to in any interval of the diatonic fcale, either above or below, as I fhall fhew in the next Chapter; and at No. 3, Canon I, the higher line contains a fubject which alfo can be replied to in various different manners, as the fucceeding Canons fhew. *Marpurg* gives an example of a Canon by *Stoelzel*, which can be refolved in more than two thoufand different ways; but as fuch Canons are more for curiofity than real ufe, I have not given any more than the faid examples of them.

II.   *Of Canons, in regard to the different Sorts of Imitation.*

§ 8. The replies of a Canon may be made in different *intervals*, with greater or leffer *flrictnefs*, in equal or contrary *motion*, with equal or different *length of notes*, and at equal or unequal *diftances*. Thefe particulars I fhall now endeavour to explain.

§ 9. In regard to the *Interval*, a Canon may be calculated for a reply in the unifon, or in any other interval, above or below, in the following manner, viz.

Firft, fo that *all* replies are in the unifon or fome other interval.

Secondly, fo that one reply is in one, and the other in fome other interval; either above, or below that, in which the fubject begins.

According to what I have faid juft now it muft be underftood, that there is a great difference between an interval above or below. For the fecond above C is D, and the fecond below C is B; and fo it is with all other intervals above or below.

§ 10. In any one interval, or in any number of different intervals, the imitation may be *flrict* or *free*.

Strict the imitation is, when a reply proceeds by the fame number of tones and femitones, as there are contained in the fubject. To effectuate this, it is neceffary, if the reply is made in a key or interval different from that of the fubject, to introduce in it fuch fharps, flats, or naturals, as are required to produce the ftrict imitation; which may be done, either by the Clef, or occafionally in the reply. Of the former or different fignatures by the Clef, fee Plate XXXI, Canon III, by Dr. *Burney*, where the fecond part is in F, and the two others in C; and two examples by *Kirnberger*, in which every part is in a clef different from the others, fee at Plate XXXI and XXXII. And equally the fame it would be, if the fharps or flats by the Clef had been introduced occafionally in the replies.

Lefs flrict is the imitation, when a reply is made according to the degrees of the diatonic fcale of the fubject, without any accidental fharps, flats, or naturals, than thofe contained in the fubject itfelf. According to this fort of imitation therefore, a reply may be made in G, the fifth of C, without a fharp, or in F, the fourth of C, without a flat.

§ 11. In regard to the different *motions* in which an imitation can be made, the reply of a Canon may be made, in equal or reverse, in retrograde or reverse retrograde motion; and in one of these motions only, or in two or more of them at the same time.

Examples of Canons in equal motion see in Canon I and II, by *Kirnberger*, at Plate XXXI and XXXII; one in contrary motion at Canon I, by Dr. *Burney*, Plate XXX; one in retrograde motion at Canon IV, Plate XXIX; and one in reverse retrograde motion, a Canon V, the same Plate.

§ 12. In regard to the *length of notes*, replies of a Canon may be made either in notes of the same length as those of the subject; or by augmentation, or diminution. Examples of the former sort, see in the Canons of Plate XXVIII, No. 2, 3; one by augmentation at Plate XXIX, Canon VI; one by double diminution is Canon VII, and by triple augmentation Canon VIII, of the same Plate.

In the above examples *every note* of the subject is imitated in the required proportion. But there are Canons found in which the reply only selects *certain notes* out of the subject, and imitates them. Or also: Canons in which the reply imitates notes of very *different* lengths, by notes of *one sort* of length. Examples see at Plate XL, Canon I, and at Plate XLI, Canon IV, V. These remarkable Canons, which might be called Canons by *selected*, and by *reduced* imitation, ought to be taken particular notice of, as they shew the way to a great number of similar but other varieties of imitation.

One sort of imitation, similar to the latter ones, is that, which *Marpurg* calls *interrupted* imitation, or in which the same notes are imitated in the same sort of length, but with interspersed rests. The opposite to it would be *contracted* imitation, or when a subject with interspersed rests is imitated without the rests, but with notes of the same length. This interruption or contraction of replies may also be varied in different manners.

Another sort of imitation, which is very curious, but related to the above *selected* imitation, is found in *Bevin*'s Canon III, at Plate XL, which will be more explained under a Survey of the Canons given; see Chap. IX. § 27.

§ 13. Respecting the *Distance* at which the reply may imitate the subject, it appears: that a Canon may be calculated for a reply at any reasonable distance. But if a Canon shall consist of more than two parts, the different replies may be made either at an *equal*, or *unequal* distance. The former is: when the third reply follows at the same distance after the second, as the second after the first, and the first after the subject; and the latter: when the first, second, and third reply do not follow at the same distance one after another, as the first does after the subject. Examples of replies at an *equal* distance, see at Plate XXVIII, No. 3, Canon I, II; and one at *unequal* distances, at Plate XXXI, Canon III, by Dr. *Burney*, where the first reply appears *one* bar after the subject, and the second reply *two* bars after the first.

But the first reply to a subject need not be made at the same *time of the measure*, as that where the subject begins, but may follow the subject *per arsin* as well as *per thesin*, or on the unaccented time as well as on the accented. And the distances of the succeeding replies may be fixed according to the same variety of accented or unaccented times. This being the same as answers in fugues by unaccented to accented, it will require no particular example.

III. *Of Canons, in regard to the Number and Quality of Parts.*

§ 14. A Canon may be fet for *two* or *more* parts without any accompaniments; or for any number of *real* parts with one or more others as *accompaniments*; or for *two* parts which may be *doubled by thirds*; or for any number of parts *to a given melody*. According to thefe particulars I fhall explain Canons in this place.

§ 15. When the fubject is calculated but for *one* reply, it produces a Canon of *two* parts; *two* replies make a Canon of *three* parts, and fo forth; which will require no farther demonftration. And if the Canon is not exprefsly intended for many refolutions, or many forts of replies in one refolution, it may be conftructed fo, as to produce a complete or fatisfactory harmony, *without any accompaniment*. Of this fort are the Canons at Plate XXVIII and XXIX.

§ 16. But when the fubject of a Canon is intended for a particular melody, or when it fhall be calculated for many forts of replies, the harmony cannot always be rendered fufficiently complete; and in fuch cafes it is good, to add to the real parts of the Canon one or more filling parts, as *accompaniments*.

The faid accompaniments may confift, either of a bafs only, or of one part between or above the Canon; or of any two, three, or four parts. And how additional parts may be fet to the real ones of a Canon, as duplicates, follows from what has been faid in Chap. V. § 20.

§ 17. Another variety in the number of parts of a Canon is: when a Canon of two parts is calculated fo, that a third and fourth part may be *added in thirds* to the above original parts; like as a double counterpoint of a fimilar nature. See my Effay on Harmony, Chap. XIV, § 8, 16, 21, and 25. And an example at Plate XXX, Canon IX, where the reply in the third above, and fixth below, are nothing elfe than the added thirds in queftion.

§ 18. The laft fort of Canons mentioned above, is that, which muft be fet to a *given melody*. It is one of the moft difficult forts of all thofe mentioned in this chapter. But *Sebaftian Bach* has fet a great number of thefe Canons; and fome of them fee at Plate XXXV, Canon II, III, IV, and at Plate XXXVI, Canon V, VI, VII. And another example fee at Plate XXX, Canon X.

CHAPTER IX.   OF THE CONSTRUCTION AND RESOLUTION OF CANONS.

I. *Of their Conftruction.*

§ 1. All the Canons I have given a defcription of in the laft Chapter, muft be conftructed either as *fimple*, or as *double* ones, and both forts with regard to all the particulars that have been mentioned in the faid Chapter. The rules which muft be attended to in their conftruction, I fhall endeavour to give in the prefent chapter.

A. OF THE CONSTRUCTION OF SIMPLE CANONS.

§ 2. I fhall endeavour to fpeak of the conftruction of the Canons in queftion, firft in regard to the *Interval* in which the reply is to be made; fecondly in regard to the *Motion* in which it fhall be made; and thirdly in regard to the *length of notes* in which it fhall appear.

I. *The Interval in which the Reply is made.*

§ 3. The eafieft forts of Canons, in regard to the Interval in which the replies fhall be made, are thofe in the *Unifon*, or the *Octave*.

They may be divided into two claffes, viz: thofe that confift of *equal* divifions; and thofe of *unequal* divifions. By the former, I mean Canons, whofe fubject confifts of as many ftrains or divifions of equal length, as their harmony contains parts; and by the latter, thofe, which are not divided into as many ftrains of equal length, as their harmony contains parts.

§ 4. An example of the *former* fort fee at Plate XXXVI, Canon VIII. Its fubject confifts of twenty-eight bars, and it is calculated for three replies in the unifon or octave; the firft reply to begin at the diftance of feven bars after the fubject, and each fucceeding reply at the fame diftance after the preceding one; fo that when the laft reply begins, the faid four equal divifions of the fubject make a regular harmony of four parts, as it appears at Plate XXXVIII, Canon VIII. Canons of this fort are contained in every regular Harmony for two, three, or more *equal* voices or inftruments; for, if the different parts of fuch a harmony are fet one after another, like as thofe of Canon VIII, Plate XXXVIII, in the fubject at Plate XXXVI, they make a Subject for a Canon in the *Unifon*; and if every part is regular as a double counterpoint to all the other parts, the replies may alfo be made in the *Octave*.

The reafon why I have required the harmonics in queftion to be for *equal* Voices or Inftruments, (i. e. for none but trebles, or none but tenors &c.) is obvious. For if it was for a treble, alto, tenor, and bafs, all the parts could not properly be written in one ftave of lines, except with the affiftance of their different clefs; nor could they be properly performed in their real place, by one and the fame voice or inftrument, as it is required in a Canon.

To demonftrate more clearly what I have faid above, I return to the example at Canon VIII, Plate XXXVIII. This is a regular harmony for four *equal* voices or inftruments; but as it is alfo a regular quadruple counterpoint of the octave, two of the parts may be performed an octave above or below the others, as the G clef on the firft line fhews, which makes the treble notes the fame as written in the bafs clef, only an octave higher. To make fuch an harmony a Canon, any of the four parts may begin, and proceed through its line by itfelf; but that which founds beft as a *folo* ought to be taken. When the firft or beginning part is thus gone through its line, its performer takes any other line of the harmony, which has the beft effect as a *duo* with the firft part, whilft another performer takes that part which made the beginning. When both parts are thus gone through their line, the firft part takes any of the two remaining lines which has the beft effect as a *trio* with

R

the

the two former ones, whilft the fecond performer takes that part which the firft had laft, and the third performer takes the beginning part. At laft the firft performer takes the laft part, the fecond performer that which the firft had laft, the third performer that which the fecond had laft, and the fourth performer the beginning part. When the firft performer has done with the laft part, he returns to that with which he made the beginning, and goes through the whole again in the former order, which all the other performers do in their turn, till they like to conclude ; and this may be done in the Canon in queftion at the note marked with a paufe in every part.

According to this defcription therefore, the loweft part of the Canon in queftion makes the beginning ; the part over it then fucceeds it : next the third part from below is annexed to the fecond ; and at laft the higheft part follows the third, as the fubject of this Canon at Plate XXXVI, Canon VIII, fhews. But if it had been thought proper, the four parts in quef- tion might have been placed one after another, in any other fucceffion, viz : in regular order downwards ; or beginning with the fecond or third part, which I hope will require no farther demonftration.

In the fame manner as above. Canons in the Unifon or Octave may be made, of all the examples of fimple counterpoint I have given in my Effay on Harmony at Plate XX, XXI, and XXII, if the bafs alone, or both the bafs and tenor, is fet an octave higher, to render the parts calculated for *equal* voices, as I have faid near the beginning of this fection.

§ 5. The fecond fort of Canons in the Unifon or Octave I have mentioned at § 3, are thofe of *unequal* divifions. They may be written in two different manners, viz. firft : fo, that all the replies are introduced at *equal* diftances, like as in the Canons of § 4, but that the harmony is continued longer than what the diftance is from one reply to another ; or fecondly fo, that the replies are introduced at *unequal* diftances.

1, The rules which muft be attended to in conftructing the faid firft fort of Canons are as follows :

Rule I. Write down a fubject as far as to the place where a reply fhall begin ; and fet the fame melody into the part of the reply, but begin where the fubject ended. If there fhall be more than one reply, you muft fet the fame part of the fubject into the part of every reply, fo that the beginning of a fucceeding reply comes in after that of a preceding one. See Plate XLII, No. 1, at a, a, a.

Rule II. Add to the beginning part, a melody of the fame length as the firft, but fo that it be perfectly harmonious to the fecond part ; and then carry the fame into the part of every reply. See the former example at b, b, b.

Rule III. Continue in this manner as long as you think proper, which in the example in queftion is done till f, f, f.

Rule IV. If the Canon fhall be *infinite*, the latter additions to the fubject muft be calcu- lated fo, that when the fubject repeats again in the firft part, it may be as regular over the others, as has been required in the above Rule II. See the example at a a, b b.

Rule V. But if the Canon fhall be *finite*, it may be concluded at the intended length ; and inftead of the repeated Subject at a a, b b, in the above example, any other addition may be made to the preceding parts, till they are as long as the part of the laft reply. An example of fuch additions fee in Dr. *Burney*'s Canon III, at Plate XXXI ; the fmall notes in the firft and fecond part. Alfo in *Bevin*'s Canon IV, Plate XLI, where the firft paufes over the fecond and fourth part fhew, with which note the fubject and replies end.

2, If the replies of a Canon are introduced at *unequal* diftances, according to the fecond

3

manner

manner of writing the Canons in queſtion, pointed out at the beginning of this §, the following rules muſt be obſerved :

Rule I. Begin the Subject with a melody as long as the *ſmalleſt* diſtance between the replies, and carry the ſame into the part of every reply, *according to the diſtance* at which they ſhall follow the Subject, as well as each other. See Plate XLII, No. 2, at a, a, a.

N. B. In this example the ſmalleſt diſtance of the replies is one bar, therefore no more than one bar is the firſt beginning ; but in the part of the ſecond reply it is ſet two bars farther than the firſt reply, according to the diſtances intended for the replies.

Rule II. Obſerve the above Rule 2, 3, 4, 5, under No. 1, of the preſent §, according to the letters b b b, c c c, d d d, &c. in the example in queſtion.

N. B. Though this example contains a reply in the fourth below, which does not belong to the Canons in queſtion ; yet it will ſhew the manner of writing them as well as if both replies were in the uniſon or octave.

§ 6. If a Canon is to be conſtructed in the *Second,* or *any other* interval, above or below, it cannot be done according to what has been ſaid in § 4, but the rules given in § 5, both under No. 1, and 2, muſt be obſerved in it.   And according to theſe rules the Canon muſt be conſtructed, not only when the replies are all in one and the ſame interval, but alſo when they are in two, or more, different intervals, with the only conſideration, that every piece of the ſubject muſt be carried into the different parts of the replies, according to the *interval* in which the reply is to be made.

An Example which contains one reply in the fifth below, and one in the octave below, we have ſeen at Plate XLII, No. 2. And the ſubject of one in eight different intervals ſtands at Plate XXXV, *Canon* 9 *in* 1, by *Marpurg,* which the Reader will be able to reſolve according to its explanation, and the marks of the replies underneath it.

§ 7. In the above ſections I have ſpoken of Canons, which, when they are repeated, begin in the *ſame* intervals again, in which the ſubject as well as every reply began at firſt ; in this place now I muſt ſhew what is to be obſerved in regard to thoſe Canons, which at every repetition begin in a certain *higher* or *lower* interval, and thus are calculated to proceed or modulate through the whole ſcale, or the whole muſical circle, according to the deſcription given of them, under Canons *per tonos,* at Chap. VIII, § 6.   The *Rule* for conſtructing them, is : obſerve the rules given in § 5, under No. 1, and 2, with the following two exceptions, viz : *firſt,* that the end of the Canon muſt be ſo, as to admit of the repetition in ſuch a higher or lower interval as intended ; *ſecondly,* that every part muſt be a regular double counterpoint of the octave, to all the others, ſo that, where it is required, the reply may be made an octave higher or lower than its reſpective interval, to prevent the parts coming too high or too low.   According to theſe rules are conſtructed, all the Canons *per tonos* in the plates, as will appear under *A Survey of all the Canons given,* at § 27.

II.   *The Motion, in which the Reply is made.*

§ 8. As the replies of a Canon may be made in equal, reverſe, retrograde, and reverſe retrograde motion, and I have yet treated but of thoſe in equal motion, I am now to give rules for thoſe in *reverſe, retrograde,* and *reverſe retrograde* motion.

§ 9. A Canon in *reverſe* motion is made as thus : Obſerve all the rules given in § 5 and 6, and only carry every piece of the ſubject *reverſed* into its reſpective places of the reply or replies.

An

An example of a Canon in *reverfe* motion fee at Plate XXXV, Canon III, and its folution at Plate XXXVII, III.

When a Canon fhall be both in *equal* and *reverfe* motion, it is conftructed according to the rules mentioned juft now, with the only difference, that every piece of the fubject muft be carried into its refpective places of the replies, in the equal or reverfe motion in which its reply fhall be made.

An example of this fort fee at Plate XXVIII, No. 3, Canon II: the replies of which are explained underneath it.

The above reverfe, and mixed right and reverfe Canons, are calculated to be *finite* or *infinite*, according to Rule IV and V, at § 5, No. 1; and if they fhall be Canons *per tonos*, the rules given in § 7, muft be attended to in conftructing them.

§ 10. To write a Canon in *retrograde* motion requires the obfervation of the following rules, viz: ·

Rule I. Write down any even number of parts, of *half* the length your whole Canon fhall be of; but fo that the whole be regular according to the rules of *retrograde* counterpoint. See my Effay on Harmony, Chap. XIV, § 35.

Rule II. Add the lower of every two parts to the higher, but *backwards*, and the Canon is completed.

An example fee at Plate XLII, No. 3, which is the original compofition of a retrograde Canon of eight parts, according to Rule I; and how every fecond part of the fame example muft be added backwards to the firft, according to Rule II, fee at Plate XXIX, Canon IV. How Canons of this fort are performed, fee under A Survey of Canons, at § 27.

§ 11. A *reverfe retrograde* Canon muft be conftructed after the following rules, viz:

Rule I. Write down any even number of parts, of *half* the length your whole Canon fhall be of; but fo that the whole be regular according to the rules of *reverfe retrograde* counterpoint. See my Effay on Harmony, Chap. XIV, § 36.

Rule II. Add the lower of every two parts to the higher, but *backwards* and *reverfed*, and the Canon is completed.

An example fee at Plate XLII, No. 4, which is the original compofition of a reverfe retrograde Canon of eight parts, according to Rule I; and how every fecond part is added, backwards as well as reverfed, to the firft, according to Rule II, fee at Plate XXIX, Canon V.

Every part of this laft example is for two performers, the one to fing or play forwards, and the other backwards and upfide down. To enable him that performs the reverfe retrogreffion, to fing or play in the right interval, proper clefs muft be placed at the end of the Canon, and upfide down.

N. B. That both retrograde and reverfe retrograde Canons may be made of *another Canon*, appears from the examples given in this, and the preceding §: for the original compofition to that at Plate XXIX, Canon IV, is nothing elfe but the refolution of the higher line of Canon I, No. 3, at Plate XXVIII; and the example at Canon V, Plate XXIX, arifes from Canon II, at Plate XXVIII, No. 3.

III. *The different Lengths of Notes, in which the Reply is made.*

§ 12. As the replies of a Canon may be made, not only with notes of *equal* length, but alfo with notes of *augmented* or *diminifhed* length, I come now to fhew the conftruction of the *two latter* forts of Canons.

In

In regard to thefe Canons it will appear, that a reply by augmentation can only imitate half the fubject, in the fame number of bars; and that a reply by diminution can imitate the whole fubject twice over, in the fame number of bars. Alfo: that by double or triple augmentation, no more than one quarter, or one eighth of the fubject can be imitated in the fame number of bars; and that by double or triple diminution the fubject may be repeated four times, or eight times, to one reply.

§ 13. The rules which muft be obferved, in conftructing a Canon by *fimple augmentation*, are as follows:

Rule I. Write down a melody of fuch a length, that it does not go farther than where the firft reply fhall begin, and (in cafe there fhall be more than one reply,) that it is no longer, than, when carried by augmentation into the part of one reply, it may reach only to the beginning of a fucceeding reply.

Rule II. Carry the faid firft piece of the fubject, by augmentation, into its refpective places as well as intervals of the replies.

Rule III. Add to the firft melody a piece, that is no longer than the firft, but of fuch a nature that it be perfectly harmonious to the parts underneath, as well as to the other parts of the Canon, when carried into its place of the replies.

Rule IV. Carry the faid addition to the firft melody, by augmentation, into its refpective place of every reply; and continue in this manner, till the Canon is as long as intended, or nearly as long.

Rule V. As this fort of Canons can only imitate one half of the beginning part, it is neceffary, when the replies go as far as you wifh to carry the Canon, to add to the preceding part or parts fuch melodies, as will agreeably accompany the laft reply to the end, without regard to the above Rule I, II, III, IV.

Rule VI. If this fort of Canons fhall be *infinite*, you muft calculate its end fo, that every part can properly return to the beginning again, according to Rule IV, at § 5, No. 1; and if it fhall be *finite* the end muft be properly conclufive. If it fhall at every repetition begin in another Key, and confequently be a Canon *per tonos*, the end muft alfo be calculated accordingly, in the fame manner as I have fhewn above at § 7. And the rules according to which it can be made a *reverfe* Canon, follow from § 9.

An example of an infinite Canon by fimple augmentation, and with reverfe imitation, fee at Plate XXXV, Canon IV. The note at which the reply ends is pointed out by a paufe over it.

Canons by *double augmentation* are conftructed exactly like the above, with the only exception that only one quarter of the firft part can be imitated by the reply. And the rules for thofe by *triple* augmentation, follow from what has been faid above.

An example of a Canon by *triple* augmentation fee at Plate XXIX, Canon VIII; in which the reply takes one half of the beginning melody, which is fet four times over to the reply, viz: twice in equal, and twice in reverfe motion. The reply therefore is eight times as long as the notes which it imitates.

§ 14. A Canon by *diminution* is conftructed according to the rules which I fhall give in this place, viz:

Rule I. Write a beginning melody as long as the diftance between the Subject and firft reply, or the fmalleft diftance between any two of the replies fhall be, and carry the fame by diminution, or double or triple diminution, into its intended places and intervals of the different replies.

s

Rule

Rule II.   Continue in this manner, till the Subject is as long as you wish the Canon to be. And as the replies imitate only one half, one quarter, or one eighth of the Subject, according to the degree of the diminution, you may calculate the Subject so, that it can be replied to twice, or four times, or eight times over, as in Canon VII, Plate XXIX, or Canon VIII of the same Plate, when (in the latter example) the reply is confidered as being the Subject, and the Subject the reply.

Rule III.   But you may alfo let the fubject be imitated but once, and afterwards add to the part of every reply, fuch melodies as will agreeably *accompany* the fubject to the end.

How Canons by all forts of diminution can be rendered infinite, or finite; remaining in the fame key, or modulating through all, or *per tonos*; in equal or reverfe motion, follows from what has been faid in the preceding fections of this Chapter.

§ 15. That Canons may be calculated for intermixed *augmented* and *diminifhed* replies, follows alfo from what I have faid above; but as they are very difficult to conftruct, I do not recollect having feen examples of them.

How only fome notes may be *felected* from the Subject, and replied to by augmentation, appears in the Canons by *Bevin* at Plate XL, and XLI.

IV.   *The Number and Quality of the Parts of a Canon.*

§ 16. How the *real* parts of a Canon muft be conftructed I have fhewn above, I therefore fhall now endeavour to fhew how fome other parts may be *added* to the real ones, either as *accompaniments*, or in *thirds*; or alfo: how a Canon may be fet fo, as to be perfectly harmonious to a *given* melody, independant of the Canon.

§ 17. When mere *accompaniments* are to be fet to a Canon, it may be done in all the different manners in which accompaniments can be fet to a Fugue, as I have fhewn in Chap. V, § 20.   This will require no farther demonftration.

§ 18.   But when a Canon of *two* parts contains no other effential notes than the Third, Fifth, and Octave, and the faid parts ftand throughout in contrary or oblique motion, a *third* part alone, or both a *third* and *fourth* part, may be added to the Canon, in *Thirds over* the original parts.   The vaft number of varieties which thus can be produced with a Canon, by inverfion, follows from what is faid in my Effay on Harmony, Chap. XIV, § 9, 16, 21, and 26.

An example of added thirds to one part of the Canon fee at Plate XXIX, Canon VIII, where the thirds are added to the bafs; and one, in which they are added both to the treble and bafs, at Plate XXX, Canon IX.

§ 19. When a Canon is to be conftructed over or to a *given melody*, it is neceffary, *firft* to obferve all the rules given before, refpecting the Canon itfelf; and *fecondly* to take care, that every piece of the fubject be perfectly harmonious, not only to thofe parts of the replies and of the given melody, which immediately belong to it, but alfo to thofe other parts of the fame to which it muft be carried, according to the faid rules, (fee § 5, & *feq.*) This renders the conftruction of the Canons in queftion very difficult.   But many difficulties can be furmounted in them by the occafional introduction of fome Refts, in places where

where they do not render the harmony too poor, nor interrupt or prevent the refolution of a diffonance.

B. OF THE CONSTRUCTION OF DOUBLE CANONS.

§ 20. By *double* Canons I here underftand thofe of two or more really *different* Subjects; and not thofe which arife merely from different forms of one and the fame fubject, though they are written in more than one line to render their folution eafier than otherwife. The general and particular fenfe in which the term *double* Canons is ufed, and the terms *triple* and *quadruple* Canons, I have explained at Chap. VIII, § 4.

§ 21. A *double* Canon, or one of two Subjects, is conftructed as thus: Either complete a fimple Canon firft, and then fet a fecond one to it, fo as to be perfect in itfelf as well as perfectly harmonious to the other: or alfo begin both Subjects at once, and proceed from piece to piece in both Canons, till they are completed.

The principal rule for this fort of Canons is: that both Subjects muft be different, in motion as well as in the forts of notes of which they confift, but that both Canons muft perfectly agree in Harmony. In all other refpects each of the two Canons belonging to the double Canon, muft be conftructed according to the rules given under Simple Canons.

An example of a double Canon fee at Plate XXVIII, No. 3, Canon I.

§ 22. A *triple* or *quadruple* Canon is fet like a double one, with the only difference, that in a triple Canon three Subjects are imitated, and in a quadruple one four Subjects. Examples of which will not be required.

§ 23. As I have in Chap. VIII, § 4, mentioned *compound* Canons, under double ones, I fhall now fay a few words refpecting their conftruction.

There are as many forts of compound Canons poffible, as there may be various combinations of more than one fort of replies in one Subject. To give the reader a little idea of this, I point out the firft Canon by *Emanuel Bach*, and three by *Fafch*, at Plate XXXIII, which will be explained at § 27. Thefe Canons are all upon one and the fame principle, but their conftruction might have been varied as thus: *Firft*, by beginning each Canon as it ends, and ending as it begins, that is to fay, on the fame principle, but not with the fame notes: *fecondly*, by replying firft with notes of *diminifhed*, and afterwards with thofe of *augmented* length, or *vice verfa*, which would anfwer the fame purpofe of making the reply as long as the Subject, as by the method ufed in the Canons in queftion; *thirdly*, by intermixing *double* and *triple* augmentation or diminution with fimple ones, on the fame principle of making the reply as long as the fubject, and in other manners, which the Reader may difcover by his own confideration.

Another fource of varieties is opened by *E. Bach*'s fecond Canon at Plate XXXIII, and its two folutions by *Kirnberger*.

Varieties on other principles again are fhewn in the Canons by *Bevin* at Plate XL, and XLI; and more forts of various combinations might be found if there was occafion for it.

§ 24. One particular fort of Canons may ftill be confidered in this place; it is that which comprehends Canons calculated for *more than one*, or for many forts of refolutions, commonly called *polymorphos*.

Thefe

Thefe Canons cannot be conftructed like others by attending to all the rules, on which every fort of refolution depends; but their fubjects muft be fought for and difcovered, in fhort felect melodies; and the beft in general are found in thofe fhort melodies, which depend on the moft *fimple harmony,* and which proceed by *gradation,* either afcending or defcending.

One example of fuch a fimple melody I have given in my ten Canons on one and the fame fubject. And an example of a Canon which can be refolved more than two thoufand different ways, is found in *Marpurg's* Abhandlung von der Fuge, Part II, being a Canon by *Stoelzel,* the author of the enharmonic fugue I give at Plate XXIV; the fubject is nothing but the diatonic fcale afcending, when all notes are quavers, except thofe of the fourth and fifth degree, which are femiquavers.

II.   *Of the Refolution of Canons.*

§ 25.   By the *refolution* of a Canon I underftand, the art of unriddling its fubject, or of difcovering the replies for which it is calculated, when the author has *not explained* it fufficiently or not at all. It affords the moft ufeful practice, not only in the ftudy of Canons, but alfo in the ftudy of harmony in general, as it requires a conftant recollecting, not only of all the rules on which each fort of Canon depends, but alfo of the rules of harmony and double counterpoint, and therefore is by no means unimportant in the ftudy of harmony and compofition.

§ 26.   But there cannot be given fuch diftinct rules for the refolution of a Canon as for its conftruction; and the only way of refolving a Canon that is without all explanation, is: to try in what intervals, at what diftances, in what motion, and by what fort of length in the notes, one can find out fome of its replies; and then to fee whether the replies difcovered make with the fubject a complete harmony or not. If they make a complete harmony the Canon is confidered as refolved, though it may admit of more refolutions; and if not, fome other refolutions muft be fought for.

To make the diligent reader more acquainted with all the examples of Canons I have given in this and the preceding chapter, than what I have been able to do in thofe places where I mentioned them, I fhall now go over them in the order in which they appear in the plates; and thereby have an opportunity to add what I ftill think neceffary.

III.   *A Survey of all the Canons given in this Work, according to the Order in which they ftand in the Plates.*

§ 27.   At Plate XXVIII, No. 2, fee a general Canon *per tonos,* to exemplify a reply in any interval above or below the unifon. The figures above and below fhew the interval, in which the reply may be made, and the mark § the note where it is to begin. At every return the beginning is made a *fecond* (or one degree) lower than before; and when the parts come too low, the reply may be made a feventh higher, inftead of a fecond lower.

A. CANONS ON THE SUBJECT OF FUGUE I, PLATE XIV.

Canon I.   The higher line is the Subject in queftion; and the lower line the initials of my three chriftian names, A, F, C, firft right and then reverfed. The harmony is nothing

3   but

but the perfect major Triad, with a tranfitory chord on every unaccented quarter of the meafure. The eight upper parts are the foundation to Canon IV, as will appear at Plate XLII, No. 3.

Canon II. This Canon is the foundation to Canon V, as will appear at Plate XLII, No. 4; but for variety's fake I have introduced four parts only inftead of eight.

Canon III. This Canon *per tonos* begins a *third* (or two degrees) lower at every return; and may alfo be inverted in the Octave, to prevent the parts from coming too low.

Canon IV, Plate XXIX. How this Canon arifes from Canon I, has been fhewn before. It may be fet in fcore fo, that every line is written twice over, viz: firft right, and then fo that the end makes the beginning, (or according to retrograde motion;) and then it may be performed like any other fcore, every line the right way.

Canon V. How this Canon arifes from Canon II, has been faid before, and will appear at Plate XLII, No. 4. It may be fet in fcore, fo that every line is written twice over, viz: firft right, and then according to reverfe retrograde motion; and afterwards it may be performed like the above Canon IV.

Canon VI. Here both parts are written in full, and the reply imitates half the Subject, according to what has been faid in § 13.

Canon VII. Here one half of the original fubject is replied to twice by the whole Subject, according to § 14.

Canon VIII. Here the Subject appears four times, viz: twice right and twice reverfed, to one half of its imitation, according to § 13; and the thirds added to the bafs muft alfo be taken notice of.

Canon IX, Plate XXX. The thirds added to both original parts are to be taken notice of here.

Canon X. The Subject in queftion is in the bafs, as a given melody, and a Canon is fet over it, according to § 19.

B. CANONS BY DR. BURNEY.

Refpecting the following Canons I muft obferve, that they are, by permiffion of their celebrated Author, tranfcribed from a collection of his manufcript Canons, containing upwards of an hundred Canons in all varieties of intervals, and in various lengths and forms; and that I have only numbered them here according to the order in which I have placed them.

Canon I, Plate XXX. This Canon might have been expreffed in one line, like that at Plate XXVIII, No. 3, Canon II. But to facilitate its refolution it is written in two lines like a double Canon. It is infinite, but calculated to conclude at the place marked with a paufe, and with thofe notes of the replies which are expreffed by fmall ones.

Canon II. This ænigmatical Canon is explained underneath by Dr. *Burney*'s own folution, which fhews: that the notes with the tails turned upwards are the firft part, thofe drawn downwards the fecond, and the middle line unifon.

Canon III, Plate XXXI. The firft and third part of this Canon is in C, and the fecond in F, which is pointed out by the flat at the clef of the fecond line; and when turned upfide down, the firft and third line is in F, and the fecond in C. It muft be performed as thus: firft, all three performers fing the right way, with the fame words; then the piece is turned upfide down, and all three performers fing again one way, and with the fame words, as it appears in the inverfion; at laft it is inverted again and fung like the firft time,

when

when the firſt and ſecond part are continued as long as the third, by the ſmall notes. This Canon therefore is different from that reverſe retrograde one I have given at Plate XXIX.

c. CANONS BY KIRNBERGER.

N. B. Theſe Canons, and the following ones by *Emanuel Bach*, and by *Faſch*, are taken from *Kirnberger*'s Kunſt des reinen Satzes, Vol. II.

Canon I, Plate XXXI. The four different Clefs and Signatures before this Canon ſhew, that it ſhall be ſtrictly imitated in three different intervals. It differs from other Canons *per tonos* in two points, viz: firſt, that it proceeds throughout in four different Keys; and ſecondly, that it need not repeat as often as there are diatonic degrees, or chromatic intervals in the ſcale, but that it divides the whole ſcale into three major thirds, C—E, E—A flat (or G ſharp,) and A flat C. See its ſolution underneath it.

Canon II. This maſterly Canon is on the ſame principle as the former, but it differs from it in one point, viz: that the ſubject does not repeat twice in its original form, but that its repetitions are varied ſo, as to become a continuation of one and the ſame ſubject throughout. Such varieties ought to be taken particular notice of by the diligent reader, becauſe they may lead him to the diſcovery of uſeful varieties in other ſorts of Canons. The ſolution of this Canon ſee underneath it.

b. CANONS BY EMANUEL BACH.

Canon I, Plate XXXIII. This curious Canon is firſt imitated with notes of equal length in the fifth below, till the ſubject is half as long as intended, and then the reply takes the ſubject again from the beginning, and imitates it by diminution, which conſequently renders the reply as long as the Subject, according to what I have ſaid in § 14. Some remarks reſpecting varieties of Canons which might be conſtructed on the ſame principle ſee at § 23.

Canon II. The apparent inſignificance of a little piece like this, would perhaps let few perſons ſuſpect, that there was any thing particular contained in it, if they were to ſee it on a piece of paper, without the name of its author, and without any explanation. But the two maſterly ſolutions *Kirnberger* has made of it, as underneath it, ſhew again, what I have ſaid before, viz: how much there depends upon the Knowledge of treating a Subject.

E. CANONS BY FASCH.

Canon I, II, *and* III, Plate XXXIV. Theſe are, as I have ſaid before, conſtructed on the ſame principle as No. 1, by *Emanuel Bach*. But the *firſt* contains a third part, by double diminution of the Subject; the *ſecond* is made conſiſting of three parts by adding thirds to the reply; and the *third* conſiſts of two ſections, the latter ſection being an inverſion of the former. Such varieties muſt again animate a diligent ſtudent to try if he can add more to them.

F. CANON BY MARPURG.

See *Canon* IX *in* I, at Plate XXXV. At the firſt note of every bar a reply begins a third lower than the former, and this Canon is remarkable for containing all the Triads which

the

the diatonic scale produces, viz : three major triads, three minor triads, and the diminished triad.   See *Marpurg*'s Abhandlung von der Fuge, Part II, Page 99.

G.   CANONS ON THE ROYAL SUBJECT, BY SEBASTIAN BACH.

Respecting the Subject in question, I have said at Chap. VI. § 10, under Rule II, that it was laid before the Author in question, by the *King of Prussia*, to extemporize upon. This he did not only in the most masterly manner, but also composed upon the same subject two Fugues, and the following Canons, which he dedicated to His Majesty, entitled, *Musicalisches Opfer*, (Musical Offering.)   The said Fugues are: the first a ricercata in three, and the second in six parts.

Canon I, Plate XXXV.   The first nine bars are the Subject in question, and the other nine a counterpoint, set first to it according to the rules of § 10, and then added to it backwards.   The second performer takes the whole line backwards, as the retrograde clef at the end shews.   See its Solution at Plate XXXVII, I.

Canon II.   The Subject in question in the bass, as a given melody, and a Canon is set over it for two violins ; the reply begins at the first note of the second bar, as the mark shews.

Canon III.   The Subject in question is the Treble, as a given melody, and a Canon in the fourth below, and in reverse imitation, is set under it.   The interval of the reply, and its reverse motion, is indicated by the reversed Clef and Flats, after the first Clef; and the distance of the reply is pointed out by the mark under the note in the middle of the first bar.   See the solution of the lower line, or Canon, at Plate XXXVII, III.

Canon IV.   The *varied* Subject in question is a given melody, and the Canon is contained in the lower line.   The reversed clef shews the interval, and the motion, in which the reply shall be made ; and the superscription tells, that it shall be by augmentation. The distance of the reply is pointed out by a mark in the first bar.   See the solution of this Canon at Plate XXXVII, IV.

Canon V, at Plate XXXVI.   Another variation of the Subject in question makes a given melody in the upper part, and the Canon is contained in the lower.   The two clefs shew the interval and the motion of the reply ; a mark under the second bar shews its distance ; and the modulation towards the end, as well as the Direct between the third and fourth line, shew that it is a Canon *per tonos*, and must begin a second higher at every return.

Canon VI.   A Variation of the Subject in question again makes a given melody in the upper part, and the Canon is contained in the lower.   The F clef on the highest line shews the interval of the reply, which is to be in equal motion with the Subject of the Canon ; and the mark in the second bar shews its distance to be one bar.   The directs at the end refer to the first note after the repeat.

Canon VII.   A variation of the Subject in question makes the beginning of the Canon, which is explained only by the two clefs.   But as the F clef is reversed, and (when turned upside downwards,) stands on the second line, it makes the reply to be reversed, and to begin on A, a third above the F clef.   The number of replies is not mentioned, nor their distance ; but I have found the said reverse reply to be two bars and a half behind the subject.   Whether this Canon is calculated for more than two parts, I have had no time to try.

Canon VIII.   A variation of the Subject in question makes the beginning.   The G clef on the first line makes its notes to be an octave higher than those of the F clef on the

fourth

fourth line. This Canon is therefore in the Unifon and Octave; and its folution at Plate XXXVIII, VIII, fhews that it has been invented according to the rules given at § 4.

Canon IX. *Fuga Canonica*, at Plate XXXVIII, *& feq.* This piece is a Canon in the form of a fugue of two parts, with an additional bafs. The G clef on the firft line fhews the interval of the reply; and the paufe near the end fhews, that its diftance fhall be ten bars from the beginning. Similar mafterly pieces are in that great Author's *Art of the Fugue.*

H. CANONS BY BEVIN.

The fcarce work from which the Canons in queftion are taken, I have mentioned at Chap. VIII, § 4; I therefore need only add, that I have numbered them here according to the order in which I give them, and not as they ftand in the above Author's work.

Canon I, Plate XL. The firft part is the Subject; the fecond part is its reply at one bar's diftance; the third part arifes by felecting only the minims out of the firft part, and making them all femibreves, which renders this a very curious fort of a Canon which may be varied in many different manners. They muft be conftructed from bar to bar, or by fmaller pieces, according to the rules given at § 5, *& feq.* The fourth part is an added melody, or accompaniment.

Canon II. This Canon *per tonos* is fet to the third part of the former, as to a *given melody*, and confequently according to the rules given at § 19. The faid given melody is the firft part, and the Canon is in the other three parts.

Canon III. This very curious ænigmatical Canon ftands in Bevin's work with red and black notes, which, as I could not have them, I have changed into large and fmall ones. The explanation over its folution at Plate XLI, fhews the meaning of this difference; and alfo that this Canon has been fet to the fame *given melody* as the former. The firft part of the faid folution therefore is the given melody; the fecond, third, and fourth part is the Canon, of which the fourth part is the Subject; and the fifth part added as an accompaniment. The *rules* according to which this Canon has been conftructed are: *Firft*, write down one bar of the fubject, fo as to be perfectly harmonious to the firft as well as the fecond bar of the given melody; *fecondly*, carry this piece of the fubject into the part of the reply, fo as to come under the fecond bar of the given melody; *thirdly*, add to the fubject a piece as long as the firft, fo that it may make a regular third part, to the reply and given melody, as well as to the firft piece of the fubject and given melody; *fourthly*, carry this fecond piece of the fubject before the fecond piece of the reply, fo as to make a third part to the fubject and given melody. In this manner two Bars of the Canon are completed. The next two bars are done in the fame manner; and the fifth and fixth bar again in the fame manner.

This Canon therefore confifts but of *two parts* fet to a given melody; and the curiofity of it arifes from the reply's being divided into two parts, with interfperfed refts, fo that it becomes a Canon of *three* parts to a given melody.

Canon IV. This Canon alfo is to the fame *given melody* to which the two former ones have been fet, but in the following very ingenious manner: *Firft*, the given melody has been made the fubject of a Canon, and has been replied to by the bafs in the octave below, with the fame intervals, but with notes of different length; *fecondly*, a real Canon of two parts, imitative of the former by reverfion, has been fet to the two former parts, like as to one given melody.

Canon

Canon V.   The former given melody is in the bafs, and a Canon of three parts has been fet to it in the very curious manner, that the Subject and one reply proceed in equal motion, and by the fame fort of notes; and that the fecond reply proceeds in contrary motion, and by a different fort of notes, being femibreves throughout.

I.   CANONS BY HANDEL.

In the laft Canon by *Sebaftian Bach* I have given an example how real Canons may be fet in the form of a Fugue.   In the two following ones by *Handel*, I fhall now fhew other forms of a fimilar nature.   Both are taken from the well known Oratorio *Jephtha*; and as the inftrumental parts are only going in the unifon or octave with the vocal parts, and with the fame forts of notes, as the laft fymphonies fhew, I have omitted them; except in a few places, where the vocal parts reft.   And the treble is written in the G clef, merely for the fake of admitting the violin notes without altering the clef.

Canon I.   See Plate XLIII, & *feq.*   The alto and the bafs fing a Canon in the octave below, till the fifteenth and fixteenth bar; and the treble and tenor fall in to relieve them in the fourteenth and fifteenth bar.   The latter two fing the fame Canon a fourth higher, like the anfwer of a Fugue to the preceding fubject, which they end in the twenty-fixth bar, and confequently make it a little fhorter than the former two parts.   In the fame bar the bafs begins the latter part of the fubject again, and the alto follows at the fame diftance as before.   In the thirtieth bar the treble begins the fubject again, but tranfpofed, and the tenor follows; but the bafs to it repeats the latter part of its words, with fuch notes as agree with the Canon in the other parts.   The judicious and fine varieties contained in the remaining part of the piece, I leave to the Reader's own examination.

Canon II, fee Plate XLV.   The beginning is made with a Tutti of four bars, when the Canon begins in the treble, and the alto replies to it in the fifth below.   In the ninth bar the tenor falls in with the firft reply, and in the tenth the bafs follows with the firft fubject, but the treble and alto fing additional parts to the Canon, inftead of refting.   In the thirteenth bar a tutti relieves the Canon.   In the twenty-eighth bar the Canon appears again, and continues in the different parts till the thirty-fixth bar, where another tutti begins, and continues till the end.

K.   CANON BY CHARLES HENRY GRAUN.

See Plate XLVII, & *feq.*   This Canon is the fecond part of a Duet in the above author's *Ifigenia in Aulide*, and I have taken it from Vol. I. of that valuable collection of Graun's works, entitled: Duetti, Terzetti, Quintetti, Seftetti, ed alcuni Chori, delle Opere del Signore Carlo Enrico Graun, Berlin, and Koenigfberg, 1773.   The whole collection makes four or fix volumes in large folio; and as Graun is univerfally acknowledged to have been one of the moft claffical Harmonifts, and yet every part of his fcores is confifting of the moft natural and pleafing melodies, there can be nothing more recommendable for ftudy, both in regard to *vocal* mufic, and to the management of *inftrumental parts*, than that collection.   Yet a ftudent fhould not confine himfelf to the works of one, if he can have thofe of more great authors.

The Canon begins in the Primo, and is replied to in the Secundo, at half a bar's diftance, and in the Unifon.   In the fixth bar an apparent beginning is made again, but without continuing the Canon.   In the thirteenth bar a fimilar beginning is made, but it alfo ter-

U   minates

minates in a mere imitation. In the fifteenth bar the latter half of the words begins again with a real Canon, till the eighteenth bar, after which the piece concludes with imitations only.

The purpofe for which I give this Canon, is to fhew: how a piece may partly confift of a ftrict Canon, and partly of imitations fimilar to a Canon. Of its melodies, and inftrumental parts, I fhall fpeak in the following Chapter.

CHAPTER X.　OF VOCAL MUSIC.

§ 1. Vocal Mufic is that fet for *Voices*, either without or with inftrumental accompaniments. It is the principal branch of mufical compofition. For, *firft*, the words give a more diftinct meaning to the founds to which they are fet, than what can be given to founds without a verbal explanation; and on that account vocal mufic has in general a greater effect upon our feelings, or is more interefting, than mere inftrumental mufic. *Secondly*, vocal mufic muft be judged of, not only according to its propriety as a piece of compofition without words, but alfo according to the manner in which it is adapted to the Character, Verfe, and Declamation, of the Text; and trefpaffes againft the true expreffion of a Text, are much more confpicuous in a mufical piece, than thofe againft many other rules.

I fhall endeavour to fpeak of the mufic in queftion, firft *in general*; and fecondly with regard to its particular qualities, as *Recitative, Air*, and *Chorus*.

I. *Of Vocal Mufic in general.*

§ 2. In all forts of vocal pieces it is neceffary to obferve the following *general rules*, viz:

Rule I. No paffages ought to be introduced in the vocal part or parts of a mufical piece, but what are calculated for Human Voices in general, both with regard to *facility*, and to the poffibility of *fetching Breath* without miffing notes.

1. In regard to facility, it will be allowed, that a paffage can be eafy or difficult, not only on account of the *Intervals* and *Sort of Notes* of which it is compofed; but alfo on account of the *Harmony* with which it is accompanied.

What *Intervals* are eafy or difficult to be fung, in themfelves, and without regard to their harmonious accompaniment, I have fhewn in my Effay on Harmony, Chap. III, § 20; and what is eafy or difficult in regard to the *Sorts of Notes*, of which a vocal paffage is compofed, follows from the nature of human voices in general, which a perfon who will compofe for them muft know, as well as the nature of an inftrument for which he intends to write. All quick paffages therefore, particularly thofe compofed of great intervals, are more or lefs difficult, and ought to be avoided in general.

That the moft eafy Intervals can be rendered difficult to fing, by the fort of *Harmony* with which they are accompanied, muft alfo be confidered. For, what can be eafier to fing than the Unifon, or the fame note again? and yet it may be rendered difficult, if not impoffible, for any Singer to hit it, even when he is prepared for it, merely by the faid harmonious accompaniment. As this may appear incredible to fome of my Readers, I will

2　　　　　　　　　　　　　　　　　　　　　　　　　　　explain

explain it by the Tune of an Hymn, the words of which stand in a book called *German Psalmody*, and begin, " Now let us praise the Lord," see Plate L, No. 1. If the first period after the Repeat is played as at No. 2, a, any singer who attends to the harmony will be inclined to begin the next line a whole tone *higher* than what he should, or as at b ; and if the second period after the Repeat is played as at No. 3, a, he will find it hardly possible to avoid beginning the next note, a whole tone *lower* than the unison, or as at b. Some very judicious remarks related to the object in question are found in *Holden's* Essay towards a rational System of Music, from Article 220 to 225. According to all the above, it is necessary to give a vocal passage, such an accompaniment as will support, but not confuse, the singer.

2. In regard to *fetching breath*, it would be easy to give a number of examples, in which it is impossible to fetch breath without missing a note. A composer therefore should also be careful in this particular.

Rule II. Every vocal part should be particularly calculated for the *Compass*, as well as the *Sort of Voice* for which it is set.

1, In regard to Compass, it must be observed, that in general a common voice cannot be considered as exceeding a Tenth, or the utmost a Twelfth ; which, if applied to the four principal parts of vocal music, fixes their compass as follows, viz :

The Bass, from F under the first line ⎫
The Tenor, from C under the first line ⎪ To the Tenth, Eleventh,
The Alto, from F on the first line ⎬   or Twelfth above.
And the Treble, from C on the first line ⎭

N. B. Though for Solo Voices, a compass of two octaves, and sometimes more may be set ; yet a composer should be careful not to go to the extreme, in general as well as in particular cases.

2, In regard to the Sort of Voice, the Bass should have bass passages ; the Treble, treble passages ; and the two middle parts, such as make a proper medium between the two extreme Parts. This is particularly required when the music is in parts, or for two and more singers ; but it should also be attended to even in Solos.

What I understand by Treble, Alto, Tenor, or Bass Passages, will follow from what I have said in my Essay on Harmony, Chap. IX, § 3, respecting the *clauses* of the said four parts of a harmony ; and in the same work at Chap. III, § 5, respecting larger or smaller intervals. The application to the four parts in question must be made as thus :

A bass part should in general contain progressions by *larger intervals* than the upper parts ; and more *bass clauses*, than other ones.

A treble part should in general proceed by smaller intervals than the lower parts ; containing more *treble clauses* than other ones.

An Alto or Tenor part should in general contain progressions, by intervals, that make a proper medium between those of a treble or bass part ; and more *alto or tenor clauses* than treble or bass ones. Yet when the alto or tenor is a Solo part, it may conclude its periods or sections with treble clauses, which are better in all the three upper parts than Bass clauses.

N. B. That the four parts of a harmony should not be confined to one sort of intervals, or each to its own sort of clauses, is naturally understood. For as all chords and cadences *may* not only be inverted, but *ought* to appear inverted as well as fundamental, if the harmony shall contain a proper variety, it follows: that all sorts of intervals and clauses

may

may be intermixed in the faid four parts, if it only is done fo, as not to deftroy their principal characteriftics, pointed out under the Rule in queftion.

Rule III.   The harmony and melody of the Mufic muft correfpond with the Text, in its *general character.*

By the *general character* of a text I underftand : that air of ferenity or melancholy, happinefs or forrow, or of any other defcription, which characterifes the whole of it ; or that variety of general characteriftics, which may change with the different Sections of the text.

The faid general characteriftics ought to be attended to, firft in regard to a *whole Opera, Oratorio,* or work which confifts of various pieces, independent of each other ; fo that the whole mufic be expreffive of the fame character as the whole text.   Secondly, in regard to every *whole piece* contained in the faid works ; fo that the mufic be adapted to the particular general fentiment contained in the text.

Contrary to this rule are in general the compofitions of thofe theatrical pieces, which have been wholly or partly compiled from the works of different compofers.   For, even when the compilation is executed with the greateft fkill and judgment, there cannot be one general character in it ; and to hear pieces of trios, quatuors, or fymphonies, torn out of their connection, mutilated, and forced to words which they are not calculated for, cannot but have a bad effect upon any perfon who attends to the propriety of the mufic.

Rule IV.   The mufic muft alfo correfpond with every *particular characteriftic* of the text.   Thefe characteriftics I fhall endeavour to confider with regard to the *metre* of the text ; its *words* ; and the *fort of letters* in every word.   See the three following fections.

§ 3.   In regard to the *metre* of a text when poetical, or, (which is the fame,) the flow of the words when profaical, I have faid in my Effay on Harmony, Chap. XII, § 24, that the *rhythmical* order of the mufic fhould exactly correfpond with the *metre* of the verfe, according to the fimilitude of the one to the other, fhewn in that chapter.

In regard to the *metre itfelf* therefore, the rhythmical order of the mufic muft correfpond with it, even when the founds are confidered as *indifferent in themfelves* ; but the ftops and cadences in it, muft be expreffed by the nature of the *mufical* founds.   Refpecting both fee the Work and Chapter mentioned juft now.

Concerning the queftion, what fort of Meafure is beft calculated for every fort of Metre? It is evident, that *in general,* and in plain melodies, thofe meafures are beft, which contain as many times in a bar or its divifions, as the text has fyllables in a foot of the verfe.   Confequently, that *common time* of two or four times in a bar, is beft for thofe verfes which confift of *two* fyllables in a foot ; and that *triple time,* or tripled common time, is beft, when a foot of the verfe confifts of *three* Syllables.   According to this obfervation, the well known fong *Rule Britannia,* is very properly compofed in common time, and *God fave the King* in triple time.

But in *particular cafes,* or for certain purpofes, it is alfo allowable, to give two times of the mufical meafure to every accented fyllable of a foot of the verfe ; or alfo, to fet two or even three fyllables to one time of the meafure.   By thefe means, metrical feet of three fyllables may be compofed in common time ; and feet of two fyllables in triple time.   The faid two fongs therefore might alfo be compofed as thus : *Rule Britannia* in triple, and *God fave the King* in common time.

Yet in all cafes, the *accented* fyllable of a metrical foot muft come on the accented time of the meafure ; and if more than one foot fhould be fet to one bar, the accented fyllables muft fall on the accented parts of every divifion of the meafure.   What muft be obferved,

when

when accented as well as unaccented fyllables fhall be fung to one and the fame time of the meafure, fee in § 22.

§ 4.   In regard to *Words*, as mentioned in Rule 4, § 2, it is not fufficient, that they are accented and expreffed according to the feet of the verfe to which they belong; for, fometimes a poet allows himfelf a little liberty in the fcanfion of his verfe, if he cannot have every foot of the metre ftrictly accented without giving up an important word or fentiment; but every principal word of the text muft be placed in fuch a part of the meafure, and expreffed with fuch a harmony and melody, as its nature requires. This rule Dr. *Arne* has very judicioufly attended to in the above mentioned fong *Rule Britannia*. For, in the third line of the firft verfe, " This was the charter of the land," the word *was* ftands on the accented part of a metrical foot; but the word *this* requires a greater accent in.the expreffion; on account of the latter therefore the compofer has taken a liberty againft the general rhythmical order of that piece, and begun the line in queftion with the accented note, inftead of the unaccented; and by this judicious liberty in the compofition he has corrected the imperfection of that line of the text.

But when *more than one* verfe fhall be fung to one and the fame melody, and the poet has not exprefsly calculated them for that purpofe, by fetting equal ftreffes upon the fame parts of every line in each verfe, the compofer ought to attend to the *firft* and *laft*, or the *firft* and *moft* verfes, in particular, and to cover the faults of the others according to what I fay in § 21.

§ 5.   The *fort of letters* in every word is the laft which muft be attended to according to Rule IV, in § 2.

This obfervation concerns the Poet as much as the Compofer; for no perfon fhould undertake to write words for mufical pieces without a perfect knowledge of what words or letters are more or lefs calculated to be fung. But as a compofer muft know to make the beft of a text, as it is, if he cannot have it corrected, I fhall attempt a few remarks, refpecting the quality of Syllables which fhall be fet to mufic, viz:

1.   In reality, nothing of a word or fyllable can be *fung*, but its Vowels, and Diphthongs; and Confonants ferve only to give vowels a greater variety of pronunciations, than what could be produced with vowels alone. But one vowel or diphthong is better calculated for finging than another, according to greater or leffer *eafe and opennefs of the mouth* with which it may be pronounced and held out.

2.   According to this remark, the letter A, when pronounced as in the French, Italian, or German language, is beft calculated for fetting holding notes or long paffages to it; and that pronounced *ay*, as in *Mary* or *Paper*, is the neareft related to it.

The next vowel in rank I fuppofe to be O; with its neareft relation the German ö, which is pronounced like the French *eux*.

The third in rank confequently is E, when pronounced *ey*, as in *Whey*.

The fourth in rank I fuppofe to be I, when pronounced *ee* as in foreign languages. For when this letter is pronounced as *Eye* in Englifh, it is in fome foreign languages a diphthong, compofed of e—i, and belongs to the above firft clafs of the vowels in queftion.

The fifth and laft in rank therefore is U, when pronounced *oo*, as in the Italian and German language, or as in the French word *gout*; and its related letter ü, as in the German language, or in the French word *rue*. But though u, when pronounced as in the Englifh words *ufe*, or *mews*, founds like a diphthong compofed of i—u, yet its latter part is heard moft, and confequently this makes no alteration in the above rule.

x

3. The

3.   The Diphthongs, which arife from the compofition of the above vowels, are more or lefs ufeful for finging according to their refemblance to one or another of them; and this refemblance muft be decided according to the divifion which they admit of, or even require, in finging.

For *oy* in the word Boy, is fung like *Bau-y*; confequently this diphthong is nearly as good as *au*.

Ou in the word *hour*, is fung like *Au-u*; and is therefore alfo fimilar to *au*.

All other diphthongs, viz : ai, au, ee, ea, eo, eu, oa, oe, ue, and ui, have in moft, or perhaps all cafes, the effect of one of the above five fimple vowels, and muft be regarded accordingly.

4.   All holding notes, figurative paffages, or fancy cadences, fhould therefore as much as poffible be given to fuch words or fyllables which contain the beft, or nearly the beft vowels or diphthongs, according to the above defcription; and if poffible to thofe which *end* with the Vowel or Diphthong, as it is difagreeable to hear a finger dwell a long while upon half a fyllable before one hears the end of it.

5.   In regard to *Confonants*, the Compofer has not fo much to obferve as the Poet and the Singer; for the Poet ought to avoid the harfher ones where they would become too crowded, and the Singer to pronounce them as gentle as plainnefs will permit. But the Compofer ought alfo to take care, that he does not fet words or letters which are difficult to pronounce, to quicker notes than what the Singer can conveniently fing with fuch words.

All the above remarks will upon examination be found ftrictly attended to by great compofers.

II.   *Of the different Sorts of Vocal Mufic.*

§ 6.   The three principal forts of vocal mufic as mentioned in § 1, are: the *Recitative,* the *Air,* and the *Chorus.* The *firft* fort comprehends mufical *declamation,* without the formality of finging the words as in lyric pieces; the *fecond* fort, melodious *finging,* principally calculated but for one performer to each vocal part; and the *third* fort, *finging in parts* calculated for a number of performers to each vocal part.

A.   OF RECITATIVES.

§ 7.   From the general definition given of recitatives, in the preceding fection, and from the term *Recitative* itfelf, which feems to denote a mere mufical reciting, follow the rules which I fhall give for this fort of mufical pieces.

§ 8.   There are two forts of Recitatives hitherto in ufe, viz: thofe with an accompaniment for a mere *Bafs or Thorough-Bafs;* and thofe with an accompaniment for *divers inftruments.* Both may be written on a text in Profe as well as in Verfe. And both forts may be occafionally intermixed one with another, as well as be interfperfed, either with vocal *Ariofos,* or with mere inftrumental periods.

§ 9.   The above *firft* fort of recitatives, or thofe with a mere *Thorough-Bafs* accompaniment, are recitatives in the ftricteft fenfe of the word. They are generally written in two staves of five lines each, the lower containing the bafs accompaniment, and the higher the vocal part; and this method of fetting the vocal part over the accompaniment, has been adapted for the purpofe of enabling the player to accompany the finger more precifely than what it would be in his power to do otherwife.

The particulars which muft be confidered in this fort of Recitatives are their *Time* and *Rhythm,* their *Modulation,* and their *Declamation.*

1. In regard to *Time,* the Recitatives in queftion are not confined to any fixed Movement or Meafure, though they are generally written in common or $\frac{4}{4}$ time, to affift the vocal and inftrumental performer in hitting together. According to this meafure every word and fyllable is placed fo as to obtain its proper *accent,* which the Singer muft ftrictly attend to; but the different *lengths of notes* the Singer need not clofely adhere to, nor to any fixed *movement,* as that would take away the required eafe of the recitative. The harmonies by which the vocal part is fupported, muft therefore be laid under it in fuch a manner, that the Player has time to attend and follow the Singer, or even to affift him in not miffing a difficult interval; but not in fo crowded a fucceffion that the Singer be confined, by keeping time with the accompaniment. How quick or how flow therefore a recitative fhall be performed, or where it fhall increafe or decreafe in quicknefs, is generally left to the difcretion of the Singer, which renders the juft performance of a recitative one of the moft difficult tafks for a Singer; but I think that the Compofer might very well affift the Performer, in that refpect, by expreffing over the Recitative how faft or flow he wifhes it to be performed, without *confining* the performer to any *fixed* movement.

The *Rhythmical Order* of the Recitatives in queftion is alfo not fo limited, as that of Airs or other vocal or inftrumental pieces. For though a good compofer would not fet one period or ftrain too unproportional to the others, yet he does not concern himfelf about beginning or ending the one on the fame time of the meafure on which he begins or ends another; and if he only attends to a good relation in the Sorts of Notes, and to the placing of every accented Syllable on an accented part of the meafure, it is fufficient.

2. The *Modulation* of thefe Recitatives alfo, does *not* depend on a certain fixed or principal *Key or Mode,* in which they fhould begin, end, and chiefly remain, like as other pieces of compofition. For, in general, neither Sharp or Flat is marked by the Clef; and the recitative may begin in any one, and end in any other key or mode. Natural and abrupt modulations may alfo be introduced in them intermixed, and without regard to the general order in which the keys and modes ought to appear, according to my Effay on Harmony, Chap. X, § 9. But the modulation ought to be reafonable in itfelf, as well as alfo and particularly adapted to the fenfe of the Text. However, in fhort recitatives, which contain but little modulation, the fignature of a certain Key is fometimes ufed by the clef, like as in *Handel's* Meffiah, the Recitative, "Behold a Virgin fhall conceive;" but the above-mentioned fignature without any fharp or flat is beft in thofe Recitatives which fhall contain a variety of modulation.

3. In regard to *Declamation,* the Recitatives in queftion cannot properly contain fuch finging progreffions, as would be like melodies of an air; but they muft be entirely conftructed upon the principle of *mufical fpeaking.* Yet as there are many different manners of declamation even in the moft artlefs fpeaking of common life, and many more in a fpeech delivered according to the rules of art, on the Stage, in the Pulpit, or at the Bar; fo the mufical declamation of a Recitative, which fhould be declamation with the higheft *grace, energy,* or *affection,* admits of more or lefs *graces,* as well as of fome *long notes,* or even fhort *tranfitory* or *figurative* paffages, according to the Style in which the Recitative is

written,

written, and to fome particular occafions offered by the nature of the Text. But in all cafes the Melody of the Recitative fhould confift of progreffions, which border more on melodious fpeaking than finging; confequently in general of no more than one note to each fyllable.

The *Claufes* with which the vocal part ends its different periods or ftrains, are therefore alfo a great object of confideration in Recitatives. For, in general, the laft note muft neither be fufpended by the preceding, nor graced by an appoggiatura; and even the progreffion by one diatonic degree to the laft note, is feldom found in recitatives by great Authors; but proceeding to it by the interval of a Third, Fourth, or Fifth, afcending or defcending, is found in moft claufes of all good recitatives.

§ 10. An Example of a regular and expreffive Recitative in the ferious ftyle fee at Plate L, No. 4, continued at Plate LI. It is taken from *Graun's* grand facred Cantata, " Der Todt Jefu," (The Death of Jefus,) and the variety, richnefs, and originality of its modulation deferve admiration. The enharmonic change at the end of the twelfth bar muft alfo be taken notice of; for fuch changes have a ftrong effect in recitatives, but they muft be introduced with great judgment, or elfe they eafily become impracticable for the Singer.

For more examples, and examples of different forts, I muft refer the Reader to the Recitatives in all the works of *Handel*; and alfo recommend the ftudy of thofe by other ftrict Authors.

§ 11. Refpecting the manner in which the Recitatives in queftion fhould be *accompanied:* it needs no demonftration, that according to the ufual manner of writing them, their proper accompaniment is one of the greateft tafks for a Thorough Bafs Player. For, the holding Bafs notes, as in the example given in § 10, fhould in general not be held to their full length; the Chords fhould fometimes be ftruck like Chords, and fometimes as Harpeggios; the Harmony fhould in fome cafes be taken in four or more, and in others but in three or two parts; the Singer fhould be affifted in difficult intervals; and wherever the Singer deviates from the ftrict length of the notes, the Player fhould precifely follow him. And all thefe particulars, moft of which are important, are in general not pointed out by the Compofer, though the Recitative in queftion has no other harmonious fupport but the one thorough bafs accompaniment; when in Sonatas, the moft infignificant graces are often carefully written down. The confequence of which is, that when the accompaniment comes under the hands of an unfkilful player, the recitative lofes all its effect; and that, as the moft able player is not always in the fame humour or fpirit, it muft fometimes fall fhort of its intended effect even under his hands.

According to thefe confiderations it might be wifhed, that Compofers, who take pains in writing recitatives, and are not indifferent about their effect, would adopt a method of rendering the accompaniment of them more diftinctly expreffed, and not leave it fo much to the ability or difcretion of the performer as is hitherto done, but without rendering it more difficult than what thorough bafs in general is.

§ 12. The *fecond* fort of recitatives mentioned in § 8, are thofe with accompaniments for *divers inftruments*, commonly called *Recitatives accompanied*, or *Accompaniments*. They are fimilar to the former in all refpects but one, viz: that the accompaniments muft be fet fo, as to be fully at eafe to attend to the liberties which the Singer takes in refpect to time; and that in thofe places where the accompaniments require it, the Singer muft more clofely

adhere

adhere to the prescribed measure and a certain movement, than in the above first sort of Recitatives.

The finest examples of this sort see in *Handel*'s Messiah, and particularly that, " Comfort ye my people ;" also in Jephtha, which is full of Recitatives, and in the other works of that great Author. From the examination of which the diligent Reader may learn, what sort of harmonies and passages have the best effect in different cases; and how instrumental periods or strains may be set between parts of the text, to give the words or sentiment some relief.

Another Author who has been great in this sort of Recitatives is *Graun*, of whom I have given an example in § 10.

§ 13. In both the above sorts of Recitatives there is sometimes introduced, an *Arioso*, being a Section or Period which must be sung and accompanied like an *Air*, and not with those liberties allowed and required in a Recitative. Of these I shall speak more in § 24.

§ 14. Though in general recitatives are only set so, that no more than *one* vocal part is heard at a time; yet *double, triple,* or *quadruple* ones might also be composed in those Scenes where sometimes two or more persons are introduced as speaking at the same time, though not the same words. But they require to be constructed, so, that every Singer is at full ease to sing or recite his respective words, and also to attend to the others ; as otherwise they would loose the effect of a Recitative.

B. OF AIRS.

§ 15. According to the definitions given in § 6, the characteristic of an *Air* is: *melodious singing*, principally calculated but for *one* performer to each vocal part ; and the particulars which I shall now endeavour to consider in regard to Airs, are: first the inventing of a proper *Melody* ; secondly, the supporting of it with a proper *Harmony* and *Accompaniment* ; thirdly, the different *Forms* in which Airs may be composed.

a. THE INVENTING OF A PROPER MELODY.

§ 16. That vocal pieces, and particularly Airs, require a more choice melody than mere instrumental pieces, follows from what I have said in § 1. For their melodies are judged of, not only with regard to their propriety as a melodious part of a composition in general, but also, and in particular, with regard to the manner in which they are adapted to the words and whole character of the Text. It is therefore necessary in inventing a melody for an Air to pay attention to the three following Rules, viz :

Rule I. Every melody of an Air must be *grammatically right* in itself. What is to be observed in regard to this rule I have shewn in my Essay on Harmony, Chap. III, § 20, to which I beg leave to refer the Reader.

Rule II. A melody must be more *easy* and *simple*, than *difficult* and *complicated*.

In which particulars a melody may be *easy* I have shewn at § 2, all of which must be attended to in an Air; but as there are different Sorts of Airs, some of which ought to be more grand and elaborate, or consist of more figurative passages than others, it follows, that some may also be much more difficult than others, and yet sufficiently easy and simple in their kind, or for their purpose. And that a noble *simplicity* is one of the greatest beauties even in the grandest bravura Song, will require no demonstration, as it appears from a number of the best airs of *Handel, Graun, Hasse*, and other great Composers.

Y   *Rule*

Rule III. A melody muſt be *ſatisfactory* and *intereſting*, even without its accompaniments.

The neceſſity of attending to this rule appears, when we conſider, that the principal melody or vocal part of an Air is not only much more attended to, than to the other parts, but alſo that it is always felt and remembered like ſomething by itſelf. But the accompaniment of a melody ſhould alſo be of ſuch a nature, as to make an intereſting addition to it, without overpowering or obſcuring it.

N. B. Beſides the above, all the general Rules given in § 2. *& ſeq.* muſt be attended to in the conſtruction of a melody, which will require no demonſtration.

b. THE SUPPORTING OF A MELODY, BY A PROPER HARMONY AND ACCOMPANIMENT.

§ 17. In my Eſſay on Harmony, Chap. XVI, § 7, *& ſeq.* I have ſhewn how one and the ſame melody may be accompanied with different *Harmonies*; and from the number and variety of Inſtruments which may be uſed in its accompaniment, it follows, that alſo a great variety of effects may be produced with every Harmony, by the ſaid *Accompaniment*. It is therefore of the higheſt importance in compoſing an Air, to know how to ſupport its melody with ſuch Harmonies, and ſuch accompaniments, as are moſt adapted to its Character, and moſt calculated to produce a good effect of the Air.

As a proper Movement, Meaſure, and Rhythmical Order of the Air, muſt have been fixed upon, before its Melody and Harmony is begun, I need not ſay any thing reſpecting theſe particulars here, but that they ought in every reſpect to correſpond with the general character, as well as with every particular characteriſtic of the Harmony and Melody.

§ 18. Reſpecting the *Harmony* of an Air, there ought to be conſidered, *firſt*, whether the character of the words requires the piece to be in major or minor, and in which major or minor key it will be beſt; and *ſecondly*, whether it ought to proceed in one uniform manner, or through a variety of paſſions, and what ſorts of chords and modulations will be beſt in every caſe. According to theſe conſiderations the whole, as well as every period and chord of the piece muſt be regulated. But the diſcerning Reader will ſee, that the obſervation of this Rule requires an intimate acquaintance with almoſt every thing I have ſaid in my Eſſay on Harmony, and a fluency in the practical application of it to every particular caſe.

N. B. Reſpecting the *Accompaniment* of an Air, ſee § 26.

c. THE DIFFERENT FORMS, IN WHICH AIRS MAY BE COMPOSED.

§ 19. An air may be compoſed, either ſo, as *ſimply to expreſs the Text*, without particular regard to figurative paſſages; or, with particular regard to *grandeur* and *brilliant paſſages*, calculated to ſhew the abilities of a Singer. In the former quality it may be compared to an inſtrumental Sonatina or Sonata, and in the latter to an inſtrumental Concerto. And in both qualities it may be ſet as a Solo, Duo, Trio, &c. without or with Accompaniments, as I ſhall endeavour to ſhew now.

§ 20. Under the *firſt* denomination of Airs mentioned in the preceding ſection, I comprehend, the *Plain Song*, as uſed for Hymns and Pſalm Tunes; and all thoſe various ſorts of
Songs.

Songs, which may be brought under the denomination of the word *Air* itself, such as Ariofos, Ariettas, fimple Arias, Romances, Ballads, Canzonetts, and fimilar forts of vocal pieces.

The firft, or *Plain Song*, is the moft fimple, and yet the moft noble fort of Airs hitherto known. Its principal melody may be fung only, either by a fingle perfon, or by a whole Congregation ; or it may be calculated for two, three, four, or more vocal parts, without or with accompaniments. And in all its forms it has the fineft effect, if properly compofed and performed. Some Examples of this fort, fee in my Effay on Harmony, from Plate XX. to XXV, and at Plate XXXVIII. & *feq.*

The fecond fort, or the *Air* itfelf, differs from the Plain Song in admitting and requiring lighter forts of Movement and Meafure, and more melodious graces or figurative paffages, than what would be proper for Plain Songs. It may be compofed for one or more vocal parts, as I fhall fhew in § 25.

§ 21. Both the Plain Song and all forts of Airs, may be compofed, either fo, that but one Text belongs to every piece of the Compofition ; or fo, that different words fhall be fung to one repeated piece of Compofition. In the former cafe there is nothing to be obferved, but what I have faid in the general Rules at § 2, 3, 4, 5, and at § 15, & *feq.*; but in the latter cafe it is required, either that the Text be calculated for the purpofe in queftion, or if not, that the compofer know, and endeavour to make the beft of the text as it is. This I have already mentioned in § 4, and fhall now endeavour to explain it.

For an example I take the words of *Pope*'s Hymn, " Father of all, in every age," &c. It confifts of two fyllables to a metrical foot, viz : firft a fhort, and then a long one. But its Author has not ftrictly attended to thefe accents in every verfe, for the very firft verfe begins with an accented fyllable before the unaccented, in the word Father ; and the fame accent is found in the verfes, " Save me alike from foolifh pride," and " Teach me to feel another's woe," though other verfes begin as they ought, with the unaccented Syllable, viz : " This day be bread and peace my lot," &c. If now every verfe of this fine Text fhall be fung without alteration, to one and the fame melody, it is required to invent a melody which begins fo, that both the right and wrong accented words may have a good effect with it, which may be done according to the Examples I give at Plate LVI, being beginnings of a German Hymn, compofed by different authors.

At No. 1, fee its beginning as compofed by *Emanuel Bach*, which is good for the laft Verfe, " Is God for me," but not for the firft, " God is my fong."

At No. 2, fee the fame period by an author not mentioned in the Collection from which I have taken it. This already is very good for both the above verfes.

At No. 3, fee the fame period by *Kirnberger*, which is undoubtedly the beft of the three, as in the firft verfe the word God has a higher note, and in the laft verfe the accent, fo that both verfes have a very good effect with this melody.

With the above examples the beginning of the faid hymn, " Father of all," may alfo be compared, and it will appear that the laft one is the beft beginning for it.

§ 22. An Air may be compofed either as a *fingle* piece by itfelf, or in *connection* with other vocal or inftrumental pieces ; and in both cafes it may be either a *Solo* or for *more vocal parts*; without or with accompaniments.

§ 23. An Air by itfelf, or a *fingle* Air, may, like a Sonatina, confift of one Section only, or of two or more fections ; it may be fet in the form of a Rondo, or any other piece ; and

3   without

without or with mere inftrumental fymphonies or Ritornells, at the beginning and the end, and between fome periods or Sentences of the Text.

An Example of an Air of *one* fection is the well known fong, " Rule Britannia;" one of *two* fections, each of which may be repeated or not, is " God fave the King;" one in the form of a Rondo is " Cupid, God of foft perfuafion," in Love in a Village ; and Examples of airs with inftrumental Symphonies or Ritornells are *Haydn*'s Canzonetts, the inftru-mental reliefs of which ferve for an agreeable variety, as well as to give a little reft to the voice of the finger.

§ 24. An Air in *connection* with other vocal or inftrumental pieces, may be compofed in all the above forms of a fingle air ; but as it is not fo independant as the faid Airs, a proper attention muft be paid to the connection in which it ftands with the preceding and the fucceeding piece, as well as to the general character of the whole work of which it is a piece, according to what has been faid in Chap. I.

If a fhort melodious ftrain like an air, is introduced in the courfe of a *Recitative*, it is called an *Ariofo*. It muft be fet to fuch words of the Recitative, which, as they are too pathetic, or too important for the mere melodious declamation of the Recitative, require a diftinct movement and meafure. But as an Ariofo is but a part of the Recitative itfelf, it ought to be fet in the moft fimple ftyle of an Air; that is to fay, with only few or no repe-titions of words, and without paffage work, as it appears in various Recitatives of great Compofers.

But when whole Airs, which are independant in themfelves, like the different move-ments of a Sonata, are fet in connection with Recitatives, Choruffes, or other Airs, as it is done in Operas, Oratorios, and fimilar pieces, the general character of the whole, as well as the proper relation with the preceding and fucceeding piece muft be attended to, accord-ing to what has been faid in the courfe of Chapter I.

§ 25. According to the number of vocal parts for which an Air may be compofed, it is either a *Solo*, or a *Duett, Tercett, Quartett*, &c.

A *Solo* is an Air fet for *one* voice, though that denomination is in general ufed for folo paffages in a piece, more than for whole vocal pieces. The rules which muft be attended to in writing a Solo air, are the fame as thofe given in § 2, and § 16, *& feq.* But as a fingle melody can and will be clofer attended to, than two or more together, it follows: that a Solo fhould in every refpect be as ftrict as poffible. Examples of this fort will not be re-quired.

An air for *two* voices is a *Duet*. It may be fet either fo as to make but a harmony of two regular parts, confequently without all accompaniments, or only with accompaniments that go in the unifon or octave with the vocal parts; or with a feparate Bafs, or other parts, which make it to confift of a harmony of *three* or *four* regular parts. Of the former fort are Canon IV, VIII, and XII, in Dr. *Burney*'s " XII Canzonetti a due voci in Canone;" with a mere bafs accompaniment, are all the other Canons of the fame work; and with more accompaniments is *Handel*'s duet in Meffiah, " O death where is thy fting." A whole collection of the moft valuable duets of the latter fort is the firft volume of the works of *Graun*, mentioned at Chap. IX, § 27, under *Canon by Graun*. The particular Rule for both the above forts of Duets is : that, though the two parts may fing different words, yet they muft reciprocally imitate each other's paffages, and confequently be equally obligato.

An air for *three* voices is a *Tercett*. It may be fet in both manners mentioned juft now

under

under Duetts.　Of the firſt fort are all Catches or Glees for three equal or different voices without accompaniments; and of the latter fort *Handel's* celebrated trio in Acis and Galatea, and *Graun's* equally admirable ones, in Vol. II. of the Collection quoted above under Duetts.

An air for *four* voices is a *Quartett*. It may be fet for four equal, or four different voices; or alfo, for two voices of one, and two of another fort; but thofe for three voices of one fort, and only one of another fort are not fo good as the above. It may alfo be fet without or with inftrumental parts, in both the fame manners as Duetts. See above in this fection.

The Quartett differs from the Chorus in two particulars, viz. *Firſt*, that its melodies are chiefly calculated but for one performer to each vocal part, and confequently may confiſt of more delicate paffages than what would be proper for more than one performer; *fecondly*, that its parts may contain different words, when thofe of a Chorus are generally on one and the fame text, though introduced in one part different from the other. The particular Rule which fhould be obferved in all regular Quartetts is: that the four parts ought to be concerting, and equally obligato. A very fine example of a Quartett with accompaniments is that in *Handel's* Jephtha: " O, fpare your daughter," where the accompaniments are four parts different from the vocal, and the whole eight real parts. More fine examples fee in the collection of *Graun's* works, quoted above in this fection.

According to the above principles, *Quintetts*, *Sextetts*, *Septetts*, and *Octetts*, may alfo be compofed, without as well as with accompaniments. But as it is almoft the fame with them as with quintuple and fextuple fugues, which are difficult to compofe, if they fhall be ftrictly regular, and difficult to attend to, if their greateft beauties fhall not be loft, they are not fo frequently compofed as Duetts, Tercetts, and Quartetts.

§ 26. With particular regard to the *Inftrumental* parts, or *Accompaniments*, which may be fet to an Air, it follows from what I have faid in § 25, that they may either be parts *different* from the vocal parts, or mere duplicates of the fame. In both cafes they may be either for one or only a few Inftruments, or alfo for a whole orcheftra, in the fame manner as the principal part or parts of a Sonata may be accompanied, according to what I have faid in Chap. II, § 11, *& feq.*; or according to what I have faid in Chap. III, § 11, *& feq.* when the vocal parts are confidered as the principal parts of a Symphony. And with all the faid varieties, the inftrumental parts may precede, occafionally relieve, and at laft fucceed the vocal parts, as Ritornells, or like Tuttis in a Concerto, as the vaft number of greater or leffer Airs hitherto publifhed fhew, and as therefore will require no example.

§ 27. The fecond fort of Airs mentioned in § 19, comprehends thofe commonly called *bravura Songs*, or which are written with particular regard to *grandeur* and *brilliant paffages*, and calculated to fhew the abilities of a Singer. They may be pieces of one or more Movements, and contain a Recitative or not. They may be compared in vocal mufic to what a Concerto is in inftrumental mufic; for they confiſt throughout of grand Solos relieved by Tuttis. Thefe pieces therefore are more properly fet with an accompaniment of divers inftruments, or of a whole Orcheftra, than with the mere accompaniment of a Harpfichord. But as Concertos may be fet in the latter form, the fongs in queſtion are alfo ufeful in the fame form. As their length and whole difpofition may be laid out according to any reafonable plan, and fhould not be confined to one general plan, I need not enlarge upon it; and therefore refer the diligent Reader to the examination of thofe bravura fongs of *Handel, Graun, Haſſe* and other great compofers, he can meet with, to fee the different

z

forms

forms in which they have been written, and thereby to conclude upon the varieties to which each form shews the way.

One particular thing in them is the *fancy* cadence, which is generally introduced in the principal movement, and which should be extemporized or previously studied according to the rules given in Chap. IV, § 10, though with regard to what the voice can execute.

If the songs in question are set for *two*, *three*, or *four* vocal performers, these parts should be concerting throughout, like the principal parts of a double, triple, or quadruple concerto, or as I have shewn under Duetts, Tercetts, and Quartetts, in § 25; to which I need only add: that if a double, triple, or quadruple *Cadence* shall be introduced in them, it must be previously written down according to the rules mentioned above, and studied by the Singers, so as to have the effect of an extempore fancy.

C. OF CHORUSSES.

§ 28. In § 6, I have said, that a Chorus is *finging in parts*, calculated for a number of performers to each part; and in § 25, I have shewn the two particulars in which a Chorus is different from a Quartett, or other air of a number of vocal parts equal to those of the Chorus, viz: first, that each part of a Chorus may be performed by more than one Person, as the above general definition also shews; and secondly, that the parts of a Quartett may contain different words, when those of a Chorus are generally on one and the same Text, though introduced in one part different from the other.

According to the said first particular therefore, the melodies of each part of a Chorus should be *more simple*, and *less figurative*, than those of an Air for four or more single Performers. And the same qualities are required on account of the general character of a Chorus, which should be *noble grandeur*, free from all those harmonious and melodious sublimities, which can only be well expressed by great and single performers to each part.

§ 29. There are two sorts of Chorusses to be distinguished, viz: the *plain* and the *imitative*.

The *first* sort comprehends those chorusses, in which all the parts sing the same words at the *same time*. An example see in *Handel*'s Messiah, " Since by Man came Death," which is of the plainest sort, and with a mere Thorough Bass accompaniment for the Organ. The words, " By Man came also the resurrection of the dead," are then set in a similar manner, but in a quicker movement, and with more accompaniments. A similar Chorus is that in the same work, to the words, " Worthy is the Lamb," as far as the Larghetto, " Blessing and Honor," where it begins to become imitative. And another one of a similar nature, that to the words " Surely he has borne our Griefs," which has only a little imitative part towards the end. An example which makes a sort of medium between plain and imitative Chorusses is, that to the words, " The Lord gave the word, great was the company of the Preachers," and also that, " Unto us a Child is born," which contains plain and imitative passages intermixed.

The *second* sort, or *imitative* Chorusses, are those, in which detached parts of the Text are imitated so as *not* to appear in all parts *at the same time*. They may be written either as mere *imitative pieces*, without particular regard to the rules of Fugues or Canon; or as proper or improper, strict or free, simple or double *Fugues* or *Canons*, in all the various manners I have mentioned in Chap. V, *& seq*. And in all the said, and many more ingenious forms, they

they are found written by *Handel*, who has been particularly great in Choruſſes, as every one knows who is acquainted with his maſterly Oratorios, particularly his Meſſiah, and Iſrael in Egypt. The ſtudy of theſe works therefore I beg leave to recommend to the diligent Reader.

§ 30. Both the above ſorts of Choruſſes may be ſet either *ſimple* or *double*.

A *ſimple* chorus is that, ſet but for *one choir of ſingers*. It may be ſet either for the four principal parts of harmony only, viz: for one Treble, one Alto, one Tenor, and one Baſs; or for five or more parts, ſo that it conſiſts of two Trebles, or two Altos, &c.; and as long as the ſaid two parts of one ſort ſerve but to ſecond each other it remains a ſimple chorus, though it conſiſt of eight real parts. The fineſt ſimple Choruſſes are thoſe mentioned above in *Handel*'s Meſſiah.

A *double* Chorus is that, ſet for *two* choirs of Singers. If it ſhall anſwer the purpoſe of a double chorus, the two choirs muſt occaſionally relieve each other; but they muſt alſo join in thoſe parts of the text which are calculated for particular grandeur. The moſt maſterly examples of double Choruſſes are found in *Handel*'s Iſrael in Egypt, the ſtudy of which I cannot too much recommend to the diligent Reader.

§ 31. When but *two parts* of the harmony are introduced according to the general definition, given of Choruſſes in § 28, it is called a *Semi Chorus*. The ſaid two parts may be either the neareſt related, ſuch as a Treble and Alto, Alto and Tenor, Tenor and Baſs; or alſo a Treble and Tenor, or an Alto and Baſs. But a Treble and Baſs cannot be properly introduced alone, becauſe the diſtance between them is too great. An example of the firſt ſort is the ſemi Chorus of Virgins in *Handel*'s Jephtha, "Welcome thou, whoſe Deeds inſpire." And more Examples will not be required.

§ 32. Though a Chorus may for certain purpoſes be ſet *without any Accompaniments*, like that "Since by Man came Death," in *Handel*'s Meſſiah, when the Organ part is omitted; yet *ſome* accompaniment is neceſſary when the Chorus is of any length, to prevent the parts getting too flat, and conſequently out of tune with the ſucceeding piece. And in general it is beſt to ſet them with the accompaniment of an *Orcheſtra*, proportional to the number of Singers employed in it.

In the latter caſe the Accompaniments may be ſet to the vocal parts in the following manners, viz: *Firſt*, as parts drawn from the vocal ones by doubling them in the Uniſon or Octave, or by ſelecting only their harmonies, like as in Chords of thorough Baſs; which latter may be done with holding notes, or with varied notes: *ſecondly*, as real obligato parts. Examples of all the ſaid ſorts will appear in the above mentioned works by *Handel*; and ſome of them in *Graun*'s Te Deum Laudamus, the beautiful firſt Chorus of which deſerves particular notice.

CHAPTER XI.   OF INSTRUMENTAL MUSIC.

§ 1. Under the denomination in queſtion I comprehend that muſic, which is compoſed either for any *ſingle* inſtrument, or for any *number* and *variety* of inſtruments; without, or with the addition of vocal parts.

I. *Of*

I. *Of Inftrumental Mufic in general.*

A. IN REGARD TO EVERY PARTICULAR INSTRUMENT.

§ 2. **To compofe** for any Inftrumeut, fo that the Compofition be not improper, or infignificant, requires a perfect knowledge of the three following particulars, viz : *firft*, its Compafs and Scale ; fecondly, the Nature of its Sounds ; and *thirdly*, the harmonious and melodious paffages for which it is calculated, according to its peculiar nature.

§ 3. Refpecting the faid *firft* particular, I will endeavour to give a fhort defcription of the Compafs and Scale of thofe inftruments which are moft in ufe, viz.

a. STRINGED BOW INSTRUMENTS.

The *Violin* begins from **G,** an octave below that line on which the **G** clef ftands, and goes three octaves and more, upwards : but in ripieno parts it is feldom ufed higher than **D,** a 19th above its graveft note.   Its fcale is the moft complete imaginable.   For a great player can execute on it not only every femitone, according to any Temperament, but alfo modify the enharmonic change fo, as to produce the effect of a progreffion by a real quarter tone.   Its paffages therefore need not be limited on account of an imperfect or incomplete fcale, like thofe for fome Wind Inftruments.

The *Viola* begins from **C,** a fifth lower than the Violin, and has about the fame Compafs as the faid Inftrument.   Its Scale alfo is equally perfect, and it admits of the fame fort of paffages, with the only confideration : that, as it is played with a heavier bow than the Violin, and its larger ftrings cannot vibrate as quick as thofe of the violin, there fhould in general be given no fuch quick paffages to it than to the faid former Inftrument.

The *Violancello* begins from **C,** an eleventh below the **F** clef, and its Compafs is four octaves and a half.   Its fcale is equally perfect than that of the two former Inftruments, and confequently is equally unlimited in regard to paffages.   But as this Inftrument is ftill larger than the Viola, no very quick paffages, or very fmall intervals, fhould in general be given to it in the loweft Octave.   See my Effay on Harmony, Chap. III, § 5.

The *Violono* commonly begins from **A,** a fixth below the **F** clef, and its notes are an octave lower (or more grave) than they are written ; but in Ripieno parts its Compafs is feldom extended above a twelfth upwards.   Its fcale has the fame perfection as that of the preceding inftruments, though the wide ftretches or fkippings of the fingers which it requires, render its temperament lefs certain, than that of the above fmaller inftruments. In general no very quick paffages, or quick progreffions by very fmall intervals, fhould be given to this inftrument, on account of what I have faid juft now under *Violoncello.* Though fome Violonos begin from **E,** a fourth lower than what I have faid, yet I believe that in general they begin from **A,** as above.

b. WIND INSTRUMENTS.

The *Hautboy* begins from **C,** on the **C** clef line, and goes to **D,** a fixteenth above ; or for Solo Players a couple of notes higher ; according to the nature of the paffage.   Its fcale contains every Semitone of the faid compafs, except **C** fharp in the loweft Octave, which

is difficult on the common Hautboy. It is one of the moſt uſeful wind inſtruments for Concerts, becauſe it can be uſed with a good effeɛt in more Keys than the Clarinett.

The *Clarinett* begins from E a ſecond below the F clef, and its Compaſs is about three
oɛtaves, or for Solo Players ſome notes more. Its ſcale contains every Semitone in the
ſaid Compaſs. But to produce its beſt effeɛt, it is in general uſed in no other Key but
C and F. If therefore it ſhall be uſed in any other Key, a Clarinett is uſed which ſtands
a note or more higher or lower than Concert Pitch. In C or F therefore, a C Clarinett is
uſed; in B flat and E flat, a B flat Clarinett; in A and D, an A Clarinett. D Clarinetts,
B Clarinetts, and G Clarinetts I have alſo heard of, but I believe they are ſeldom uſed.

N. B. a C Clarinett is: when its C is equal in pitch to C of other inſtruments; a B flat
Clarinett, when its C is equal to B flat of other inſtruments, &c. If therefore a piece is
ſet in F, it is calculated for the C Clarinett, and written in F as uſual. But in E flat, it is
calculated for the B flat Clarinett; and as that ſtands a whole tone *lower* than C, the piece
muſt be written a whole tone *higher* than E flat, or in F. A piece in D conſequently is
calculated for the A Clarinet, and as that ſtands a third lower than C, it is written a third
higher than A, or alſo in F. Exceptions from the above can only be made by thoſe who
are perfeɛtly acquainted with the Clarinett.

The *German Flute* begins from D, a ſecond above the C clef, and its compaſs is two
oɛtaves, or for Solo Players, a few notes more, according to the paſſages in which they
occur. It contains every ſemitone in the ſaid compaſs, and is of the ſame general uſe
as the Hautboy, though not without regard to the particular qualities of both theſe inſtruments.

The *Baſſoon* begins from B flat, a twelfth below the F clef, and goes as far as F an
oɛtave above the ſaid clef, or for Solo Players a third or fourth higher. Its ſcale contains
every Semitone in the ſaid compaſs; and this inſtrument is of the ſame utility for Baſs paſſages, as the Hautboy is for treble paſſages.

The *Serpent* begins from C, two oɛtaves below the C clef, and is ſet in general no higher
than G, a twelfth above. But a perſon who knows how to manage it may produce B flat,
a ſecond below the ſaid C; and Solo Players may go a good deal higher than the above
compaſs. Its ſcale alſo contains every ſemitone of the ſaid compaſs.

N. B. Its ſounds are equal in pitch to thoſe of the *Violono*, or an oɛtave lower than
what they are written.

The *Trumpet* produces as natural or eaſy ſounds, thoſe I have ſhewn in my Eſſay on
Harmony, at Chap. I, § 2, under the ratios $1, \frac{1}{2}, \frac{1}{3}, \frac{1}{4}$, &c. to $\frac{1}{16}$; but according to our
modern diatonic chromatic Scale, its ſcale muſt be conſidered as thus: G, (an oɛtave
below the G clef,) C, E, G, C, D, E, F, G, A, B, C. In *Solos* for the Trumpet, B flat, (a
third above the G clef,) and F ſharp, (a ſeventh above that Clef,) may alſo be uſed; and
what other intervals are praɛticable, requires a particular knowledge of that Inſtrument.

The *French Horn*, has exaɛtly the ſame natural Scale as the Trumpet; but as it gives
every note an oɛtave lower ⁊. more grave than the Trumpet, it is alſo more manageable
than that inſtrument, and therefore *Albrechtſberger* gives the following Scale for the French
Horn: viz.

The *firſt* Horn: C, (a fifth below the G clef,) E, F. F ſharp, G, and then every ſemitone upwards.

The *ſecond* Horn: C, (a fourth below the F clef,) E, F, F ſharp, G, A flat, B, C, D, E flat,
E, F, F ſharp, G, (on the G clef line,) and then every ſemitone up to the Oɛtave or Ninth
of this G.

But

But though all the above intervals may be practicable for Solo Players, yet it requires a particular knowledge of the Horn, to difcern in what paffages each of them is good, and which are calculated to be held on with certainty or not.

The *Trombono* muft be confidered as that for the *Bafs*, for the *Tenor*, and for the *Alto*. The Bafs Trombono begins from **G**, a feventh below the F clef, and produces every Semi-tone up to **C**, the eleventh of the faid G. The Tenor Trombono begins from **A**, a tenth below the C clef, and produces every femitone up to the fifteenth above. And the Alto Trombono begins a third higher than the Tenor one, producing alfo every femitone up to the fifteenth above. From thefe fcales it follows, that Trombonos are particularly ufeful in thofe full harmonies by plain notes, where the Trumpets and Horns are not fufficiently calculated to produce the chromatic intervals.

§ 4. The above inftruments are in general written in the following Clefs, viz :

The Violins, German Flutes, Hautboys, Clarinetts, Trumpets, and French Horns, are written in the *G clef*, placed on the fecond line from below. But where the Clarinetts go too low for that Clef the paffage is fet an octave higher, with the word *chalumeaux* over or under it, which denotes that it fhall be played an octave lower than what it ftands. And if the fecond Horn goes too low, the Bafs clef may be introduced in its line, or the notes may be written an octave higher, and the words *in the lower octave* be fet to them, in the fame manner as chalumeaux to the Clarinett notes.

The Viola and Alto Trombono are written in the *C clef*, placed on the third line from below ; and the Tenor Trombono in the fame Clef, placed on the fourth line from below.

The Violoncello and Violono, and the Baffoon, Serpent, and Bafs Trombono, are written in the *F clef*, placed on the fourth line from below. But where the Violoncello goes too high for that Clef, the Tenor clef, or even the Violin clef is fubftituted in its line as long as required.

§ 5. The *fecond* particular pointed out in § 2, is : the *nature of the Sounds* of every particular Inftrument. In regard to which there muft be confidered, whether they are *continuing* or *ceafing* ; *loud* or *foft* ; *harfh* or *mild* ; *grave* or *acute*.

1. *Continuing* founds are thofe which do not diminifh in ftrength, as long as they are held : fuch as thofe of the Organ, the other Wind Inftruments, and the Bow Inftruments. *Ceafing* founds therefore are, thofe of the Harpfichord or Piano Forte, the Harp, the Guittar, and the Bells.

2. The *Loudnefs* or *Softnefs* of founds, may in fome Inftruments be varied by the fort of performance, like as on the Violin or Violoncello, the Piano Forte, the Harp, and other Inftruments ; yet the natural found of the Trumpet, Trombono, or Bugle Horn, is louder than that of the French Horn ; that of a Serpent, louder than that of a Baffoon ; and that of moft wind or bow inftruments, louder than that of a moderate Piano Forte.

3. *Harfh* in found, are the Serpent and the Trombono ; *milder*, the Trumpet, Hautboy, and Baffoon ; and *mildeft*, the Clarinett, French Horn, and German Flute. And the inftru-ments which can be humoured more than the above, into all forts of effects, are : the Vio-loncello, Violin, Piano Forte, and Harp ; but above all, a fine large Organ with a good Swell may be ufed fo as to produce many different effects.

4. *Grave* in found are : the Violono, the Serpent, the double Baffoon, and the French Horn, all of which give their notes an octave lower than what they are written ; and acute in comparifon to the faid inftruments, are thofe which give their notes in that octave in which they are written, fuch as the Trumpet, the Violoncello, and the Baffoon.

2

§ 6. The

§ 6. The *third* particular mentioned in § 2, is: the harmonious and melodious *paſſages,* for which every particular Inſtrument is calculated. In regard to this, the Organ is beſt calculated for full harmonies, and ſuch ſinging paſſages which require continuing ſounds ; the Piano Forte alſo for fullneſs, but for ſuch paſſages which are enlivened by the ſort of touch, and the encreaſing or decreaſing ſtrength that is produced by it ; the Violin, Viola, and Violoncello, are calculated for leſs fullneſs of harmony than Keyed Inſtruments, but for more ſinging paſſages than the Piano Forte, and for the higheſt degree of taſteful and delicate expreſſion. The Trumpet is calculated more for ſhort and pointed notes than the French Horn, and this latter inſtrument more for holding notes than the former. The Flute, Hautboy, and Clarinett, are moſt calculated to imitate human treble or alto Voices, though with thoſe liberties their Compaſs and Execution allow ; and the Baſſoon, human baſs voices, with the ſame liberties.

But all theſe conſiderations, added to the greateſt knowledge of Harmony as well as the nature and qualities of the Pieces to be compoſed, cannot enable a Compoſer to write for every inſtrument paſſages that are particularly adapted to it, (that is to ſay, paſſages which ſhew the powers and qualities of an inſtrument to advantage, and yet are not awk-- ward to perform on it:) if he is not himſelf a tolerable player on that inſtrument. This every compoſer knows from experience ; and it is confirmed by the inſtrumental compo- ſitions of thoſe Authors, who were great on one Inſtrument, but wrote obligato for others which they did not ſufficiently know. If therefore a compoſer will write for Inſtruments he is not intimately acquainted with, he muſt aim more at the *effect* of the *whole,* than *paſſage work* for ſuch inſtruments ; but if he cannot well avoid attempting the latter, to conſult a judicious player on ſuch inſtruments, reſpecting the paſſages he intends to in- troduce.

B. OF THE COMBINATION OF DIFFERENT INSTRUMENTS.

§ 7. If two or more Inſtruments ſhall be introduced together in a piece or movement, there muſt be conſidered ; firſt, which inſtruments *agree* together ; and ſecondly, which produce the beſt *variety* in their combination.

§ 8. In regard to the ſaid *firſt* particular, it is natural, that inſtruments of the *ſame* or a *ſimilar* nature agree moſt ; and that thoſe of a *different* nature agree only in proportion to the greater or leſſer *relation* between them. According to this obſervation therefore, Violins agree beſt with Violins, and Bow Inſtruments with Bow Inſtruments ; or Flutes with Flutes, and Wind Inſtruments with Wind Inſtruments, &c.

But thoſe Inſtruments which *agree moſt* will often agree *too much,* or ſo much that the paſſages of the one cannot be diſtinguiſhed from thoſe of the other, by which the beſt of their effect is loſt ; it is therefore neceſſary to aim at a judicious *variety,* between thoſe in- ſtruments which ſhall be introduced together, being the ſecond particular pointed out in § 7.

§ 9. The beſt *variety* is produced by a *regular intermixture* of a well agreeing and well connected inſtruments ; and this requires either an *equal number* of the different inſtru- ments which ſhall play together, or a good *proportion* between their *unequal* numbers.

By an *equal* number of combined inſtruments, I underſtand : when the piece is written for no more inſtruments of one ſort than of another, e. g. for one Violin, one Tenor, and one Baſs ; or for two Violins and two Baſſes. And by an *unequal* number : when it

is

is fet for more inftruments of one fort, than of another, e. g. for two Violins, one Tenor, and one Bafs.

But as I have faid in this §, that a regular combination of inftruments requires alfo a proper *connection* between them, it follows: that the above combination of two Violins, (being Treble inftruments,) and two Baffes, is not fo good as if a Tenor had been introduced between them; becaufe Trebles and Baffes are not fo well connected, as Trebles, Tenor, and Baffes.

And refpecting the faid good *proportion* between the unequal number of different inftruments, it is neceffary: that if there are more of one fort than of another, the greater number fhould be of fuch a nature as not to overpower or obfcure the leffer number. One of the beft combinations of inftruments therefore, according to this obfervation, is: two Violins, a Tenor or Viola, and a Bafs or Violoncello. And more ufeful varieties for Trios, Quatuors, or any other fort of mufical pieces, will follow from what I have faid, fo that I need not farther enlarge upon this fubject.

II. *Of certain Sorts of Inftrumental Mufic in particular.*

A. OF THAT FOR AN ORCHESTRA.

§ 10. Mufic for an Orcheftra is that, which is fet for *moft* or *all inftruments* required for a Concert, and calculated for more than one performer to every part, in thofe paffages called Tuttis.

It may be fet without formal Solos, as in Symphonies; or with intermixed Solos, as in Concertos; or with added or intermixed Vocal Parts, as in Operas, Oratorios, fingle Songs, or other vocal pieces. As I have treated of all thefe pieces before, and have alfo fhewn the diftribution of the harmony between the feveral parts, (fee Chap. III, § 13,) and what is to be confidered in regard to the Nature, Relation, and Variety, of the Inftruments which may be ufed in an Orcheftra, (fee from § 2 to § 9 of this chapter,) I need only add here fome Remarks refpecting the following two particulars which I have not yet fufficiently touched, viz: *firft*, what Harmonies, Melodies, and Paffages, are proper for an Orcheftra; and *fecondly*, what combinations of Inftruments are good in the whole, as well as in particular Paffages.

§ 11. Refpecting the *Harmony* which is proper for an Orcheftra, that is to fay for Tuttis in which all or moft Inftruments and Performers are employed, it is natural: that the more it is plain, and the lefs complicated or divided into quick and delicate harmonious progreffions, the better it is. For, the mufic of an Orcheftra has upon our ears an effect, fimilar to that which a grand Picture has upon our Eyes: and both require to be heard or viewed at fome *Diftance*, if the effect of the whole fhall not be loft. A snow that diftance requires more *grand* varieties of Shades, Lights, Colours, and Figures, in the faid fort of paintings, than what would be proper in a fmall picture, calculated to be looked at clofe by; fo it requires alfo grander and more diftinct harmonies and modulations, in the mufical pieces in queftion, than what would be proper for thofe coming under the denomination of Sonatas, (See Chap. II.) But as a grand Picture is alfo executed with larger brufhes, than a delicate one or a miniature, and confequently is compofed of larger and more bold *Strokes* than the lattter; fo a piece for an Orcheftra even refembles it in that refpect, for it is performed by at leaft feveral players to each part, and confequently

with

with heavier founds than thofe of a high finifhed Sonata or Quartett, and its harmonies muft be calculated accordingly.

But in thofe paffages where only a few fingle Inftruments relieve the Tuttis of the whole Orcheftra, the harmonies and harmonious progreffions may be more delicate, and fimilar to thofe of pieces comprehended under the denomination of Sonatas; in the fame manner as fome of the moft diftinguifhed parts of a picture are alfo finifhed with more nicety than other parts.

That a harmony can be very plain, and proceed as it were by manly ftrides, and yet be exceeding *rich in modulation*, and productive of the fineft effects, appears from almoft all the Overtures, and particularly from the Choruffes of *Handel*, and will require no demonftration.

From the above obfervations refpecting Harmony, the qualities of *Melodies*, and melodious *Paffages*, proper for Orcheftra Pieces, will alfo follow. For, in both it muft be confidered that every part is to be performed by more than one Player, and that confequently all thofe melodious niceties, and all thofe quick figurative paffages, which cannot be executed in the greateft perfection by perfons playing together, are loft, or even produce a confufed effect. This might be eafily proved, by having fome of *Haydn*'s grand Symphonies, written for fuch able Performers to every inftrument, and for fuch great Leaders, as there are found in the principal concerts of this Metropolis, performed in an indifferent manner. For as they are in many Harmonies, Melodies, and Paffages, fublime and finifhed to a high degree of nicety, they cannot but loofe more in effect, by a deficient performance, than lefs intricate and yet good pieces.

§ 12. The *fecond* particular mentioned in § 10, is: what *Combinations of Inftruments* are good, in the *whole*, as well as in *particular Paffages*, of a Piece for an Orcheftra. Of this I fhall endeavour to fpeak here.

1. In the *whole*, the four *Principal Parts* of modern pieces for an Orcheftra are: The firft Violin; the fecond Violin; the Tenor, or Viola; and the Bafs, or Violoncello and Violono. Of thefe the Viola is generally written as Primo and Secondo, but both in the Unifon, in all places, where not a fort of Solo paffage renders the diftinction of a firft and fecond Tenor neceffary. The faid principal parts are expected to be doubled, in proportion to the number of other parts which fhall be introduced with them.

The *Wind Inftruments* which may be ufed in an Orcheftra encreafe from the fofter or milder, to the louder and harfher ones, till they are all united in the grandeft Orcheftra; but in general they are introduced by *two* and *two*, fuch as two Trebles and two Baffes.

The firft clafs of wind inftruments therefore, which may be introduced in a fmall Orcheftra, are: two German Flutes, and two French Horns; and inftead of the Flutes, Hautboys may alfo be taken.

To the above may be added as a fecond clafs, two Hautboys, and two Baffoons; or the firft clafs may alfo be omitted, and this fecond only be introduced.—N. B. Inftead of the Hautboys or German Flutes, Clarinetts may alfo be ufed, according to circumftances, or alfo with them, if the Baffes are fufficiently doubled. A third clafs comprehends two or three trumpets, and two or three Kettle Drums.—N. B. Though the latter are no Wind Inftruments, I mention them here as the ufual fupport of the Trumpets.

As a fourth Clafs, one, two, or three Trombonos, may be ufed, fo as to take the principal notes of the harmony in Tuttis; and a Double Baffoon, and Serpent, may be added to the Bafs, to give the whole a fufficient fupport.

　　　　　　　　　　　　　　　　　　　　　　　　　　　　　　How

How the Harmony may be diftributed among all the faid inftruments, I have fhewn in Chap. III, § 13.

2. In *particular paffages*, any *two* equal inftruments, or any of the faid claffes of *four* inftruments, or alfo any *fingle* one of the above Wind Inftruments, may be introduced as Solo, or in a predominant paffage, in the following manner, viz:

Two Flutes, or two Hautboys, or two Clarinetts, or two Horns, or two Trumpets, or two Baffoons, alone; or any two of them, with thofe two placed above in the fame clafs with them; or alfo, any two of one clafs, with two of fuch another clafs, which are neither too much like them, nor too different from them. According to this laft remark, two Flutes and two Clarinetts would be too much alike ; and two Trumpets and two Baffoons, too different from each other.

The above principles I hope the diligent Reader will be found attended to, in the Scores of all great Compofers.

B. OF PIECES FOR A MILITARY BAND.

§ 13. The noble fort of mufic in queftion, differs from other mufic in being calculated chiefly to be played *out of doors*, or in the open field. I fhall endeavour to fpeak of it, firft *in general*; and fecondly with regard to the particular forts of *pieces* ufed in it.

§ 14. *In general* I fhall confider: *firft*, the diftribution of the Harmony among the different inftruments; and *fecondly*, the ufe that may be made of the different Inftruments.

1. The *diftribution of the harmony* among the different Inftruments, might in all refpects be like that for an Orcheftra, of which I have fpoken in Chap. III, § 13, if a military band had always four principal inftruments, of an equal or proportional ftrength, like the two Violins, Tenor, and Bafs, of an Orcheftra. For, then the two Clarinetts or Hautboys might take the firft and fecond, and the two Baffoons the third and fourth part of the Harmony; and the other parts might be added to them in the unifon or octave, or by felecting only thofe notes of the harmony, which can be doubled moft according to what I have faid in my Effay on Harmony, Chap. III, § 4.

But, as in general a larger band has the two Clarinetts doubled, the firft Baffoon fingle, and only the fecond Baffoon, fupported by a Serpent, which renders the firft Baffoon unequal in ftrength to the other parts, it requires a good deal of Knowledge and Judgment to fupport the firft Baffoon with the Horns, in fuch a manner, that its part may be heard as well as the other parts. For, as the Horns fhould as much as poffible have parts different from thofe of the other inftruments; and as alfo they do not naturally produce every Interval, the faid manner of letting them fupport the firft Baffoon is not fo eafy as it might at firft appear.

The above difficulty may be overcome by making the harmony confift but of *three* principal parts, fo that the two firft parts are played by the Clarinetts, and the third part by both Baffoons in the Unifon or in Octaves. In this cafe the Clarinett parts may be doubled or fupported with Hautboys or Flutes, and the Baffoon part with a Serpent; and the Horns and Trumpets may be added in the fame manner fhewn above in this fection, but fo as to give the harmony an effect equal to that of four or five principal parts. This diftribution of the harmony therefore is the eafieft, and yet it has a good effect, becaufe it renders the Bafs more fupporting to the other parts than the above firft diftribution; and it alfo fhews the Horns and Trumpets to more advantage than the former diftribution.

All the above muſt be underſtood of the *Tuttis* of a military piece only; for in thoſe paſſages where one or two inſtruments ſhall be introduced with *Solo* parts, the diſtribution of the harmony may be varied in different manners, according to what I have ſaid in Chap. III, § 13, No. 3.

2. The uſe that may be made of the different *Inſtruments*, follows from what I have ſaid above in this ſection, and in § 12. For, in *Tuttis* the three or four *principal* parts of the Harmony ſhould be given to the moſt perfect Inſtruments, being Clarinetts, Hautboys, Flutes, Baſſoons, and the Serpent; and the *filling* parts to the Horns and Trumpets, with the addition of Fifes, Drums, and Cymbals, where it is required. But in *Solos*, any one Inſtrument, or any two which properly agree according to what has been ſaid in § 7, *& ſeq.* may take principal parts, and the others may accompany them, ſo as not to over-power them.

Reſpecting the latter, or Solos, I have found, that when there are in a Band ſome Players of extraordinary abilities, they will now and then perform parts which were not written for their Inſtrument. This may properly be done only in thoſe caſes, where the original and the ſubſtituted Inſtrument are of a ſimilar nature, that is to ſay, calculated to execute the part in the *ſame octave*; but a Baſſoon or French Horn cannot properly take an upper part, and perform it an *octave lower*, if the accompaniments are not originally cal-culated, or altered for that purpoſe.

§ 15. *The Pieces* which are ſet for a Military Band, may be divided into *Pieces of Duty*, and *Occaſional Pieces*.

1. Under the *former* I comprehend: The *March*, the *Quick March*, and the *Troop*.

A military *March*, is a piece, calculated to mark the ſteps of Infantry, when marching in Parade; and at the ſame time to afford an agreeable entertainment to the hearers. Its character is or ought to be Boldneſs and Grandeur, without Wildneſs or extravagant mo-dulation. It is generally written in four Crotchet time, but marked with a C and a down-ſtroke through it, to ſhew, that it conſiſts but of *two times* in a Bar like $\frac{2}{2}$, (ſee my Eſſay on Harmony, Chap. XI, § 8, b:) and in marching it requires *two ſteps* to a bar. It has ori-ginally been compoſed but of two Sections, each of eight bars; but at preſent it is written of three or four ſections, as well as of twelve, ſixteen, or even more bars in a Section; and the Plan for it muſt be made according to Chap. I. If Marches are compoſed for other purpoſes than the above, ſuch as for ſolemn or joyful Scenes on the Stage, or as Dead Marches, they muſt be particularly calculated for the Occaſion.

A *Quick March* is a piece, calculated to mark the common walking ſtep, and thereby alſo to entertain the hearers. It may be written in $\frac{2}{4}$ or $\frac{6}{8}$ time, and conſiſt of two, three, or four Sections, from eight to ſixteen bars; and it muſt be played ſo as to take two of the ſaid ſteps in each bar. As it is played in marching, it ought to be eaſy, and conſiſt of ſimple but bold Paſſages and Modulations. Cotillions, or Country Dances are often uſed for the Marches in queſtion, when they are played no faſter than the Step permits.

A *Troop* is that piece, with which a Military Band alone marches up and down before the front of its Corps, on the Parade. It conſiſts of an Introduction, and the Troop or Marching Piece itſelf. The *Introduction* generally begins with a Tutti of a few ſlow notes in any Meaſure, and then continues with ſhort Solos and Tuttis, and with occaſional changes of the Movement and Meaſure, through about eight, twelve, or ſixteen Bars, when it concludes with a Pauſe. The *Marching Piece* may be written in $\frac{2}{4}$ or $\frac{6}{8}$ time, but muſt be played ſo as to take *two ſlow ſteps* in a bar. It may be of two, three, or four Sections, of eight, twelve, or ſixteen bars each: but the latter only when it conſiſts of two Sections, as otherwife it would become too long for the purpofe. The whole of it, but particularly the Introduction, is calculated to fhew the Powers and Effects of the Band, and as there is great attention paid to it, it affords the Compofer a good opportunity to fhew his talents as harmonift, and his judgment in the introduction of the various Inftruments.

2. By the *latter*, or the *occafional pieces* mentioned at the beginning of this fection, I underftand thofe, which are played to fill up fome intervals in the time of duty, or on other occafions, I fhould have nothing to fay refpecting the pieces in queftion, but that they may be fet of any fort and form, as fancy and opportunity will require and admit, if it was not for one obfervation which I beg leave to make, viz : that I have not yet found any collection of the pieces in queftion, exprefsly calculated for Sundays. For, though it would be imprudent to arrange *facred* pieces for fo public an occafion as the Parade ; yet I conceive that fanciful Adagios, Fugettas, and other entertaining pieces, which have not been compofed for the Stage, for Dances, or as Songs, would equally entertain moft hearers, aud lefs offend fome, than the faid latter pieces, which now and then are played among the others, becaufe they are not feparated from them. The pieces in queftion therefore deferve the attention of thofe who compofe for military Bands, or who choofe the mufic to be played by them.

C. OF PIECES FOR THE ORGAN.

§ 16. A good and large *Organ* is the grandeft and moft important mufical inftrument hitherto known, becaufe it is calculated to produce the effects of many fingle Inftruments, as well as of fuch inftruments playing together. Writing for it therefore, fo that its powers are fhewn to the beft advantage is one of the moft valuable branches of mufical compofition.

§ 17. The qualities required in true *Organ Pieces*, follow from the nature of *Organ Sounds*; from the temperament of its *Scale*; from the conftruction of its *Fingerboard*; and from its different *Sets of Keys*. Thefe particulars therefore I fhall endeavour to fpeak of in the following fections.

§ 18. With regard to Organ *Sounds*, we find that they *continue* with *equal ftrength*, as long as the Key is held down ; but that they may be *varied* in ftrength, acutenefs, and the fort of tone, by Stops.

From the *former* of thefe qualities, or their continuance with equal ftrength, it follows : *firft*, that the Organ is very much calculated for playing with long and holding notes ; *fecondly*, that it is not calculated for thofe paffages, which obtain life from the fofter or harder, encreafing or decreafing, touch and preffure of the Finger. Yet both thefe remarks do not preclude from Organ Pieces fuch figurative melodies, which can be executed with nicety, and do not require the faid humouring touch of the finger.

From the *latter* of the above mentioned qualities, or that Organ Sounds may be varied in ftrength, &c. it follows : that paffages, which are proper for the Organ in general, are not equally good for the different varieties of its Stops. For, fome are more calculated for a *full* Organ ; others more for lefs ftrong but *prompt fpeaking* ftops ; and ftill others more for Flutes, Reed Works, or other *particular* combined or Solo Stops. And under all the above confiderations there alfo depends much upon the *acutenefs* of the Stop for which the paffage is calculated ; as fome are better for a *fixteen foot* ftop, others for an *eight* foot, &c.

N. B. Re-

N. B. Refpecting the terms fixteen foot, eight foot, &c. I muft obferve: that in Germany any Stop of the fame pitch or acutenefs as the *Diapafon*, is called an *eight* foot ftop; thofe which give every note an octave lower or more grave than the Diapafon, are called *fixteen* foot ftops; every note two octaves lower than the Diapafon makes a *thirty-two* foot ftop; every note one octave higher than the Diapafon makes a *four* foot ftop; two octaves higher, a *two* foot; three octaves higher, a *one* foot; and a twelfth higher, a *three* foot. Thefe denominations have been adopted according to the length of the largeft pipe of fome ftops, in antient organs; but at prefent they denote only the above pitch of every Stop. According to them one fays a Trumpet thirty-two foot, fixteen foot, eight foot, or four foot; inftead of a Double-Double Trumpet, Double Trumpet, Trumpet, and Clarion. I thought it neceffary to give this little explanation of the above names of the ftops, on account of thofe Readers who might meet with German Treatifes of Mufic, where they are ufed. The names of every Stop in the large Organ at *Haerlem*, according to the above defcription, fee in Dr. Burney's Prefent State of Mufic in Germany, &c. Vol. II. Page 306.

§ 19. The *temperament of the Scale* is the fecond particular mentioned in § 18. This ought to be confidered in two refpects, viz: firft, whether it is *properly* tempered, according to the equal or a good unequal temperament, and after which; fecondly, whether it is fo *improperly* tempered, as it is ftill found in too many Organs.

A *proper* temperament I call that, which modifies the diatonic chromatic Scale fo, as to render it *perfectly tolerable* in every Key and Mode. How this may be done I have fhewn in my Effay on Harmony, Chap. I, § 5, *& feq.* If it is thus tempered according to an *equal* diftribution of what one calls its imperfection, pieces for it may be fet in any key with nearly the fame effect; though the acutenefs makes alfo a little difference even in an equally tempered inftrument. But if it is tempered according to a good *unequal* diftribution, a piece has a different effect in every Key, though it muft found tolerable in any; and the different effects it has according to *Kirnberger*'s Temperament, I have fhewn in the quoted place. The fame confiderations are required in compofing for Stringed Keyed Inftruments; but as their bad temperament is not fo ftriking as that of the Organ, I fpeak of the Organ in particular.

An *improper* temperament I call that, in which the imperfection, which arifes when the whole Scale is tuned by perfect Fifths and Octaves, is *not fufficiently diftributed* among the different Keys. That this temperament frequently arifes from tuning fifths more fharp than perfect, I have alfo obferved in the place quoted above; and how horrid it renders even the perfect Triad in fome Keys, muft have been felt by every perfon who attends to mufic. In regard to this temperament, (which, as I have before obferved, is ftill too frequently met with,) every Organ Compofer fhould write like a Beginner, who when he modulates towards many Sharps or Flats, cannot find his way through them, and therefore avoids them.

§ 20. But when the Organ is tuned properly, the conftruction of its *Fingerboard*, mentioned in § 17, or in other words, *what is applicable* in every Key, comes alfo into confideration. For, what is applicable in E, is feldom fo in E flat, or in F; except the paffages be very fimple. And equally fo it is in other Keys.

§ 21. The three particulars mentioned above in § 18, 19, and 20, have been attended to in *Sebaftian Bach*'s work, entitled *Wohl temperirtes, Clavier*, (well tempered Harpfichord, or Keyed Inftrument in general,) confifting of twice twenty four **Preludes and** Fugues, or

c c   two

two in every major and minor Key. Every Prelude and Fugue may be confidered as a Sonata of two Movements, each of which can be ufed as a piece by itfelf. This moft ingenious, moft learned, and yet practicable work, is fo highly efteemed by all who can judge of it, that as it is grown fcarce, I intend to offer it to the public analyzed. The firft Prelude and Fugue of it, fee at Plate LII, *& feq.*

§ 22. The fourth particular mentioned in § 17, is: the different *fets of Keys* of an Organ; and thefe may be divided into *Manuals* or *Pedals*. The former are thofe which muft be played on with the Hands; and the latter thofe for the Feet.

As Pedals are ftill as far as I know not very frequently met with in this Country, I will endeavour to fhew their nature, and the ufe that can be made of them in Organ Mufic.

§ 23. A fet of Pedals fhould contain at leaft *two complete octaves*, viz: from the graveft C to its double octave, and have its feparate ftops, like a fet of Keys independant of the others. But in new Organs they are often found to go a third or fourth higher than two octaves.

The *Ufe* of Pedals is: *firft* to fupply the place of a Double Bafs, without which a grand Organ has as poor an effect, as an Orcheftra without double baffes; *fecondly*, to carry occafionally fome obligato paffages, or even a whole obligato part.

§ 24. That the want of a fupporting or *double bafs* is felt by almoft every Organ Player, who has no Pedals to make ufe of, appears from the methods which are but too frequently adopted to fupply its place. For, Organ Pieces are not only met with, in which the left hand has almoft throughout to play in Octaves, or with rumbling baffes of broken chords; but one particularly unharmonious and melodious Bafs Grace, (being that of holding the lower femitone down with the Bafs note, inftead of a Beat on it,) feems to have been invented for the purpofe of rendering the Bafs more ftrong than otherwife.

But playing in *Octaves* prevents the left hand from executing fluent melodious paffages, as well as from taking a middle part; both of which is very material in good organ playing. Baffes by *broken chords* are alfo very injudicious in organ mufic in general; becaufe, firft they bring the harmony too clofely together in the lower parts, which is contrary to what I have faid in my Effay on Harmony, Chap. III, § 5; and fecondly they alfo prevent the left hand from playing one or two melodious obligato parts, which is one of the greateft beauties in organ playing. And the above mentioned *Bafs Grace*, or a note and its fubfemitone held down together, cannot have a good effect upon a mufical ear.

§ 25. An example of an organ piece with a mere fupporting bafs for Pedals, fee at Plate LVI, *& feq. Allegro* by *Hæfsler*. The places where the Pedals fall in, either by fingle notes or in octaves, are pointed out. But the Pedals fhould have a fixteen foot ftop if the Manuels have but eight foot ftops; and if the Manuals have fixteen foot ftops, the Pedals may have a thirty two foot one if the Organ contains it, or otherwife alfo fixteen foot ftops. See the N. B. under § 18.

From the above piece it will follow in what manner the Pedals may come into *Bach's* Prelude and Fugue at Plate LII, and LIV.

§ 26. The fecond fort of ufe that may be made of Pedals, as mentioned in § 23, is: to carry occafionally fome *obligato paffages*, or even a whole *obligato part*.

A fmall fpecimen of the *former* fort fee at Plate LVIII, *Spiritofo* by *Hæfsler*. The fhort

1   Solos

Solos which are to be played on the Pedals only, and the places where the Pedals join in the Tuttis, are marked as in the preceding example; and the Pedals fhould alfo have a double bafs ftop, as I have faid in the laft fection.

N. B. This and the preceding example are taken from *Hæfsler's* Small Organ Pieces, firft fet; the whole making three fets of twelve pieces each.

An example of the *latter* fort, or of a piece with a whole *obligato part* for Pedals, fee at Plate LVIII, *Trio* by *Sebaftian Bach*. This piece is taken from the faid great Author's collection of Organ Trios, and is calculated to be performed by one Perfon, on two fets of Manuals, and the Pedals. The Manuals fhould have ftops different in found, but of equal ftrength, and the Pedals a Double Bafs Stop, but the latter fhould alfo not be too ftrong for the former. That pieces of this kind, when properly performed, exceed every thing elfe in the art of Organ playing, will require no demonftration. To hear the effect of this Trio on an Organ with two fets of Keys, but without Pedals, it may be played by two performers as thus: the Bafs and the Treble by one performer, on one and the fame fet of keys; and the middle part by another performer on a fecond fet of Keys. This diftribution of the parts is better than playing the two lower, or the two higher parts, on the fame fet of keys, becaufe the parts crofs in fome places, or run one into another, by which they would not remain fo diftinct as in the propofed diftribution.

§ 27. But Pedals are ufed not only to carry an obligato *Bafs*, but alfo an obligato *middle* part. This is often done in giving out the melody of an Hymn or Pfalm Tune, on two fets of Manuals and Pedals. For when the melody has been carried through the treble with the right hand, and the Organift will fhew his abilities, he draws for the Pedals no larger but four foot ftops, (fee the N. B. under § 18,) but a tender Reed Stop among them, and then plays the principal melody on the Pedals, which, as the ftops make it found an octave above the Diapafon, renders it a middle part. The bafs then is played with the left hand on a fecond fet of Keys.

In the fame manner as carrying the principal melody by the Pedals, as faid above, it is alfo done with the left hand on the fecond fet of Manuals, fo as to make a middle part; when the Pedals carry the Bafs accompaniment. And alfo in the fame manner as the Pedals may carry the melody as a middle part, they may carry it as a Bafs Part, both which will require no demonftration.

In the abovementioned forts of giving out a Pfalm Tune to a Congregation, the accompaniments to the principal melody, or Plain Song, are made to confift of fuch figurative obligato melodies, imitations, and double counterpoints, as are moft adapted to the character of the Text to be fung. And when the Organ has three or four fets of Manuals befides the Pedals, the Introduction to the chief Melody, and the Interludes between its different Strains, are fometimes made on other fets of Keys than the Accompaniment to it.

§ 28. That regular Organ Trios may be compofed for *one Set of Keys*, I have endeavoured to exemplify by my Fugue for three hands, at Plate XVIII. But the faid piece may alfo be performed on two fets of Keys, in the fame manner as I have fhewn under *Bach's* Organ Trio in § 26.

§ 29. The laft particular I have to mention refpecting Organ Pieces, is the ufe of the *Swell*. That very excellent effects can be produced with it, we have heard in the performances, and may ftill find in the Compofitions of *Stanley*. But nothing can be more injudicious, than to ufe it almoft perpetually, and without any reafon, as fome Organ

Players do. For then it produces very bad effects, and makes the Organ found as if it gets faint, or like a perfon who fings when he is out of breath.

CHAPTER XII.   OF STYLE AND NATIONAL MUSIC.

§ 1. In Chap. I, § 20, I have mentioned, that attention muft be paid in compofing a mufical piece, to the particular *Place* and *Occafion* for which it is intended; and of this I fhall endeavour to fpeak a little more in the prefent Chapter.

§ 2. The *Places* for which mufic is compofed, are in general divided into the *Church*, the *Chamber*, and the *Theatre*; to which I add the *open Field*. As each of the faid places requires a particular manner of compofing for it, that manner is called a *Style*, and confequently there ought to be known what is the Church Style, the Chamber Style, the Theatrical Style, and Open Field Style, with all their branches.

I.   *Of the different Styles of Compofition.*

§ 3. The *Church Style* is the manner of writing properly for the Church, or other places of Divine worfhip. The pieces that are fet in this ftyle are: the Plain Song and Figurative Pieces.

1. The *Plain Song* comprehends the melodies of Hymns and Pfalms, with their harmonious accompaniment. One of the firft rules of the Antients refpecting thefe pieces has been: that they fhould be fet in one of the ancient ecclefiaftical Modes, of which I have treated in my Effay on Harmony, Chap. XVIII. And this rule has been ftill attended to by *Sebaftian Bach*; who in other cafes has fo boldly and fuccefsfully broke through the limits of unneceffary rules, for moft or all his Catechifm Hymns are written in the faid modes. And *Rouffeau* in his Dictionaire de Mufique, Artic. *Plainchant*, is alfo ftill of the fame opinion. But as thefe modes are become fo much out of fafhion in modern mufic, that it can hardly be expected any thing will at prefent be compofed in them, an Author fhould only know and confider the meaning of the above Rule, which was: that none but the moft *plain* and moft *folid* harmonies and melodies ought to be introduced in the pieces in queftion; and that all the luxuries of vain modulation, melodious graces and paffage work, which do not fupport but interrupted votion fhould be fo carefully avoided in them, as if we were ftill limited to the imperfect fcales of the Antients. And to this I muft add an obfervation by *Burmann*, which *Kühmau* gives at the end of his Pfalmody (Choralbuch) in four parts, viz: that the principal reafon why modern compofitions of Pfalmody have in general a poor effect in comparifon to antient ones, feems to be, that the Antients have written with more truly religious feelings than modern Compofers.

But it is not only the Hymn or Pfalm Tune itfelf, which fhould be properly compofed, and performed when fung; it is alfo the introduction to it, or the Prelude before it, and the Voluntary after it, which fhould be played in the Church Style, or with fuch harmonies, melodies, and Paffages, which are adapted to the facred Place as well as the Sentiment of the Hymn and the Sermon.

2. The

2. The *figurative* pieces which are compofed for the Church are either Services, Anthems, Motetts, Cantatas, and fimilar vocal pieces; or mere Organ or Inftrumental pieces. If both forts fhall not be unfit for a place of Divine Worfhip, they ought alfo to be written in a far more folid ftyle, than fimilar pieces for other occafions; and with true feelings for religion and the facred places of Divine Worfhip; as well as theatrical pieces muft be written with lively feelings for the objects to which they fhall be adapted.

In the figurative pieces in queftion may be included *Oratorios*, as a medium between Church Mufic, and Theatrical Mufic. Of thefe *Handel* has given a number of inimitable patterns, which are in moft inftances truly *folemn*, and fit to be ufed at facred places.

§ 4. The *Chamber Style* is the manner of writing properly for Concerts, and for private practice and amufement. The pieces that are written in this ftyle, are all thofe which come under the denomination of Sonatas, and Concertos, according to Chap. II. and IV; and thofe Symphonies which are no Overtures to facred or theatrical pieces. Alfo thofe vocal pieces which are neither facred nor dramatical; fuch as Catches, Glees, Bravura, or other Songs, vocal Duetts, Tercetts, Quartetts, or even Choruffes.

In the Inftrumental pieces written in this Style, one of the principal qualities is: to fhew the abilities of the Compofer and Performer, and thereby to entertain both the Performer and Hearer. Therefore all forts of modulation, and of paffages which are not irregular or injudicious, may be introduced in this ftyle.

In the Vocal pieces written in this Style, no other but the *general* rules given in Chap. X. need be obferved. For all thofe rules which relate to the nature of facred, or of theatrical pieces, do not concern the pieces in queftion.

§ 5. The *Theatrical Style* teaches to write properly for the Stage; and as theatrical pieces confift not only of Operas, but alfo of Pantomimes and Dances, all the mufic belonging to them muft be written in this Style. The principal quality of it is: that the mufic muft as much as poffible exprefs, not only the *character* of the Text or Action to which it is fet, but alfo the *action* itfelf. Some hints refpecting the means by which this may be effected, fee in Chap. I, § 15. On a fimilar principle as theatrical dances therefore, all other dances fhould be compofed, though with the difference, that the former muft be related to the whole piece to which they belong, and the latter are independant of other pieces.

§ 6. Pieces for the *open Field* require the fourth fort of the Styles mentioned in § 2. They comprehend Military Pieces, Hunting Pieces, Water Pieces, Serenatas, and fimilar pieces calculated to be played in a Foreft, a Garden, or (as it is the cuftom abroad,) under the Window of an efteemed Perfon, or Friend. The former, or Military Pieces, I have fpoken of in Chap. XI, § 13, *& feq.*; and the latter require each their particular characteriftics, according to the Purpofe for which they are fet, which will require no demonftration.

§ 7. The *fecond* particular mentioned in § 1, is the *Occafion* for which a Piece is compofed. And here it muft be obferved: that under each of the above Styles a piece can be compofed for different occafions as well: as alfo, that pieces compofed in one of the above Styles can be intermixed with thofe in another Style.

Refpecting the former we know, that an Opera may be tragic, ferious, comic, or of a mixed character; and refpecting the latter, that in a Concert, Pieces may be introduced which have been written for the Church, the Theatre, or the open Field. It is therefore

neceffary :

neceffary: firft, to know how to write according to each of the above Styles; and fecondly, how to choofe pieces of different Styles fo, that when they are introduced one among the other, the contraft may not be too ftriking. This laft is particularly neceffary in thofe Concerts called mifcellaneous ones.

§ 8.   The different Styles mentioned above, with their varieties, may alfo be confidered as the *antient*, and the *modern* Style of each fort; the Style, or better the Manner, of different *Compofers*; and the Style that is ufed by different *Nations*.

According to the above, there is: firft, the antient or modern Church Style, Theatrical Style, &c.; fecondly, the Style of *Handel*, *Haydn*, and others that are great enough to claim their own original ftyle; and thirdly, the Style of Italy, of Germany, of France, of England, or other Nations.   Of the laft, I fhall endeavour to fpeak in the following fections.

II.   *Of National Mufic.*

§ 9.   By National Mufic I underftand that *Style* of Compofition, and thofe *Forms of Pieces*, which are peculiar to fome particular Nation.   On the former I fhall endeavour to make fuch *general*, and on the latter fuch *particular* remarks, as I think moft ufeful for the ftudy of Practical Compofition.

A.   OF NATIONAL MUSIC IN GENERAL.

§ 10.   The moft mufical Nations of the prefent age I fuppofe to be thofe mentioned in § 8, viz: the Italian, the German, the French, and the Englifh; and what I have to obferve refpecting their different Styles of Compofition is as follows:

The *Italian* Mufic in general is the moft melodious, and moft graceful; but frequently neglected in point of rich elaboration.

The *German* is in general the moft rich and elaborate; but often neglected in point of foft flowing melodioufnefs.

The *French* feems in general to be the foremoft in lively imagination, and brilliant; but often deficient in point of juft harmony, and degenerated into mere paffage work.

Though I cannot fay to have found a particular national ftyle of compofition in *England*, where fome of the greateft muficians of all nations refide, and where confequently all Styles are fo much intermixed, as hardly to leave room for an original Englifh ftyle; yet the *Scotch* ftyle is fo much at home in England, that it may at prefent be confidered as belonging nearly equal to both Nations; and this is to my feelings the moft original, and a very energetic ftyle, though in fome collections of Scotch pieces which are rather ancient, we meet with modulations that are too hard and abrupt for modern mufical ears.

The above obfervations I have made chiefly for the fake of drawing from them the following conclufion, viz: that the more a Compofer endeavours to become acquainted with the good qualities of every Style, and the more he improves his own Style after them, without adopting alfo their faults, the better his compofition will be.   For, the Italian Style, enriched by good German elaboration, or the German Style foftened by good Italian melodioufnefs, cannot fail to have a better effect, than each of the faid Styles in the extremity of its national characteriftics.   And the fame it is with all other national Styles; which I prefume, will require no demonftration.

B.   OF CHARACTERISTIC NATIONAL PIECES, IN PARTICULAR.

§ 11.   The fecond particular which I have mentioned in § 9, is: thofe *forms of pieces*, which are peculiar to fome particular Nation.

2

That

That moſt Nations have ſome *Dance Tunes*, or *National Songs*, of a particular Rhyth-mical Form, or with ſome particular Harmonious or Melodious turns in them, is well known; and I have been happy to learn from Dr. *Burney*, that he has collected them from all parts of the World where they could be found, which valuable collection I hope he will not be diſinclined ſoon to preſent to the Public.

§ 12.　The ſtudy of the ſaid National Pieces, and their characteriſtics, has always been thought important for a young Compoſer, particularly by *Kirnberger*, who recommends it in his " Kunſt des reinen Satzes," Vol. I, Part II, Page 106.　The reaſon of this is obvious. For, what renders moſt modern compoſitions ſo barren of Rhythmical characteriſtics, as well as Rythmical varieties, but the neglect of all the national Dance Tunes, which were uſed in the compoſitions of the Antients, particularly at the Time of *Handel* and *Sebaſtian Bach*. And what can furniſh a compoſer with more uſeful rhythmical varieties, than an intimate acquaintance with the characteriſtics of the ſaid National Pieces, added to all the liberties he has beſides, to invent ſuch forms and varieties as he thinks proper? Theſe being con-ſiderations of importance, I ſhall endeavour to give them a little more explanation.

Every national or other characteriſtic piece, may be written, either in its original Form and Character; or with ſome judicious liberties in the former, as well as the latter.　A *Mi-nuett* therefore, may be written either in its original form of a ſlowiſh Dance Tune, in two or four Sections of eight bars each, and with ſimple harmonies and melodies, calculated to mark the time, and ſuit to the graceful motions of the Dance; or in more and longer Sec-tions, with any ſort of Modulations and Paſſages, without or with Variations, and in a more lively Movement than what would be proper for a Minuett to dance by.　In all the latter and more different forms, Minuetts are found in modern Symphonies, as well as in Sonatas; and in the latter they are ſometimes introduced as the firſt, or alſo as the ſecond, or laſt Movement.

In the ſame manner now as Minuetts, *Sarabands*, and all other characteriſtic or national pieces may be uſed either ſtrictly, or with all the liberties mentioned juſt now, which fur-niſhes a compoſer who is acquainted with them, with a great number of uſeful muſical varieties, that are hidden from before thoſe who are unacquainted with the ſaid pieces. And to this muſt be added; that a compoſer who ſometimes does not find himſelf ſufficiently in a humour, or as it is generally called, inſpired, freely to invent a movement of ſuch a cha-racter as he ſhould like it to be, can even aſſiſt his inventive Genius, by fixing upon ſome one or other of the pieces in queſtion, and elaborating them in a manner or form in which he has not yet found them.

From what I have ſaid in this ſection, I preſume it will follow, that the ſtudy of charac-teriſtic National Pieces is by no means unimportant in the ſtudy of muſical Compoſition; and I do not doubt, that if great Compoſers were to add to every piece they compoſe, a ſhort account of the model or idea according to which they have formed the plan of it, like as Haydn has done to the laſt movement in his Op. 75, called *Preſto in the German ſtyle*, and being a ſort of a quick Waltzer, we ſhould be able to trace many of their moſt ſucceſsful elaborations, back to ſome of the Pieces in queſtion. I ſhall therefore now endea-vour to give a deſcription of thoſe I have moſt frequently met with; and introduce them in alphabetical order.

§ 13.　The *Allemande* is a piece in common or $\frac{4}{4}$ time, in a moderate movement, and in a ſolid ſtyle.　*Handel* has written a good number of them in his Suites pour le Clavecin, Vol. I, II, and III; moſt of which are full of imitations in the **Fugue** ſtyle, but otherwiſe
like

like an Allegro, and of various lengths. They begin with a crotchet or three femiquavers *in arfi*, or at the lifting up of the hand.

§ 14. The *Bouree*, is a lively piece in common or $\frac{4}{4}$ time, of two times in a meafure, and much refembles a Gavotte; but it begins with the laft quarter of the meafure, when the Gavotte begins with the laft half or two quarters. It is generally written in Crotchets and Quavers, and performed a little lighter and more fluent than a Gavotte. Two examples of this fort of pieces ftand in *Sebaft. Bach*'s Violin Solos without a Bafs; the one being in $\frac{2}{4}$, and yet four crotchets in a bar, and the other in $\frac{2}{2}$. Another Example fee in Handel's Overture in Paftor Fido, the laft Movement.

§ 15. The *Ciaconne* or *Chaconne*, is a piece of moderate $\frac{3}{4}$ time, and the firft crotchet is particularly accented, and commonly prolonged by a dot. *Handel* has introduced two of thefe pieces in the fecond Volume of his Suites, each being but one fection of eight bars, but with a number of variations added to them. They feem to refemble the Saraband, but ftill differ from it in the faid accent on the firft crotchet, or rather prolongation of it, when the Saraband generally has the Dot after the fecond time of the meafure; and they are alfo not of fo ferious a character as the faid latter piece.

§ 16. The *Courante* or *Corrente*, is written in triple time, and *Handel* has introduced feveral in the faid *Suites* in $\frac{3}{4}$, and one in $\frac{3}{8}$. They generally begin with the laft quaver, or the three laft quavers of the bar; and that in $\frac{3}{8}$, begins with the three laft femiquavers. The movement of this piece fhould be moderate, but as its Style is imitative, and obligato paffages are fet in all parts, it fhould be performed with a firm touch, like Organ Pieces.

§ 17. The *Gavotte* is written in $\frac{4}{4}$ time, and begins with the two laft crotchets of the meafure. Its movement is rather quick, but as it is generally written only in Crotchets and Quavers, it ought not to be performed with that lightnefs, as if it was fet in fmaller forts of notes. An Example may be found in *Handel*'s Organ Concertos, Set. III, No. 5, the laft Movement; and feveral fhorter ones, in his Leffons, Book IV. Refpecting the relation between a Gavotte and a Bouree, fee § 14.

§ 18. The *Gique* or *Jig*, is written in quick triple time of three or fix times in a fimple meafure. Both forts of meafure are found written in Quavers, or Semiquavers; and both *Handel* has introduced in fimple, compound, and double compound meafures. A Gique in fimple triple trime, fee in Vol. II, of his Suites, Page 50; being in $\frac{3}{8}$. One in fimple $\frac{6}{8}$ time, in Suite VIII, of Vol. I. One in compound $\frac{6}{8}$, in Vol. II, Page 20. One in double compound $\frac{3}{16}$, or $\frac{12}{16}$, in Vol. II, Page 28; being that, mentioned in my Effay on Harmony, Chap. XI, § 14, at the end. And one in double compound $\frac{6}{16}$ or $\frac{24}{16}$, in Vol. II, Page 31.

Refpecting fimple, compound, and double compound meafures, and the characteriftics by which each of them is diftinguifhed from the reft, fee the quoted Chapter XI, in my former Effay. The Character of Giques in all the above meafures is mirth and cheerfulnefs; though I do not find it fo much in the double compound, as in the fimple, or fimple compound meafures.

§ 19. The *Loure* is a piece in $\frac{3}{4}$, of a flow movement and a pathetic or majeftic character. It refembles the Ciaconne in having generally a dot after the firft crotchet of a bar.

But

But it differs from the said piece, in beginning with the three laſt quavers of the meaſure, when the Ciaconne begins with the full bar; and alſo in requiring a flower and more marqued performance than that piece. The only example of a Loure which I recollect ſtands in *Sebaſt. Bach*'s Solos for a Violin without a Baſs, and is in $\frac{6}{4}$; but *Sultzer* ſays of this meaſure when found in the pieces in queſtion, that it muſt be conſidered as $\frac{3}{2}$. Yet according to what I have ſaid reſpecting ſimple and compound meaſure, in Chap. XI, of my Eſſay on Harmony, theſe pieces might perhaps be alſo written in $\frac{6}{4}$ as compound $\frac{3}{4}$, without loſing their character; and with regard to this obſervation the diligent reader may examine thoſe Loures he finds in other works.

§ 20. The *Paſſacaille* is written in $\frac{3}{4}$, and begins with the third crotchet. Its movement is moderate, and its character a ſerious Tenderneſs. It generally conſiſt but of one Section of eight bars, to which variations are made. *Sultzer* mentions thoſe in the Operas *Armide* and *Iſſe* as celebrated in France; and one written in common time, which begins with the full bar, and conſequently deviates from the above deſcription, in two particulars, ſee in *Handel*'s Suites, Vol. I, Suite 7.

§ 21. The *Paſſepied* is written in $\frac{3}{4}$ or $\frac{3}{8}$, and much reſembles a Minuett; but its character is a little more lively than that of the latter piece, and it ſhould be performed accordingly.

§ 22. The *Paſtorale* is written in $\frac{6}{8}$, its character is rural innocence, and it much reſembles the *Muſette* of which I have not given a deſcription above. Some Paſtorales are found in *Shobert*'s works for the Harpſichord, and a Muſette ſee in *Handel*'s Overture in Alcina.

§ 23. The *Polonoiſe* is a particularly characteriſtic piece in $\frac{3}{4}$ time; and its Movement like a majeſtic but fluent Andante or Andantino. It deviates from the general rule reſpecting ſimple meaſure, in making every rhythmical cæſure, not on the firſt, but on the laſt time or crotchet of the bar, ſo that every bar is ſimilar to a ſtrain of three bars in $\frac{2}{8}$ time. It is generally written in two or four Sections, of ſix, eight, or a few more bars, like one, or two alternate Minuetts. *Sultzer* gives a deſcription of the other characteriſtics which are required in this piece, if it ſhall have its true national originality. An example ſee in No. 3, of *Handel*'s twelve Grand Concertos.

§ 24. The *Rigaudon* is written in $\frac{1}{2}$, or Common time of two times in a meaſure, and begins with the laſt crotchet. Its character is lively happineſs. It commonly conſiſts but of two ſections, of eight bars each; and its ſmalleſt notes are Quavers. This deſcription ſhews, that the piece in queſtion is much like the Bouree.

§ 25. The *Sarabande* is written in $\frac{3}{2}$ or $\frac{3}{4}$ time, and its character is expreſſive and majeſtic. Its movement therefore muſt be rather ſlow, and the Dot which is commonly added to the ſecond minim in $\frac{3}{2}$, or the ſecond crotchet in $\frac{3}{4}$ time, gives it an air of dignity. Its Modulation ſhould be rich, but not too abrupt; and all paſſage work ſhould be avoided in it. The reſemblance between a Sarabande and a Ciaconne I have ſhewn in § 15. An Example in $\frac{3}{2}$, ſee in *Handel*'s Suites, Vol. I, Suite 1; and one in $\frac{3}{4}$, in Suite 4 of the ſame work. This noble ſort of pieces ſhould not be entirely neglected, and I think that a Tempo di Sarabande might now and then be introduced with a good effect, in modern Sonatas.

§ 26. The

§ 26. The *Siciliano* is generally written in $\frac{6}{8}$. It commonly begins with the laſt quaver, and has a Dot after the firſt and fourth quaver. Its character is innocence, and therefore its Movements moderate. An Example in $\frac{12}{8}$ ſee in *Handel's* Organ Concertos, firſt ſett, No. 5.

§ 27. The *Waltzer*, is written in $\frac{3}{8}$, and its movement ſhould be Moderato or Allegretto. As it is the tune to one of the moſt ſimple Dances, originally uſed in Swabia, its principal characteriſtic ſhould be to mark the time of that dance, by well accenting every bar. Its modulations as a Dance Tune ſhould therefore be ſimple, and not much paſſage work be introduced in it. As an Example I mention again the laſt Movement in *Vanhall's* Opera XXXII, quoted at Chap. I, § 10. And one of the moſt ingenious elaborations in the ſtyle of a very quick Waltzer is the laſt Movement in *Haydn's* three Sonatas, Op. 75.

§ 28. To the deſcription of the above Pieces I might ſtill have added, that of the *Hornpipe*, the *Strathſpey*, the *Reel*, and of a number of leſs known pieces, mentioned by *Türk* in his very valuable work, entitled *Clavierſchule* (being the moſt compleat Guide to the art of playing on Keyed Inſtruments hitherto known,) Leipzig and Halle, 1789. But as the former three are ſufficiently known in this country ; and as I do not doubt that Mr. *Callcott* will, in his announced Dictionary of Muſic, give an hiſtorical account of thoſe I have explained above, as well as a compleſe liſt, and ſome deſcription of all the ſorts of pieces hitherto known, I need not attempt to enlarge upon them.

§ 29. I conclude this ſecond Eſſay, and with it my Eſſay on the Science of Muſic in general ; and wiſh that the diſcerning Reader may not find himſelf diſappointed in his juſt expectations from this work.

FINIS.

ERRATA.

A LIST OF THE OTHER WORKS

PUBLISHED BY

A. F. C. KOLLMANN.

	£.	s.	d.
SECHS Geiſtliche, Lieder, &c. Six German Hymns in Four Parts, and alſo with the mere Thorough Baſs. (AUTHOR) – – – – – – – – – – – – –	o	2	o
Four Sonatas for the Piano Forte, with an Accompaniment for a Violin ad libitum, Op. II. (AUTHOR) – – – – – – – – – – – – – – – –	o	7	6
An Introduction to the Art of Preluding and Extemporizing, in Six Leſſons for the Harpſichord or Harp, Op. III. (WORNUM) – – – – – – – – –	o	5	o
Six Sonatinas for the Piano Forte, Op. IV. (WORNUM) – – – – – – –	o	4	o
The firſt Beginning on the Piano Forte, according to an improved Method of teaching Beginners, Op. V. (AUTHOR) – – – – – – – – – – –	o	6	o

> N. B. The ſaid Method is that, of uniting the Study of the Rudiments and the Practice of Playing, in ſuch a manner, that the Pupil may at the very firſt attempt begin to enjoy the latter, without neglecting the former; according to which Method he makes a regular progreſs in playing, without perceiving, as it may be ſaid, that he learns the Notes, Time, Characters, &c. See the Introduction of the preſent Eſſay on Compoſition, § 3.

	£.	s.	d.
The Shipwreck, or Loſs of the Halſewell Eaſt-Indiaman, Piano Forte, Violin, and Violoncello, Op. VI. (AUTHOR) – – – – – – – – – – – – – –	o	4	o
A Symphony for the Piano Forte, a Violin, and a Violoncello, with Analytical Explanations of the Subjects and Imitations, the Modulations, the Counterpoint Inverſions, and the Rhythmical order it contains. Op. **VII.** (AUTHOR) –	o	4	o
An Eſſay on Muſical Harmony. (DALE, *and the* AUTHOR) – – – – – –	1	1	o

Modul: from G to D

D major

Modul: from D

lead: Ch: to
G minor

to G minor

NB. G minor skipped.   Bb major as a related

Key to G minor.

Modul: through other Keys related to G minor, to the

lead: Chord of G major .

Lead: Chord to G major

p

pp *f*

G major

ten:

B minor is related to G major

mf

p

Modul to C major

Volti Subito

V.S.

Fuga III a 4,

Fuga a 6 Soggetti   C.C .Hachmeister

Alla Breve

inter

inter

inter   revers

4 by dim

* NB. S signifies the Principal Subject;   A its Answer; and 2, 3, 4, 5, 6, the other Subjects.

IX. in the 8 below, 3 above, & 6 below.

X. a 2, in the 7 below, over a given melody.

subject

I. 4 in 2   Canons by Dr. Burney

alla rovescio, in the unis.

II. Communis est via. a 2

III in ogni modo   l'ultima volta

I believe in God, believe in God the Fa_ther Almighty.

I believe in God believe in God the Fa - ther Almighty.

Canons by Kirnberger

I. 4 in 1, per tonos by 5ths

Solution of I.

I Continued .

II. to be resolved exactly like the above

Solution of II .

(33)

Canons by Eman. Bach

I
first equal
length and
then by dimin:

II

78 D.C.

Kirnberger

First Solut:
of N.° II

D.C.

Kirnberger

Second Solut.
of N.° II

Volti Subito

I Canons by Fasch

II

III

(35)

(37)

Some Solutions of the preceding Canons by Sebast: Bach

IX Fuga canonica in the 5.th above

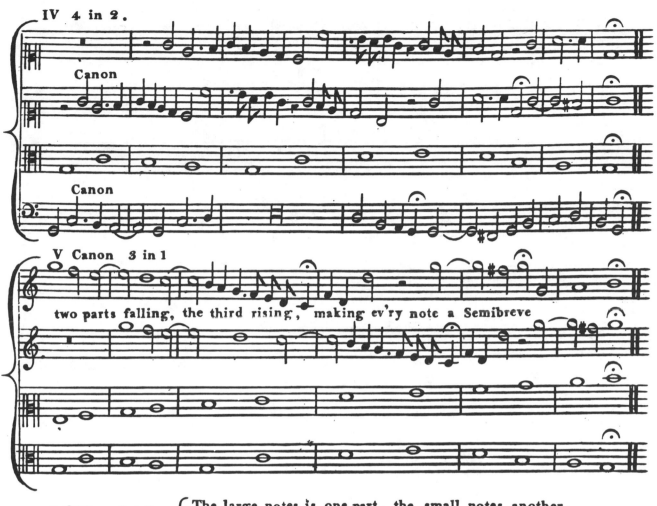

IV 4 in 2.

Canon

Canon

V Canon 3 in 1

two parts falling, the third rising, making ev'ry note a Semibreve

No. III explain'd { The large notes is one part, the small notes another, the third singeth both sorts of notes, leaving all the rests.

Solution

Canons by Handel.

Larghetto

All our joys to sorrow turning, and our Triumphs into Mourning

All our joys to sorrow turning, and our Triumphs in _to

all our joys to sorrow turning

As the Night succeeds the Day, as the night succeeds the Day.

all our joys to _ sorrow

Mourning   As the Night succeeds the Day, as the night succeeds the Day.

and our triumphs in_to mourning,   as the night succeeds succeeds the

turning,   and our triumphs in_to mourning,   as the night succeeds the

Night suc_ceeds suc_ceeds the Day,　as the Night suc_ceeds the

_ceeds as the Night suc_ceeds the Day,　as the Night suc_ceeds the

as the Night suc_ceeds the Day,　as the Night suc_ceeds the

Night　suc_ceeds the Day,　as the Night suc_ceeds the

Viol.1

Day.

Viol.2

Day.

Viola

Day.

Basso

Day.

II.　Handel

Freed from War's de_structive Sword: Peace her plen_ty round shall

Freed from War's de_structive Sword:　Peace her plen_ty

Freed from War's de_structive Sword:

Freed from War's de_structive Sword:　organ

peace her plenty round shall spread, peace her plen_ty round shall spread,

round shall spread _ _ _, peace her plenty round shall spread round shall spread,

plenty round shall spread peace her plenty round shall spread round shall spread,

peace her plen_ty round shall spread _ _ _

while in virtues path you tread.

Violin Primo

while in virtues path you tread.

Violin Secondo

while in virtues path you tread.

Viola

while in virtues path you tread.

Basso

Canon by C.H.Graun.

Viol. 1

Viol. 2

Viola

col Basso

I_lio ca_da, e'l Re_ _ _ge altero: E poi vegga il passaggiero sol ro vine e solo or_

I_lio ca_da, e'l Re_ge altero: E poi vegga il passaggiero sol ro

ro _ _ _ _ _ ri, o _ ve Troja or _ po _ sa il pie, or po _ _ _ _

vine e solo or ro _ _ _ ri, o ve Troja or _ po _ sa il piè, or po _

_ _ _ _ _ sa or po _ sa il pie, I _ lio ca _ da, e'l

_ _ _ _ sa or po _ sa il pie, I _ _ lio

Re ge altero: e poi veggail passaggiero sol rovine, e solo or ro

cada, e'l Re ge al tero, e poi veggaïl passaggiero sol ro rovine e solo orro

ri, o ve Tro ja or po sa il pie, or po sa il pie.

ri, o ve Tro ja or po sa il pie, or po sa il pie.

Prelude

Sebast: Bach (52)

Volti Subito

Fuga a 3.

Adagio